The Man Who Stopped The Sultan

To my mother, Paolina Perello Albert

EDOARDO ALBERT

THE MAN WHO STOPPED THE SULTAN

GABRIELE TADINO & THE DEFENCE OF EUROPE

OSPREY PUBLISHING
Bloomsbury Publishing Plc
Kemp House, Chawley Park, Cumnor Hill, Oxford OX2 9PH, UK
Bloomsbury Publishing Ireland Limited,
29 Earlsfort Terrace, Dublin 2, D02 AY28, Ireland

Bloomsbury Publishing Inc.
1359 Broadway, 12th Floor, New York, NY 10018, USA
E-mail: info@ospreypublishing.com
www.ospreypublishing.com

OSPREY is a trademark of Osprey Publishing Ltd

First published in Great Britain in 2026

© Edoardo Albert, 2026

Edoardo Albert has asserted his right under the Copyright, Designs and Patents Act, 1988, to be identified as Author of this work.

For legal purposes the Acknowledgements on pp. 297–98 constitute an extension of this copyright page.

All rights reserved. No part of this publication may be: i) reproduced or transmitted in any form, electronic or mechanical, including photocopying, recording or by means of any information storage or retrieval system without prior permission in writing from the publishers; or ii) used or reproduced in any way for the training, development or operation of artificial intelligence (AI) technologies, including generative AI technologies. The rights holders expressly reserve this publication from the text and data mining exception as per Article 4(3) of the Digital Single Market Directive (EU) 2019/790

A catalogue record for this book is available from the British Library.

ISBN:		
	HB:	978-1-4728-6999-9
	eBook:	978-1-4728-6997-5
	ePDF:	978-1-4728-6995-1
	XML:	978-1-4728-6996-8
	Audio:	978-1-4728-6998-2

26 27 28 29 30 10 9 8 7 6 5 4 3 2 1

Plate section image credits and captions are given in full in the List of Illustrations and Maps (pp. 7–9).
Artwork by Brian Delf in pp. 1–3 of the plate section previously published in FOR 96: *The Fortress of Rhodes 1309–1522*.
Text permission acknowledgements are given in the Notes.

Maps by www.bounford.com
Index by Mark Swift
Typeset by Lumina Datamatics Ltd
Printed and bound in Great Britain by Clays Ltd, Elcograf S.p.A.

Osprey Publishing supports the Woodland Trust, the UK's leading woodland conservation charity.

To find out more about our authors and books visit www.ospreypublishing.com. Here you will find extracts, author interviews, details of forthcoming events and the option to sign up for our newsletter.

For product safety related questions contact productsafety@bloomsbury.com

CONTENTS

List of Illustrations and Maps   7
Chronology   13

1. The War for the Heart of the World   17
2. A Boy's Life   24
3. The Tadini of Martinengo   31
4. Short and Ugly   35
5. Bringing a Cannon to a Sword Fight   41
6. The New Ways of War   49
7. The Education of a Military Engineer   51
8. A Peach, Ripe for Plucking   56
9. A Life Without Women   60
10. The Italian Wars Kick into High Gear   65
11. Why Everyone was Fighting Everyone Else   69
12. The Warrior Pope   72
13. The Patron Pope   77
14. First Blood at Agnadello   82
15. The Siege of Padua   86
16. Whispers and Gossip   92
17. The Sack of Brescia   98
18. A Life like Lightning   104
19. A Not-So-Romantic Interlude   110
20. The Dregs of War   120

21	A Military Engineer Abroad	129
22	How Venice Became Rich	132
23	Venice and the Ottomans	136
24	The World Gets Bigger	145
25	Suleiman	150
26	The Other Emperor	160
27	The Last Knight of Christendom	165
28	A Short History of the Knights Hospitaller	171
29	How to Get into a Besieged City	177
30	War Underground	185
31	War Overground	195
32	An Eye for an Arquebus	206
33	Facing General Winter	212
34	The Chancellor's Downfall	216
35	'Nothing in the world was ever so well lost…'	220
36	The Emperor's New Man	226
37	Long Nose Versus Big Jaw, or 'All is lost save life and honour'	235
38	A Famous Victory and a Forgotten Siege	246
39	Two Emperors is One Too Many	255
40	When an Old Soldier Leaves the Field	265
41	The Last Knight of Christendom: The First Man of the Modern World	278

Notes	286
Bibliography	291
Acknowledgements	297
Index	299

LIST OF ILLUSTRATIONS AND MAPS

PLATE SECTION ILLUSTRATIONS

The freestanding bastion protecting the post of Auvergne allowed the Knights to pour enfilading fire along the length of the curtain wall and the moat. Note the low *fausse braye* in front of the main curtain. (Artwork by Brian Delf © Osprey Publishing)

The post of Italy was protected by the substantial *tenaille* in front of the curtain. The inner face of the *tenaille* shows the width of the original moat and how much it was widened. (Artwork by Brian Delf © Osprey Publishing)

The defences of the post of England in 1480 and 1522. Note how narrow the original moat was. The curtain was thickened, a substantial bastion built to provide enfilading fire and a *tenaille* to protect the curtain was produced when the moat was widened. (Artwork by Brian Delf © Osprey Publishing)

The upgraded defences for the post of Provence follow the same theme: a widening of the moat, thickening of the walls and the building of a bastion to ensure the moat becomes a killing zone. (Artwork by Brian Delf © Osprey Publishing)

The negotiations between Suleiman and the Knights Hospitaller lasted for 16 days and included three face-to-face meetings between the sultan and the Grand Master. (Photo by adoc-photos/Corbis via Getty Images)

There are few paintings of the siege in Ottoman sources. This one depicts well the distinctive uniform and head dress worn by Suleiman's Janissaries. (Photo by Universal History Archive/Getty Images)

Francis I, king from 1515 to 1547, was the first Renaissance ruler of France, presiding over a glittering court that included Leonardo da Vinci, while France also became the first European country to enter into a formal treaty with a Muslim state. (Photo by Heritage Art/Heritage Images via Getty Images)

Charles V, king of Spain and Holy Roman Emperor, ruled over the world's first truly trans-oceanic empire, his writ extending from the Balkans to South America. (Photo by Fine Art Images/Heritage Images/Getty Images)

This famous portrait of Suleiman is attributed to Titian and his workshop (Titian worked with assistants who would block out and do much of the actual painting for him, leaving the master to add the finishing touches). Titian never met Suleiman. The portrait is probably based on descriptions by Venetian ambassadors and Ottoman medals. (Photo by Fine Art Images/Heritage Images via Getty Images)

Titian and his busy workshop were also responsible for this portrait of Gabriele Tadino, painted in 1538. Tadino is wearing the robes of the Religion and, in the background, Titian added a row of cannon pointing offset to represent the artillery that had been his main concern. (piemags/Alamy)

Charles VIII was not a Habsburg but, looking at his portraits, it's clear that the pile-up of genetic defects that result from royal inbreeding affected his development. Just how much was never made clear, as he died young, aged 27. (brandstaetter images/Getty Images)

This painting of the Battle of Pavia does a good job of showing the crucial importance of the walls around the Visconti Park in the battle. (Photo by Fine Art Images/Heritage Images/Getty Images)

Gaston de Foix is one of history's great might-have-beens. If he had not rashly charged a group of retreating Spanish soldiers, the Italian Wars might have ended very differently. (Photo by Apic/Getty Images)

The soldiers of the 16th century, such as the *Landsknechte* shown here, did not bother with camouflage: they were peacocks on and off the battlefield, their garish uniforms a way of establishing who was friend and who enemy amid the chaos and swirling smoke. (Photo by: Bildagentur-online/Universal Images Group via Getty Images)

European visitors to the Sublime Porte were always impressed by the discipline and silence that surrounded the sultan – very different from European courts. (Photo by DeAgostini/Getty Images)

It was not only German *Landsknechte* who wore multi-coloured outfits; if anything, Italian *condottieri* were even more eye catching. (Photo by: Danilo Donadoni/REDA/Universal Images Group via Getty Images)

The names, design, barrel lengths and bore of cannon were far from standardised during the Italian Wars, and the names were often as exotic as the guns: bombard, serpentine, basilisk, culverin and falconet, among others. (Bettmann/Getty Images)

It was not only the infantry who wore striking outfits; the artillerymen did too, making for spectacular, if increasingly lethal, battles. (Photo by: PHAS/Universal Images Group via Getty Images)

MAPS

The Italian States, 1494	10
The Siege of Rhodes, June–December 1522	11
Ottoman Frontier: The Mediterranean Sea, *c.*1450–1600	12

MAPS

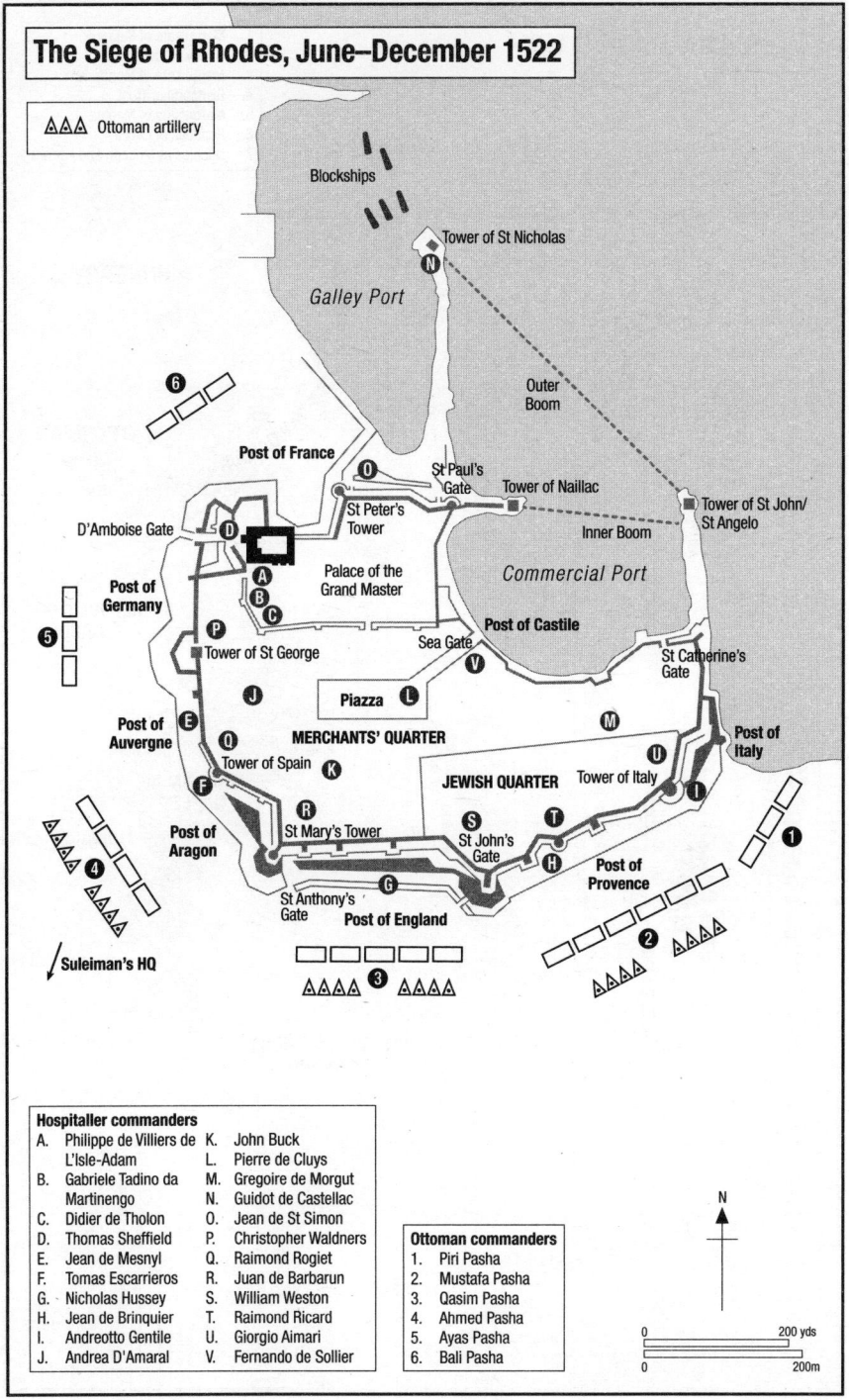

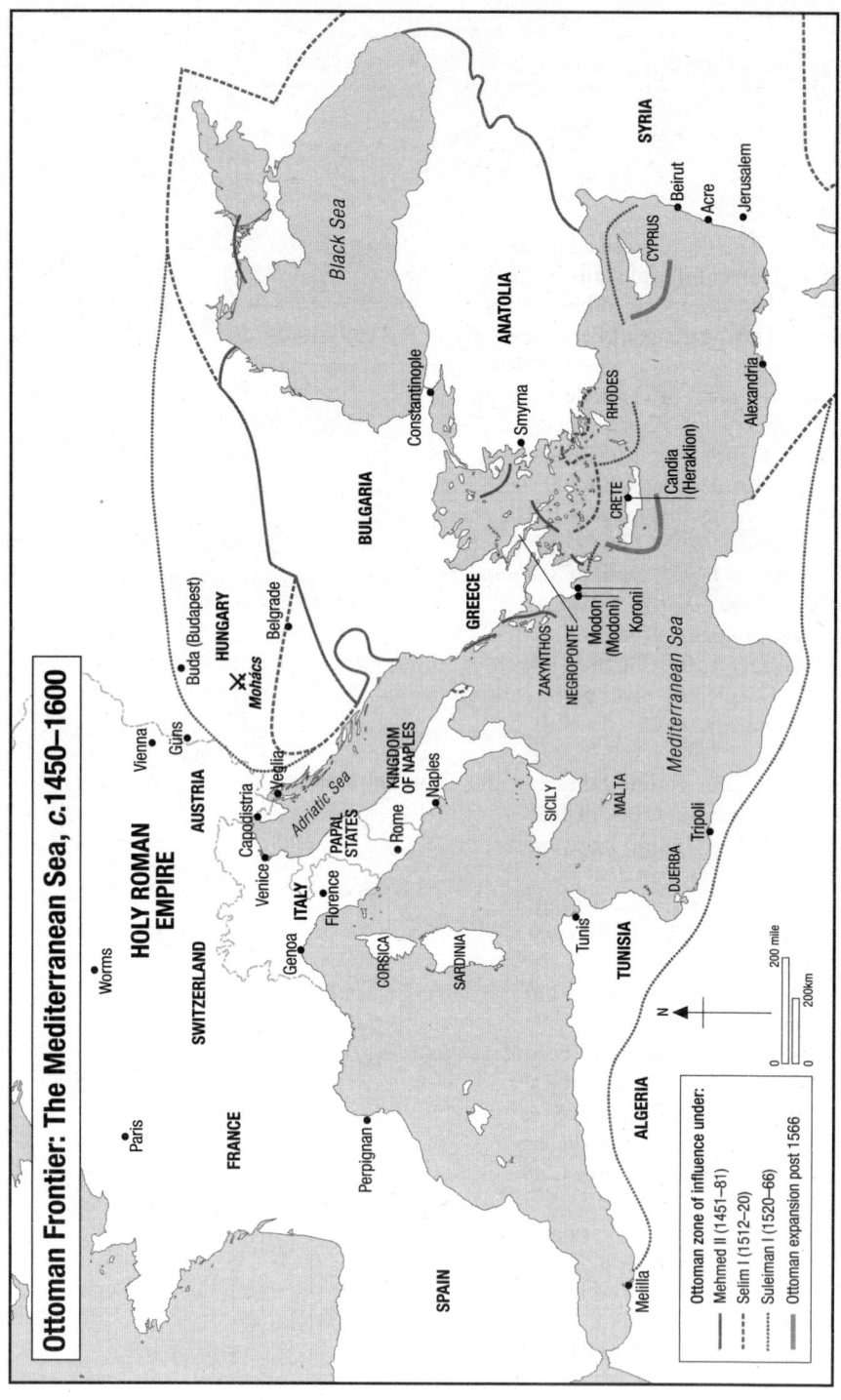

CHRONOLOGY

*c.*1450 The Portuguese adapt the caravel for use in the Atlantic Ocean.
1453 Constantinople falls to Mehmed the Conqueror.
1456 The Gutenberg Bible is printed.
1469 The marriage of Ferdinand and Isabella unites the crowns of Castile and Aragon.
1476–80 Birth of Gabriele Tadino.
4 February 1488 Bartolomeu Dias rounds the Cape of Good Hope.
1490s Gabriele goes to Bergamo to study under a French military engineer.
1492 Christopher Columbus arrives in the Americas.
1494 Charles VIII invades Italy to claim Naples.
12 September 1494 Birth of Francis I, future king of France.
6 November 1494 Birth of Suleiman, future sultan of the Ottoman Empire.
20 May 1498 Vasco da Gama arrives in India, opening up a new trade route to the Indies bypassing Venice.
24 February 1500 Birth of Charles V, future Holy Roman Emperor.
1508 Gabriele receives permission from his father to enlist in the Venetian army.
April 1508 Michelangelo starts working on the Sistine Chapel.
14 May 1509 Tadino takes part in the Battle of Agnadello.
15–30 September 1509 The siege of Padua.
August 1511 Tadino fights in the company of the condottiero Renzo di Ceri during the defence of Treviso.
Autumn 1511 Tadino is accused of conspiring against Venice.
18 February 1512 Tadino is wounded and taken prisoner following the fall and sack of Brescia.
March 1513 Venice enters into an alliance with France and all prisoners are released, including Tadino.
1 January 1515 Francis I becomes king of France.
24 January 1517 End of the War of the League of Cambrai which had started in February 1508. The peace treaty essentially returns everything to the state of affairs before the start of the war.
31 October 1517 Martin Luther nails a list of 95 theses to the door of the church in Wittenberg.
April 1518 Tadino takes part in the kidnapping of Francesca Averoldi.
23 June 1518 Kidnapping trial concludes. Tadino and co-defendants are banned from Verona and its environs. Tadino's contract with Venice is also terminated.
End June 1518 Tadino flees to Ferrara following his release from gaol.

Rest of 1518 and 1519 Influential friends of Tadino work to have him, and the other accused, pardoned and this eventually succeeds.
December 1519 Tadino goes to Venice and is acquitted by the Council of Ten.
1520 Tadino returns to the service of Venice.
May 1520 Tadino is given the governorship of Cyprus, then part of the Venetian trade empire.
June 1520 However, before Tadino can take up the governorship of Cyprus, his appointment is changed to Crete (then called Candia), another Venetian possession.
30 September 1520 Suleiman becomes sultan of the Ottoman Empire.
23 October 1520 Charles is crowned Holy Roman Emperor.
April 1521 Tadino sends report of his actions in Candia (Crete) to Venice.
24 August 1521 Suleiman captures Belgrade.
July 1522 Fra' Antonio Bosio persuades Gabriele to come to the defence of Rhodes.
1 August 1522 Tadino is inducted into the Hospitallers on Rhodes.
September 1522 Ottoman attacks on Rhodes reach a climax; a general assault on 24 September is beaten back.
11 October 1522 Tadino is shot through the eye during the siege.
20 December 1522 Hospitallers agree in principle to surrender to Suleiman.
1 January 1523 The Knights leave Rhodes. Tadino had probably departed a few days earlier.
5 January 1523 Tadino arrives on the Greek island of Zakynthos.
11 January 1523 Tadino arrives in Gallipoli.
Early 1523 Tadino arrives in Naples.
Early 1523 The Knights arrive on Crete (Candia).
Spring 1523 Tadino goes to Rome.
August 1523 The Grand Master arrives at Civitavecchia, the port of Rome, which becomes temporary HQ of the Knights.
1 September 1523 The Grand Master meets Pope Adrian in private audience.
8 October 1523 Tadino leaves Rome as part of a delegation to Emperor Charles V.
4 December 1523 The embassy, with Tadino, arrives in Pamplona where they meet the Emperor.
Early 1524 Tadino has many audiences with Charles V. In the end, Charles V offers him the position of general commander of the Spanish artillery.
Spring 1524 Tadino returns to Rome to ask permission of the Grand Master to take up the position offered to him by Charles V.
Beginning May 1524 Tadino leaves Rome to return to Spain with permission to take up the post.
3 July 1524 Official proclamation of Tadino as general commander of the Spanish artillery.
August 1524 Tadino takes part in the siege of Marseille.
Autumn and winter 1524 Tadino takes part in the defence of Pavia.
24 February 1525 The Battle of Pavia. Tadino leads the garrison out from the city to attack the French rearguard.

CHRONOLOGY

5 April 1525 The promulgation of the *Segunda ordenanza de las Guardas*, which lays out standard features for the manufacture of Spanish artillery.
1525 Tadino is appointed prior of Barletta.
February 1526 Tadino travels to Barletta to take possession of the priory there.
29 August 1526 Suleiman is victorious at the Battle of Mohács, killing the Hungarian king.
31 August 1526 Charles V writes to Tadino, telling them that he is urgently needed to take command of the defences of Genoa, upon which a French attack is imminently expected.
By 15 September 1526 Tadino reaches Genoa before this date, having sailed there on a fast felucca. He rapidly oversees the buildings of bastions and defences.
6 May 1527 Imperial troops sack Rome.
Winter and spring 1527 The siege of Genoa drags on, with the Spanish unable to relieve the defenders.
August 1527 The siege comes to an end. Tadino is taken prisoner.
End August 1527 Tadino is taken as prisoner to the castle of Cremona.
May 1528 Tadino is transferred to the castle of Brescia.
October 1528 Tadino is finally released from captivity.
End August 1529 Tadino confers with Charles V on the necessary artillery preparations to face the Ottomans.
27 September–14 October 1529 First siege of Vienna.
February 1530 Gabriele is in Bologna for the coronation of Charles V as Holy Roman Emperor.
July 1532 Tadino works on the defence of Austria against a fresh Ottoman attack.
23 September 1532 Charles V arrives in Vienna, Tadino among the captains with him.
Autumn 1532 At Tadino's request, Charles V writes to Venice asking La Signoria to forgive Tadino for deserting his post in Candia (Crete), a grudge that has endured for ten years. Venice agrees.
8 April 1533 In Genoa, Charles V signs the document giving Tadino leave to retire from his service and stipulating his pension.
June 1533 Tadino retires to Martinengo.
1535 Charles V recalls Tadino to be an advisor in the preparations for the attack on Tunis.
1536 Tadino returns to Martinengo.
1537 onwards Tadino settles in Venice. Renews his friendship with the mathematician Niccolo Tartaglia.
1538 Titian paints Tadino's portrait. A medal is also minted with Tadino's effigy in profile.
30 May 1543 Tadino writes his will.
4 June 1543 Tadino dies. He is buried in a marble tomb in the church of S. Giovanni e Paolo but the church was later remodelled and the tomb lost.

1

The War for the Heart of the World

10 August 1522, beneath the city of Rhodes.
The drum began to chime.

This was unusual. Drums don't normally chime. But this was no ordinary drum. Set into its rim was a series of silver bells, attached by an ingenious mechanism to the drum skin so that when the skin vibrated the bells would ring. One after another, the bells began to sound, making an incongruously bright and cheerful peal in the quiet dark of the tunnel.

Gabriele Tadino, the Italian military engineer holding the drum to the wall of the tunnel, looked to the boy crouched beside him. The boy's eyes were fixed upon the bells sending up their silvery peal. Tadino held his finger to his lips.

In the tunnels, they must be silent, always silent, so that the Turks would not hear them through the rock.

The man and the boy sat listening to the silvery peal of bells, trying not to cough from the bad air and dust.

Then, the ringing stopped.

They both stared at the bells. Still, they did not ring.

Moving slowly, Tadino laid the drum carefully down on the floor of the tunnel and then placed his ear against the side of the tunnel, flat against the rock. He crouched, listening, for a long time. He moved his head, listening in different places, even lying down so that he could put his ear on the floor.

The drum lay on the floor, its bells still.

Tadino pointed back down the tunnel and the boy nodded, understanding the instruction. He turned and made his way along the tunnel to where its entrance shaft ran up to the blessed air outside. Tadino followed, hunched over where the boy walked upright.

The boy leading, they climbed the ladder up the shaft, the daylight dazzling their tunnel-dark eyes but the air sweet in lungs that had been breathing the bad air in the tunnels.

Standing by the shaft entrance, Tadino grabbed the boy. 'Run and bring the Grand Master. Tell him to hurry. It will not be long.'

Now, out of the tunnels, there was no longer any need of silence.

The boy, one of the children the Italian had trained to use the vibration detection devices – everyone but Gabriele called them 'Tadino's ears' – ran off towards the Master's palace.

Out in the plain air, Tadino could hear the sounds of the siege. For two months the city of Rhodes had lain under the cannon of the Ottoman Empire. For two months, Turkish sappers had been digging under the great ditch that surrounded the city, trying to tunnel under the city to plant mines and breach its walls. Then the Grand Turk's men, the Janissaries in their disciplined columns and the wild akinji, *would come pouring into the city. The inhabitants of a city under siege taken by storm knew not to expect mercy from the victors. For three days, Rhodes would suffer rapine, the survivors taken as slaves.*

But for the last two weeks Tadino had been directing the counter-mining operation, digging a ring of tunnels around the city from which his boys, using the devices he had invented, listened for the tell-tale scrape of Turkish tunnellers. Whenever they detected a tunnel, Tadino would carefully direct his own miners to dig a counter-tunnel under the Ottoman tunnel. Then, when the tunnel was dug, he would set a carefully calculated charge into the tunnel head and detonate the mine, collapsing the Ottoman tunnel and killing the miners.

It was war underground. It was war conducted in a darkness lit only by lamps, fought by men who returned above ground limed white as if they were walking corpses. Tadino's ears, his drum detection devices, were the means by which he sought to discover the Ottoman tunnellers and stop them before they could mine the city's walls.

In most cases they had succeeded, but this tunnel had penetrated right under the post of Aragon, the section of the defences manned by brother knights from Aragon. It had been too late to counter-mine. But Tadino hoped that the measures he had taken would save the wall when the mine exploded. The silence underground indicated that the Turks were pulling their miners out of the tunnels before detonating the mine.

They would all know soon enough if he had done enough to save the city's wall.

Tadino made his way the short distance to the command post of Fra' Juan de Barbaran, captain of the post of Aragon.

As he walked in the shadow of the wall, Tadino heard the cough of one of the Ottoman cannon. Without thinking, he turned his head, listening for the sound of its impact. The sharp crack came from the far side of the thick city wall and, hearing it, he did not pause to go and inspect the damage. The impact sound had told him that the cannon, one of the wide mouthed bombards, had shot a stone ball at its target. The ball had shattered on hitting the wall, causing little more than a few cracks. It was the sharp bright sound of metal striking stone that made Tadino stop and inspect the damage, for the iron cannonballs, though smaller, were fired from cannon with longer muzzles and a greater charge of gunpowder, giving them much greater velocity which, coupled with the hardness of iron, would often shatter the stone they struck.

Reaching the command post, Tadino found Fra' Juan de Barbaran directing some of his arquebusiers to new positions in the Bastion of St George. Seeing Tadino, Fra' Juan de Barbaran stood up.

'Is it soon?'

'Yes,' said Tadino.

'Reserves?'

'Have them ready.'

'They are.'

'Then come and see. I have sent for the Grand Master too.'

Fra' Juan de Barbaran, wearing breast and back plate but without the full armour worn by a knight for battle, followed Tadino back along the wall.

They reached the tunnel shaft at the same time as the Grand Master arrived with his servant-at-arms, Fra' Antonio Bassi.

Fra' Philippe Villiers de L'Isle-Adam, the Grand Master of the Order of Knights of the Hospital of St John of Jerusalem, the Knights Hospitaller, appeared to be less certain of the outcome: he was wearing full armour, although Fra' Antonio Bassi was carrying his helmet.

'Soon?' asked Fra' Philippe when Tadino joined him.
'Yes,' said Tadino.
'Where?'
'Here.'
The men waited, looking around but always towards the ground.
'Are you sure those will be enough?' Fra' Philippe pointed at the holes drilled into the wall in front of them.
'They will be enough,' said Tadino.
When he had learned of the Ottoman tunnel it had been too late to counter-mine it. The only chance was to vent the explosion upwards. So he had ordered holes drilled into the city wall above where he judged the mine would explode. If he had judged correctly, the force of the explosion would be dissipated up and out through the holes, leaving the wall intact.

If not...

'Where is the reserve?' Tadino asked Fra' Juan de Barbaran.
The commander of the post of Aragon pointed to the approaching men, a mixture of mercenaries, men-at-arms and a handful of brother knights, fully armoured.
'Tell them to wait there,' said Tadino, and Fra' Juan de Barbaran ordered his men to rest in the shade.
Fra' Philippe looked up towards the sun. It was beginning to dip down from its zenith but the day was still warm: it was 10 August in the year of Our Lord 1522 and summer's heat lay heavy on the day.
The Grand Master turned to Tadino. 'How much long...'
The mine exploded.
They felt the ground beneath them shake, like a dog shaking water from its fur, but before the walls could shiver and break, gouts of stone and air and dust vomited from the holes in the wall, spreading grit and earth over the watching men.
The ground settled.
The three men, Tadino, Fra' Philippe and Fra' Jean, stared at the wall. It stood. Cracked in one or two places, but it still stood.
Tadino turned to Fra' Jean. 'The arquebusiers are in position?'
Fra' Jean nodded.
'Then they should find good sport among the Janissaries waiting for the wall to fall.'

As Tadino spoke, they heard the crack of arquebuses firing and, from the other side of the wall, the cries of men struck.

Fra' Philippe turned to the Italian.

'We endure, thanks to you.'

Tadino shook his head. 'Not just to me, but to all here fighting the Grand Turk.'

The island of Rhodes was the pivot upon which Gabriele Tadino's life turned. When he arrived on the island at the end of July in 1522 he was a military engineer of some limited renown, known for his work during the interminable Italian Wars. When he left the island at the end of the year, he was a brother of the Knights Hospitaller, his reputation such that he had to be smuggled away lest Sultan Suleiman press him into his employment, willing or not.

Rhodes is both island and city. As an island, it rises from the eastern Mediterranean some ten miles from the mainland. As a city, it had been the headquarters and fortress of the Order of the Knights of the Hospital of St John of Jerusalem, better known as the Knights Hospitaller, since 1310. Unlike their rivals, the Knights Templar, the Knights Hospitaller had survived the fall of the Crusader kingdoms. They had set up their base on the island of Rhodes where they sat astride the sea lanes running from Constantinople to the Holy Land. When Constantinople was the Christian continuation of the Roman Empire, this was not a problem. But after 1453, when the Muslim Ottoman Turks conquered Constantinople, the presence of the Knights so close to the heartland of the Ottoman Empire proved a sore trial to the sultans.

In 1480, Mehmed, the sultan who had conquered Constantinople and brought the final end to the Roman Empire, tried and failed to take Rhodes, the Knights enduring 86 days of siege before the Ottomans called off the attack.

Forty-two years later, Mehmed's great-grandson Suleiman landed on the island with an army numbering in the region of a hundred thousand men.

Facing him were 700 Knights and a few thousand mercenaries and Rhodians. On the face of it, this was not a match but a massacre waiting to happen.

But among the defenders of Rhodes was a man who had only arrived on the island at the end of July, when Suleiman's forces were still landing.

The newcomer was an Italian, Gabriele Tadino, from Martinengo in the province of Bergamo.

Presenting himself to Fra' Philippe, Gabriele Tadino appeared as an answer to unanswered prayers. Knowing that they were shortly to face the might of the Ottoman Empire, Fra' Philippe had sent out appeals to the princes of Christendom, requesting their aid in the coming struggle with the Turks. The princes, Charles V, king of Spain, Francis I, king of France and Henry VIII, king of England, had all replied fulsomely, promising aid to the brave knights, the bulwarks of Christendom, against the Muslim onslaught. But though their replies were ornate with flowery rhetoric and promises, their words were empty. Charles and Francis were preoccupied with their struggle for control of Italy while Henry was laying the foundations of the obsession that would split his realm from the wider Christian world.

Reading their letters, Fra' Philippe knew they would not come.

He had hoped for more from Genoa and, in particular, from Venice. Both these maritime republics had seen their profits shrink as the Ottomans gradually took control of the ports of the eastern Mediterranean. But the Venetians were loath to provoke the Ottomans, their biggest rivals but also their largest trading partner. So they pointedly refused to send any soldiers to help defend Rhodes, despite the suspicion that their own colonies on Crete, Cyprus and other islands in the Aegean might be next.

When the Knights Hospitaller scaled down their requests from squadrons of galleys and battalions of soldiers to a single man, La Serenissima still refused: Gabriele Tadino was too valuable.

Gabriele Tadino was too valuable because he was a master of the new discipline of military engineering. The invention of gunpowder, and its wholesale adoption by the Christian states of Europe as well as by the Muslim Ottomans, was beginning to change the nature of warfare. It was the cannon that Mehmed hauled overland to Constantinople that had battered a breach into walls that had stood for a thousand years. Cannon, firing balls of stone or metal, would bring down the walls that had protected castles and cities for the previous five hundred years.

In response, a new breed of soldier, the military engineer, had overseen the construction of a new style of fortifications: walls became low and squat, the better to absorb and deflect the impact of cannonballs, while bastions were built to provide flanking fire against the enemy foot soldiers trying to climb through breaches in these walls. For along with cannon, defenders and attackers now had smaller gunpowder weapons: arquebuses.

Gabriele Tadino had made his reputation during the Italian Wars that had ravaged Italy for the last 30 years. He learned how to muster guns to defend a breach, how to build and bolster defences, where to site cannon and how to hide them. In particular, he learned about underground warfare, of tunnelling and mining and how to ventilate shafts so that men might not suffocate when digging tunnels. In these small battles, Tadino became a master of the new arts of war.

But Tadino was a romantic as well as an engineer. When he heard tell of the Knights' defiance of the sultan's demand that they leave Rhodes, and of their request that he might be released from his employment by Venice to aid them, he decided to ignore his employer's refusal. Tadino took ship himself, arriving on Rhodes as the Ottoman blockade was being established.

So pleased was Fra' Philippe, the Grand Master, to have Tadino in the city that, on 1 August 1522, he received the Italian as a Knight of Magistral Grace, investing him with the Grand Cross.

It must have been a brief ceremony: Tadino was already busy. He was overseeing the digging of counter-mining tunnels, training teams of Rhodians, mostly boys too young to fight, in the use of his mining detectors, overseeing the repair of the fortifications damaged by the Ottoman artillery and constructing retrenchments to cover the places where it looked likely the Turkish cannon would breach the walls.

Gabriele Tadino would remain a brother of the Order of the Knights of the Hospital of St John of Jerusalem for the rest of his life. How long that life would be depended upon the outcome of the siege of Rhodes.

2

A Boy's Life

23 October 1494, Martinengo, Italy.
'Gabriele, what are you doing?'

Gabriele dropped his pen and tried to cover the paper. But it was too late. His father stood over him, looking down at the table and his drawings.

'Did I not tell you to stop making these ridiculous drawings of cannon and bastions?'

'Er, sì, papa.'

'Did I not also tell you to concentrate on your studies?'

Gabriele dropped his head.

'Sì, papa.'

'Then what are these?' He pointed at the drawings on the table.

'I – I was drawing new defences for Florence, papa.'

His father shook his head. 'Florence? Why Florence? We are Martinenghesi. We have nothing to do with Florence.'

'I heard you talking about what would happen if the king of France decided to come with his army to claim the throne of Naples. You said that he would have to conquer Florence on the way. So I thought I would make some defences that his cannon could not knock down.'

Gabriele's father shook his head. 'I am a doctor. My father was a doctor. You will be a doctor. Our job is to put together the men who draw the attention of kings, not find new ways of killing them.'

'Sì, papa, but with these defences, not so many of them would be hurt when the cannon fire.'

'Enough.'

A hand swept the paper and quill from the table. The pages floated like they were leaves, drifting from the autumn trees.

'Enough of your stupid scribblings. We have a patient to see.'
'Sì, papa, I am sorry.' Gabriele stood up.
'You should want to hurry.'
'Papa?'
'It is your friend, Giuseppe, the son of the captain.'
'Giuseppe? What is wrong with him?'
'Fever. High fever. Come, let us do the work of healing. Bring my bag.'
'Sì, papa.'

Leaving the drawings where they lay on the floor, the boy, now on the verge of manhood, rushed after his father, picking up the bag as he went.

His father was already striding down the street, passers-by calling out greetings as he went.

'Buongiorno, Dottore Clemente!'
'Com'è sta, Signore Clemente?'
'Dov'è va, Dottore?'

To these greetings and questions, Clemente di Michele Tadino gave reply according to the degree of the man asking the question: to those of quality, the popolo grasso, he stopped to pass a few words, to ask after wife and children before passing on; to those from the popolo minuto he nodded gravely and answered in kind but did not stop to speak. To the rest, he nodded, and sometimes offered a smile, but did not speak.

Gabriele, following in his father's wake, did much the same, although the men of the great guilds that made up the popolo grasso did not speak much to third sons nor expect the third sons to speak back. However, the shopkeepers and bakers and butchers, the popolo minuto, were happy to talk, even with a third son, and Gabriele was normally happy to speak back. But not when his father was hurrying to reach a patient.

And particularly not this patient.

Father and son hurried along the street, the arches of the portici that ran along the street marching alongside them. From some of the arches, grocers and bakers called out to the people passing by but Clemente and Gabriele Tadino paid them no heed, turning instead through the gate that led to their destination.

The castello *of the Colleoni. The boys in Martinengo called it La Casa del Capitano.*

Gabriele stopped, as he always stopped, when the tower came into view: it rose higher than the tallest tree, its red brick exterior blank and forbidding low down and with only a few window slits, set high in the tower, to allow archers to cover the street below the tower.

The castle's walls wrapped around the courtyard, the tower watching inside the castle as well as outside.

Signor Clemente walked up to the gate where two soldiers dressed in the red, white and yellow of the Colleoni, slouched, their tunics unbuttoned that they might enjoy the October sun before winter arrived and the sun lost his power. They were soldati di ventura, *soldiers of fortune, who had decided that their fortune largely lay in taking the coin of the Colleoni.*

'I am here to see the captain's son. I am the doctor.'

The soldati, *galvanised from their midday stupor by the invocation of the name of their* condottiero, *stood aside, the more slovenly of the pair even adjusting his tunic so that it covered his substantial belly.*

'Per favore,' said the slimmer of the pair, gesturing for Dr Tadino and his son to pass through the gate. 'The boy is not well.'

'That,' said Dr Tadino as he went past them, 'is why I am here.'

With Gabriele scurrying behind, Dr Tadino strode through the gatehouse and into the castle courtyard.

The red and grey bricks of the walls rose high around them. The sun, not so high as it had been through the summer, now lit only part of the courtyard and Dr Tadino walked in shadow as he marched across the straw-strewn tiles towards the door to the captain's private quarters.

'Dottore! Come quickly.' Another soldato *gestured for them to hurry and Dr Tadino strode faster with Gabriele trotting to keep up with his father.*

They went through the door and the shade within wrapped around them. With the soldato *leading, they made their way up the stairs to the captain's private apartment. A fourth* soldato *was standing outside the door and, seeing them coming, he pushed it open.*

'Dottore, please.'

Dr Tadino swept past him and into the captain's private chamber with Gabriele following.

Entering the room, Gabriele squinted, trying to see, for the shutters were closed and the room was wreathed in a fug of smoke from the fire that was burning in the grate. He coughed, his eyes watering, but as his eyes cleared he saw the captain, standing by the bed.

And then he saw his friend.

'Giuseppe,' he gasped.

The boy lay in the bed, his shift stained with sweat and his eyes hollow and fever ridden. Two of his father's soldati were attending him, one wiping a wet cloth over the boy's forehead, the other trying to get him to drink from the flagon he was pushing to his lips.

Dr Tadino pushed the soldati away from the boy.

'Open the shutters, get some air in here. And bank the fire, are you trying to roast him?'

The captain raised his hand. 'But Dottore, for fever you should heat, no? That is why I told my men to close the shutters and bank the fire.'

'No, captain, no, not for this fever.'

Captain Colleoni, his face stricken, looked from his son and back to the doctor. 'He will be all right?'

'It is good that you called me now. Open the windows, let the good air in and the bad air out.' Dr Tadino turned to his son. 'Gabriele, my bag.'

Gabriele put the bag on the floor next to his father but as he did so, the boy turned his head and vomited, violently, over the side of the bed and onto Gabriele's legs.

Gabriele felt the warm, wet whip and jumped back but too late: the vomit was dripping down his legs. He let out a cry of disgust and tried to move further back, out of range of another vomit but his father, seeing him, gestured him forward.

'As a doctor, you must accept such baths as a part of the job.'

Gabriele, struggling not to gag himself, was unable to move any closer. He stood there, shaking his head.

'You do not have to fear, Gabriele. Giuseppe has cleared the excess bile from his body. He will not vomit again. At least, not for many hours.'

'I – I will open the windows, papa.'

His father glanced at him, then turned back to his patient. 'You do that.'

Trying not to feel the way his vomit-wet hose clung to his legs, Gabriele made his way, stiff-legged, towards the windows and, unlatching the shutters, pushed them open to allow the cool October air into the pestiferous room.

Trying to escape the smell, Gabriele stuck his head out of the window. As he did so, he saw a man running across the courtyard towards him. From his mud- and sweat-stained garb, Gabriele could see that he had travelled long and fast. The man, feeling Gabriele's regard, looked up and saw him.

'The captain?' he called up to him.

'In here...' Before Gabriele could go on to say that the captain's son was too ill for visitors, the man had disappeared beneath him.

'A messenger is coming,' Gabriele said to Captain Colleoni.

'Did he say what he wants?'

'No,' said Gabriele.

'Tell him to go away.'

But before Gabriele could get to the door, he heard the sound of steps running up the stairs.

The urgency with which the man was coming told Gabriele that there must be great and terrible news to tell.

The man burst into the room. He wore red and gold, the colours of the Republic, La Serenissima, although the dust of the road dimmed the colours.

Seeing the boy lying on his bed, attended by the doctor, the messenger suddenly stopped his mouth from speaking.

It was the captain who spoke.

'My son is ill. Tell your message, tell it quick and be gone.'

The messenger bowed, his breath rasping from his running, and then straightened.

'Captain Colleoni. The Signoria asks you to make your men ready. Charles, the king of France, has marched with many men into Piedmont. He has taken the fortress of Mordano. He now marches on Florence. He has many cannon; they knocked down the walls of Mordano within two days. None can withstand their fire.

The Signoria calls upon you to prepare for war.' The messenger bowed again, his message complete.

Captain Colleoni stared at the messenger.

'Two days you say? The French destroyed the walls of Mordano in two days? There was no treachery?'

'No, Captain. The captain tried to defend the fortress but in two days the French artillery breached the walls and the French broke through the defences. There was a great massacre.'

'Two days? You are certain.'

'Sì, Captain, I am sure.'

Captain Colleoni shook his head. 'Then nothing is secure any longer. You say that Charles marches to Florence?'

'Sì, Captain.'

'With such cannon, the Republic cannot withstand the French. They will sue for peace. Then the way lies open to Rome and Naples.'

'That is what the Signoria fears, Captain.'

'And then his attention may turn to Venice?'

'The Signoria fears that also, Captain.'

Captain Colleoni shook his head. 'These are new times we live in. What was once secure is so no longer.' He looked to the messenger. 'Take my message back to the Signoria. I will be ready when they have need of me. But for now I must tend to my son.'

The messenger bowed.

'My men will see that you have food and drink, and your horse is stabled, fed and watered ready for you to return with my answer.'

'Thank you, Captain.'

The messenger made his dusty way from the room.

Captain Colleoni turned back to Clemente Tadino, who had been tending to his son while he spoke with the messenger.

'Will Giuseppe be all right, Doctor?'

Dr Tadino slowly stood up. 'I must bleed him a little to relieve the fever, but I believe he will be all right with rest and good air.' He nodded towards the windows. 'The shutters must be kept open, even during the coolest part of the day. Have your servants fan the bad air from the room when there is no breeze.'

'I feel a bit better already, papa,' said Giuseppe. His voice was weak but his words were clear.

Captain Colleoni went down on his knees beside his son, holding his hand in his own.

'It's cool,' he said. He looked up at Dr Tadino. 'The fever has left him.'

Dr Tadino nodded. 'I think he will do well.'

Captain Colleoni stood back up.

'As you have done this for my son, Dr Tadino, I will do the same for your son. Giuseppe has told me of his interest in the arts of war, and he showed me some of the drawings he has done of forts and fortifications. For one so young, they show great skill. So, I will send your son to Bergamo, to be apprenticed to the engineer there, that he may learn the skills necessary to defend against the new weapons of war.' Captain Colleoni gestured towards the door through which the messenger had departed. 'As you heard, there will be much call for knowledge such as this in the years to come.'

Dr Tadino nodded, but did not say anything.

Captain Colleoni looked askance at him. 'Is there something wrong with this? I do your son great honour.'

'No, I thank you, gracious captain, most sincerely. I – it was only that I had hoped that Gabriele would become a doctor, as I am and my father before me.'

Captain Colleoni laughed. 'Did you not see how he flinched when my boy vomited? Your son is not meant for the trials of a doctor, for the vomit, the bile and the shit. Send him to Bergamo, let him learn the arts of war, and he will make such a name for himself that the house of Tadino will be known through all the kingdoms of Europe.' The captain stared at Dr Tadino. 'What do you say?'

'I – I don't know what to say,' said Dr Tadino.

'Then let's ask Gabriele.' Captain Colleoni turned to the boy. 'What say you? Do you want to go to Bergamo and study the arts of war?'

'Can I?' asked Gabriele. 'Can I really?'

'With your father's permission, you can,' said Captain Colleoni. 'Doctor?'

For what seemed forever but was actually only two or three seconds, Clemente Tadino made no reply. Then, finally, he looked at Gabriele.

'Go with God, Gabriele, and bring honour to your family.'

'Thank you, papa,' cried Gabriele. 'Oh, thank you, thank you.'

3

The Tadini of Martinengo

In 1494, Gabriele Tadino was in his teens. We don't know exactly when he was born but it was between 1476 and 1480, with 1478 being the most likely date. If that was the year he was born, then he was 16 when the news of the French invasion reached his hometown.

Gabriele was the third of five children born to Clemente Tadino, a doctor in Martinengo, a town that was home, then, to a few thousand people, lying ten miles south of Bergamo.

Martinengo is situated about 30 miles east of Milan and in the 14th century it fell under the control of the Visconti family, the dukes of Milan. However, Milan and Venice came into conflict at the start of the 15th century and, on the signing of the Peace of Ferrara on 5 May 1428, Martinengo passed under the control of the Venetian Republic.

One of the greatest servants of La Serenissima during the middle of the 15th century was the mercenary captain, or *condottiero*, Bartolomeo Colleoni, and in reward for his faithful service the Republic granted Martinengo to him in 1454. That didn't mean Colleoni owned the town. However, he became both its master and its guardian. As master of Martinengo, Colleoni could gather the revenue due to him, including taxes such as the *capitazione* (head tax) and the *fuocatico* (hearth tax), dues on farm produce that were paid in kind, and the fines levied on subjects who had broken the law. As its guardian, he was responsible for its defence, as well as serving as its chief magistrate.

To keep an eye on his new domain, as well as to carry out his duties, Colleoni built a house there, the tower of which survives today. As the town's guardian, and thus the man responsible for its spiritual wellbeing as well as its physical defence, he founded a Franciscan monastery and convent, as well as improving and reinforcing the town walls in light of the changing arts of war.

The first Tadino of whom we have a record was Stefano Tadino who, in 1340, lived in Caravaggio, a town eight miles south-west of Martinengo. (If you're wondering, yes, Caravaggio the artist did spend his early years in Caravaggio a hundred years after the birth of Gabriele Tadino.) Stefano Tadino had a son, Cristoforo, who continued to live in Caravaggio and who in turn had two sons, Michele and, somewhat confusingly, Tadino (who presumably would have been known as Tadino Tadino).

The two brothers divided their inheritance, with Tadino taking the family properties in Caravaggio and Fornovo, while to Michele went the family properties in Bergamo, Crema and Brescia.

However, Michele had also studied medicine and in May 1434 he moved to Martinengo because he had been appointed as the town doctor and the post strictly required that he live in the town.

Michele did well for himself in Martinengo, and in 1468 he commissioned a new tabernacle in St Agatha's Church in gratitude for his good fortune. The main altarpiece was carved from Candoglia marble and it remained in place for 250 years until the church was remodelled in the early 1700s. Michele's donation was taken apart and the carved altarpiece was embedded into a building on Via Cucchi Marcantonio, where it can still be seen at the junction with Via L. Odasio. The wall below is covered with posters announcing the deaths of local residents.

As well as fortune, Michele was blessed with family: Felice, Clemente and Stefano. Felice and Clemente continued the family business, practising medicine in Martinengo.

Doctor Clemente Tadino had his first child, Gian Francesco, in 1474. Gian Francesco was followed by Gerolamo, then Gabriele, and two younger siblings, Michele and Tranquilla.

For two generations at least the Tadini had been a medical family. They had done well from medicine and there was every expectation that Clemente's sons would follow in his footsteps. However, the world was changing and, in the end, of the four boys only Michele took on his father's profession: Gian Francesco, Girolamo and Gabriele all became soldiers.

As for their sister, Tranquilla, she is one of those figures who slides into the historical shadows, appearing only twice in the surviving records: in Gabriele Tadino's will, which at least indicates that she outlived her three military brothers, and before that in documents relating to Gabriele's captivity between September 1527 and October 1528, when she was part of the efforts to secure Gabriele's release.*

The refusal of the three eldest of Dr Tadino's sons to follow their father's calling is all the odder since they were well placed to do the studies necessary to become doctors. Italy was the leading centre of medical education in Europe, and had been since the 9th century, when the first institution that could be called a medical school was established in Salerno, on the Amalfi coast south of Naples.

The Schola Medica Salernitana became known throughout Europe for its teaching, with students travelling there from all over the continent to enrol on its medical programme. This required eight years of study: three years of training in logic and then five years of medical training, followed by a practical year under the direction of an experienced physician. As well as dissecting pigs, which were thought to be closest to humans in their internal structure, the school benefited from a lessening in the old Classical prohibition against human dissections. The professors there performed a human dissection every five years. While this was inadequate, it prepared the way for the new universities that began to be established in Europe from the 11th century onwards.

The Schola Medica Salernitana never broadened its curriculum to include the range of subjects that were taught at the medieval universities, so it is not counted as the first of them, although it predates the University of Bologna by at least 150 years.

The University of Bologna, which was probably where Clemente Tadino studied medicine, was founded in 1088, although it only became a fully-fledged university a century later, followed in the 13th century by the universities of Oxford, Paris and Cambridge. Along with teaching canon law, theology and philosophy, these early universities also taught medicine, producing qualified physicians who, by

---

*For details, see Chapter 19: A Not-So-Romantic Interlude.

virtue of their years of study, quickly became the top of the medieval medical tree.

The University of Bologna was an early example of pupil power: the students there banded together to run the university, voting through their representatives on whom to hire as teachers, how much to pay the professors and the content of the courses. There was even a committee, called the 'Denouncers of Professors', to which students could report teachers who did not keep time or who failed to teach all their classes during a term.

At Bologna, the study of medicine lasted for four years. During that time, the student physician attended 46 lectures, each lecture based upon a text by one or other of the Classical authorities, in particular Hippocrates and Galen, plus lectures on the work of the Persian polymath Avicenna (Ibn Sina), whose *Canon of Medicine*, written in 1025, was the single most influential medical textbook of the time. The students' study was, at least in its initial stages, highly theoretical, revolving around careful logical analysis of the chosen texts, with relatively little practical work. However, the practice of careful description and analysis led to physicians writing detailed descriptions of the course of diseases, laying the foundations for medicine to move gradually towards an evidence-based appraisal of treatments. Although it did little to stop the spread of the disease, physicians around Europe wrote accurate descriptions of the symptoms of the bubonic plague, allowing us now to accurately measure its spread and identify the cause.

As well as teaching medicine, these early medical schools put in place the professional standards that still govern how doctors treat their patients. That doctors should strive to heal their patients, respecting their confidences and treating the poor as well as the rich with no regard for relative wealth comes directly from the ethics inculcated by these first medical schools. We have a lot to thank them for.

But despite the family's close connections to medicine and the relatively easy journey to Bologna, Gian Francesco, Girolamo and Gabriele Tadino all decided to ignore family tradition and become soldiers.

Charles VIII, king of France, was the reason for their decision.

4

SHORT AND UGLY

Charles VIII, the king of France, didn't mean to end the Middle Ages. All he really wanted was the Kingdom of Naples and a little respect. But when, on 3 September 1494 he crossed the border at Montgenèvre into Piedmont in Italy, ending the Middle Ages is what he and the 30,000 soldiers he brought with him unwittingly did.[1]

There had been other tidings of change in the previous decades. Constantinople, the last link to the Roman Empire, had fallen in 1453 to the Ottomans. In 1492, Christopher Columbus landed in the Bahamas, but it would be a few years before the full significance of his discovery would be appreciated. By the start of the 16th century the Age of Discovery was under full sail. On 31 October 1517, Martin Luther nailed his theses to the door of the church in Wittenberg, starting the Reformation. In 1543 Copernicus published his theory that the earth and the other planets circled around the sun.

The world was changing, physically, spiritually and philosophically.

But before all of these changes, Charles VIII had crashed through Italy, transforming the dynamics of power that had held Italy in relative peace for the previous 50 years. The *adventus Carolus* transformed the balances that had held Europe in check, setting the stage for a new era in war and lowering the curtain on the martial values of the Middle Ages. Now, a gun fired by a peasant or a cannon manned by hired soldiers could kill a knight who could trace his blood back 500 years and who was wearing armour costing a year's wages.

That it was Charles who set these changes in motion was a surprise though. He wasn't even supposed to be king. But his parents, King

Louis XI and Charlotte of Savoy, had desperately bad luck with their children, even in an age of high infant mortality. Charlotte gave birth to eight children, five boys and three girls, with Charles the seventh of her children. But all Charles's brothers died as infants, leaving Charles as the only heir to his father.

It must have seemed likely that Charles would go the same way as his brothers. He was a sickly child and, frankly, ugly too. His head was too big for his body, his nose was huge even in comparison to his already outsized head, he had a short trunk and stubby legs. The courtiers, looking at this ill-shapen boy and the mortality that had tracked his family, assumed he would die before he reached ten.

But Charles survived. He was often sick, but he recovered each time. His father, fearful of losing his only surviving son, prescribed an easier education than he had received himself: no need for Charles to begin to learn Latin at six.

To the courtiers, Charles was a pleasant but foolish child, little suited to the exigencies of kingship. Charles's father shared the views of his courtiers. Suffering from ill health, and knowing that he probably did not have much time left to live, Louis amended his will so that, should he die when Charles was still young, then his elder sister, Anne, would rule as regent.

While Louis thought his son a fool, he knew Anne for the formidably intelligent woman she was, labelling her 'the least foolish woman in France'.

Louis, a shrewd but little-loved king,[2] died when Charles was 13. According to the terms of his will, Anne became regent, wielding power while Charles grew to his majority. Anne, called 'Madame la Grande' during her regency, skilfully navigated the difficulties of her years in charge, dealing with the magnates whom Louis had variously betrayed, backstabbed and sidelined while still ensuring that power remained concentrated under the crown. It was no easy path Anne had to navigate: the war with the barons, which the crown fought between 1485 and 1488, was called the Mad War, which Anne won through her customary mixture of gentle and tough diplomacy backed up, finally, by force.

So when Anne handed the kingdom to her younger brother in 1491, as Charles turned 21, she gave him a realm in which royal authority was increasingly assured while the power of regional barons had been effectively subdued. The young Charles really was king of France, rather than simply being one among a collection of rival magnates, nominally their ruler but in practice subject to coalitions of his barons wielding more power than he.

Adulthood had done nothing to make Charles more pleasing to the eye. Even the royal portraits reveal a man with a quite extraordinarily large nose and weak eyes. What they don't reveal was how short he was: just over 5 feet or about 160 cm. While that was not extraordinarily short for the time, kings, who had a better diet than anyone else, were not expected to be so short.

What the portraits also conceal was Charles's unexpected cunning. His courtiers thought him feeble and feeble minded but, upon ascending the throne, Charles proved to be as effective a ruler as his father.

This was shown most clearly in his wooing of and marriage to the most eligible woman in France, another Anne, but in this case she was the duchess of Brittany. The dukes of Brittany had been amongst the most obstinately independent of the great French magnates. Francis, the duke of Brittany, had no sons so he officially recognised Anne as his heir, assuming that he could arrange her a suitable marriage that would secure the dukedom. However, Francis died from injuries he suffered after falling from his horse. As he lay dying, Francis called Anne to his side and made her promise that she would never allow the duchy to become subject to the kings of France.

Although Anne was only 11 when she made this vow, she took her promise seriously.

Nevertheless, the death of Francis meant that Anne, now the duchess of Brittany, had become the greatest marriage prize in France. And she was a prize that Charles intended to claim. Unfortunately for Charles, there were two obstacles in the way. Firstly, he was already engaged to Margaret of Austria, the daughter of the Holy Roman Emperor, Maximilian I. Secondly, Anne had herself already married, by proxy, Margaret's father, the same Holy Roman Emperor, Maximilian I. If this all seems ludicrously tangled, it's important to bear in mind that the marriages of kings were not affairs of the heart but political deals.

Obviously, reneging on his commitment to marry Maximilian's daughter while also pinching his fiancée would cause problems between Charles and the Holy Roman Emperor. But if he allowed

Maximilian to marry Anne, then he would find his own territory boxed in, to west and east, by lands controlled by the emperor. This was not something Charles was prepared to countenance, even at the risk of war with Maximilian.

But luckily for Charles, Maximilian was engaged elsewhere, putting down problems in Hungary, while the marriage itself had never been consummated since the couple had not yet met each other.

So the French marched into Brittany and lay siege to Rennes. Anne held out in her city for two months, hoping that aid would come to help her escape her suitor. The kingdoms of Castile and England both sent contingents of soldiers to help the defender, but neither wanted war with France, while Maximilian's Hungarian problems precluded him from attacking from the west.

As Charles was seeking a bride so that he might claim Brittany by marriage rather than conquest, the French conducted the siege with greater circumspection than they would show three years later when they invaded Italy: Charles did not employ his cannon to batter down the walls of Rennes.

The city endured the siege for two months. Archaeologists digging on the former Convent of the Jacobins before its conversion to a congress centre found two mass graves, one containing the bodies of Bretons and the other of French soldiers dating from the time of the siege.[*] The bodies were all of young men who had died from stab wounds, indicating the vicious and personal nature of the fighting during the siege.

Anne was 14. Her people were dying for her. Her sister, Isabelle, died too, and it was becoming increasingly clear that there was no prospect of her supposed husband, the emperor Maximilian, coming to her rescue.

So Anne decided to take matters into her own hands. She might not be able to refuse Charles's marriage demands, but she could negotiate the terms under which she would enter into this marriage.

By November 1491, both parties began talks over the marriage contract. On 15 November, Charles was allowed into the city. Negotiations continued, with Anne pushing for guarantees of Breton independence while Charles attempted to draw the duchy more firmly under his control.

---

[*] The dig took place between 2011 and 2013.

While medieval royal women were accorded high status, when it came to the task of producing heirs to the throne, they were subject to the most humiliating examinations. One example comes from what Anne had to endure. Before Charles agreed to enter into marriage with her – and remember she was only 14 at the time – the French required that she prove that she would be able to produce children for the king. To that end, Anne had to parade naked before the king's commissioners: Anne, Charles's elder sister, and two male advisers. Having inspected the naked duchess as one would inspect a brood mare, the commissioners wrote a report that noted Anne had a congenital limp but concluded that she would be capable of bearing children.

In the end, the Treaty of Rennes stipulated that both Anne and Charles give up their claim to Brittany. Furthermore, if Charles died without a male heir, then Anne was bound to marry his successor as king of France. However, the dukedom would revert to Anne on Charles's death and remain hers even though she would have to marry another French king.

As unlikely as these string of events might seem, they all came to pass and Anne did become duchess of Brittany again.

However, that was all still in the future.

What lay in the present was marriage to the king.

Anne's view of the union was made clear on her wedding day: she arrived with two beds.

But within the calculus of royal marriages, physical attraction was of little concern, at least so far as the women were concerned. They had to do their duty and provide heirs to the throne.

Anne did her duty. She spent most of her married life pregnant, producing six children, none of whom survived infancy.

As for Charles, it turned out that he was something of a libertine. At first, he confined his attentions to his queen but as they spent more time apart, except for those meetings required to make her pregnant again, Charles became notorious for the attentions he paid to other women, whether they wanted them or not.

Of course, while Charles and Anne were now married, there was still the problem that Anne had already married, albeit by proxy, Maximilian, the Holy Roman Emperor, and that Charles was engaged to Maximilian's daughter.

This called for some urgent politicking on Charles's part. Unless he could get the pope to officially annul Anne's previous marriage, the union would be on sticky matrimonial ground. As no one was claiming that Anne and Maximilian had consummated their marriage – they had never met in person – it didn't prove too difficult to persuade the pope to agree the annulment, which was granted on 15 February 1492. At the same time, the pope also gave them permission to marry despite Charles and Anne being technically too closely related to marry, being in the fourth degree of consanguinity. Thus the marriage was recognised by the church.

However, by stealing Maximilian's bride and spurning his daughter, Charles had turned the Holy Roman Emperor into his sworn enemy. This enmity would continue for the next half century, long after the men who started the feud were dead. Unfortunately for Italy, rather than engaging each other directly, the kings of France and the Holy Roman Emperors mainly confronted each other in Italy.

Although Anne was clearly repulsed by her husband, she knew well what was required of her as queen of France, the only title Charles would allow her as he had taken away her title of duchess of Brittany. Their first child, a son, was born on 11 October 1492. Since Anne and Charles had married on 6 December 1491, Anne must have fallen pregnant almost immediately.

Having produced a male heir, and having taken Brittany, which for so long had defied the claims of the French crown, Charles was beginning to prove his worth as monarch. In 1492, Charles was still only 22. While officially he had been king since 1483, his sister had held power until 1491, so he had only been king in reality for two years. But already he was staking a claim to be taken seriously among the ranks of European royalty.

Charles was well aware of the whispers that had surrounded him since he was a child, courtier stories that branded him feeble and weak minded, some even saying that he resembled an ogre. Most of these stories had their origin in people's response to his physical appearance: in person, he was the opposite of kingly, an early example of how aristocratic inbreeding could produce disastrous results. But while his body might have been ill-shapen, it is clear that Charles's mind was turning towards proving that, in deeds, he was greater than his appearance.

About the best that the courtiers to the young prince could say of him was that he was of a pleasant disposition. Being nice was not a kingly characteristic. And it was one that Charles was determined to shed.

5

Bringing a Cannon to a Sword Fight

Growing up, Charles had learned of his father's claim to the kingdom of Naples. This claim dated back to the 13th century when Charles of Anjou, brother of King Louis IX of France, became king of Naples. The House of Anjou continued to rule Naples until 1382. The last reigning Anjou monarch was Queen Joanna, who, despite marrying four times, had no children. Joanna wanted Louis I, Duke of Anjou and brother of King Charles V of France, to inherit the crown on her death, but the rival claimant, Charles of Durazzo, who had the backing of the pope, invaded, captured Joanna, murdered her and took the crown.

The kings of France maintained their formal claim to the throne of Naples throughout the 14th and into the 15th century, even though by 1442 the kings of Aragon had seized Naples and taken the crown. These kings proved competent rulers and by the end of the 15th century Naples had a population of somewhere between 100,000 and 150,000, making it the biggest city in Europe. This was in large part due to the rule of Ferdinand I, who had been king of Naples since 1458. Having seen off his challengers during the early years of his rule, Ferdinand Ferrante had presided over 20 years of prosperity and growth.

However, when Ferdinand died, Charles saw his chance. Ferdinand's son, Alfonso, was loathed by many Neapolitans. Ludovico Sforza, the Duke of Milan, saw an opportunity to drive a wedge into the wall of alliances and enmities that kept all the north Italian states at rough parity, and invited Charles both to reassert his claim and to come to claim it.

The problem was how to claim it. There was no one in Naples with sufficient strength to withstand the king of France, so long as Charles could bring his army there to back up his claim. But the question was how to get there.

A marine operation, sending a fleet from Marseille across the Ligurian and Tyrrhenian seas, would be a frightfully risky proposition, although it had the advantage of depositing his army where it needed to be.

The alternative land route meant that Charles would have to cross the Alps and march down through much of Italy, crossing various republics and duchies, as well as the Papal States, before getting to Naples.

None of those republics, duchies or states were going to be happy about having a large French army marching across their territory. The long supply route would also leave his army's logistics dangerously exposed, particularly if they had to waste time laying siege to obdurate fortresses along the way.

Charles chose the land route.

At the start, no one was too worried. Other armies had tried such tactics, only to become bogged down while investing one after another of the fortresses and fortified towns and cities that studded Italy. Then, the hot Italian summer, disease and uncertain logistics went to work, ensuring that the invading army, after some show of victory, returned the way it had come.

Italy is protected by the Alps, mountain ramparts as formidable as those of Mordor. To enter Italy, Charles marched over the Col de Montgenèvre. This is the lowest pass through the Alps (and one used definitely by Julius Caesar and possibly by Hannibal) but it still rises to over 6,000 feet (1,860 metres), making it a difficult route for an army bringing heavy ordnance with it.

For the French were bringing cannon too.

By this point, at the end of the 15th century, gunpowder weapons had featured on the battlefields of Europe for nearly two centuries. The first depiction of one comes from an English book from 1326 which shows something that looks like an urn spouting fire. Through the 15th century, gunpowder weapons featured regularly during sieges but only rarely proved decisive. While cannon breached the walls of Harfleur in 1415, Constantinople in 1453 and Krems in 1477, there were many other sieges where they proved surprisingly ineffective.

These 'great gonnes' were big, heavy and expensive. It was really only kings who could afford to indulge in the trial-and-error experimentation that went on during this period, as smiths tried out different forging techniques and trialled varying bores. Because they were such large pieces of metal, the only craftsmen who had experience of working at such scale were, curiously, bell founders. Indeed, the man who cast the cannon that cracked the walls of Constantinople was originally a Hungarian bell founder. Orban initially offered to make cannon for the Byzantines but the cash-strapped emperor, Constantine XI, couldn't meet his wage demands. Unfortunately for Constantine, Orban promptly left Constantinople and made his way into Ottoman territory. In his meeting with Sultan Mehmed Orban claimed that his cannon could bring down the walls of Babylon, never mind Constantinople. Mehmed, who suffered none of the financial embarrassment that plagued Constantine, promptly employed Orban, who went on to cast the huge siege cannon that breached the previously impregnable walls of the city. However, Orban did not get to enjoy the fruits of his wages for he and his crew were all killed when one of their cannon exploded.

This was one of the major drawbacks of early cannon: their tendency to explode. Their other great problem was their size and weight. The Ottomans managed to drag the vast siege cannon to Constantinople by employing huge teams of men and 60 oxen, but for most military campaigns it was just not possible to move cannon over the terrain the army needed to cover. They were simply too heavy and too unwieldy.

But up in the north of France, the gunmakers employed by the kings of France had been busy. It was their cannon that had broken down the walls of the last English fortresses in France, ending the Hundred Years' War. In the years after the end of the long war, French bell founders worked hard on improving the design of their weapons and, by 1490, they had created a cannon that was the prototype of the weapon that would dominate European and world battlefields for the next four centuries.

The first cannon were large, wide-bore objects that fired carefully carved stone balls. They were placed in solid wooden blocks that were dug into the earth; moving them required the gunners to hoist the barrel onto a wagon. With solid suspension and hard wheels, these wagons, with their top-heavy loads, ran the risk of toppling over wherever part of the road surface fell away – a not uncommon feature of medieval roads.

Another disadvantage of these early bombards was their ammunition. Stone masons, among the most skilled and high status medieval craftsmen, had an instinctive dislike for carefully carving stone into smooth round balls, only for them to be loaded into a bombard and flung through the air to explode into fragments against the ramparts of a fortress. They did work to last for centuries, not seconds.

However, these problems were solved by the French cannon makers of the second half of the 15th century.

Bronze, although a more expensive material than iron, did not explode but rather cracked, leaving the gun crew to fire another day. Longer, narrower barrels allowed the cannon to fire smaller, but heavier and denser, iron cannonballs. While stone masons might cavil at carving stone balls, foundry workers had no problem with casting iron balls.

Being lighter, these bronze cannon could be fixed to two-wheeled gun carriages. Moreover, the barrels could be easily elevated or depressed because they were attached to their carriage via two trunnions, prongs forged into the body of the cannon just forward of its centre of gravity. The cannon itself could be traversed by simply lifting the end of the gun carriage and moving it round.

The cannon that King Charles brought with him into Italy were lighter and more mobile than anything that had been seen in Italy before. They predominantly fired heavy, dense iron balls. And they could travel at the same pace as the French king's army.

However, the smart money was on Charles's advance stalling as he tried to make his way south through Italy. It was a long way to go and there were many fortresses and fortified cities and towns along the way, all of which Charles would have to subdue to ensure his lines of communication were kept open.

The smart money proved stupid.

Charles set off down the Apennines, the mountain range that runs down the length of Italy's boot. The first of the Italian city states in his way was Florence. Through the 15th and 16th centuries, Florence oscillated between being a republic and a duchy under the rule of the Medici. When news arrived of the French advance, however, Florence was in the midst of one of its periodic bouts of puritanism, driven by the preaching of the Dominican friar Girolamo Savonarola. After much prayer, Savonarola had decided that Charles was God's scourge, sent to whip the Italians back into line, and he urged the Florentines not to stand in his way. The Florentines, and their duke, Pietro de' Medici, had further reason to stand aside from the French march when they heard that the French had made short work of the border fortress at Fivizzano, demolishing its walls in a few short and fierce bombardments. With Savonarola's encouragement, Pietro de'Medici decided to throw in his lot with Charles.

On 17 November 1494, Charles VIII rode into Florence, lance balanced upon his thigh, the image of the conquering medieval king. Arriving on horseback also allowed Charles to conceal his own lack of stature: in France, he had many soubriquets, including 'the Short', 'the Ugly' and 'the Fool'.

The next significant obstacle were the Papal States. Their line of territory ran right across Charles's line of advance. But a terrified Pope Alexander VI, hearing of the destruction the French artillery wrought upon any fortress that defied them, promptly offered Charles free passage through his territory.

That left the border of the Kingdom of Naples open, save for its own fortresses. The garrison of Monte San Giovanni, on the border, bravely tried to resist but the French cannon took only eight hours to breach its walls. The French poured in and massacred the defenders.

News of this transfixed and terrified all the Italian states. Monte San Giovanni had previously stood impregnable, on one occasion surviving a seven-year siege.

All the old certainties were tumbling down.

It seemed nothing could survive the terrifying power of the French artillery: no city, no stronghold, no fortress.

On 22 February 1495, Charles VIII rode into Naples, lance once again propped upon his thigh, the new ruler of the Kingdom of Naples.

It had taken Charles less than half a year to march through Italy and conquer an entire kingdom. Campaigns, which had previously taken years, he had conducted in days, sometimes even hours.

Nothing was safe any longer.

Now the king of Naples, Charles was faced with a question: what to do with the place. It's clear that he had not given much thought to ruling, as opposed to conquering, the kingdom. While he heard petitions and attempted to deal with some local grievances, his attempts at bringing Naples under his control mainly involved giving the chief offices of state to his nobles – who promptly set about turning these benefices into cash or kind. While the king might maintain the fiction that he would remain king of Naples, clearly his men were less confident that he could retain his hold on a kingdom so distant from their own – and few of them were willing to remain in Naples when the king decided to return home.

However, before his return, Charles decided to enjoy Naples. The city was famous throughout Europe both for its own beauty and for the beauty of its women. Charles, enamoured with both, wrote that all the city needed to make it Eden would be for Adam and Eve to make an appearance.

Italian chroniclers scribbled scandalised stories of Charles forcing himself upon virgins and wives, while others spread rumours that, in addition to his other deformities, Charles also had an extra toe on each foot. There's no definitive proof of Charles's polydactyly, but he did wear unusually broad duckbill shoes.

With the shock of the French march through Italy slowly wearing off, the northern Italian city states began to realise that when Charles decided to return to France he would have to go back the way he had come. But it was not just the Italian states who were disturbed by the French rampage: Ferdinand of Aragon, whose possessions in Sicily were now under French threat, as well as the Holy Roman Emperor both saw the French attack as a direct assault on their areas of interest.

In response, Milan and Venice, together with Aragon, the Holy Roman Emperor and the pope, signed an agreement on 31 March 1495 to create a defensive league for the mutual protection of their territories in Italy against any attacks.

Charles was now boxed into Italy's boot.

There was some talk among Charles's advisors about him returning to France by ship. But having won the renown he had previously lacked through his advance into Italy, Charles refused to scuttle away by sea, leaving his army to make its way home without him. Charles decided that, if necessary, he would fight his way back to France.

It was 20 May 1495 when Charles rode out of Naples. The French army made their way north, following the same route they had taken on their way south: through the Papal States, stopping in Rome for two days (Pope Alexander VI had prudently withdrawn to Orvieto before Charles arrived in Rome), up past Siena and Pisa and then on towards Parma.

It was there that the French found an army waiting for them. The League had gathered a formidable army of 20,000 men, commanded by a distinguished *condottiero*, Francesco II Gonzaga, the Duke of Mantua. They outnumbered the French two to one and, as the armies faced each other, had an excellent position on the right bank of the River Taro.

The strategic aim of the League army was nothing less than the destruction of the French expedition. For the French, the key outcome was to clear the way for their retreat from Italy.

Unfortunately for the later history of Italy, Francesco devised a complicated plan with his forces crossing the river at four different places. But heavy overnight rain meant that only two crossing points were possible, allowing the French to concentrate their forces and repel the Italian advance, while those men who did get across became completely distracted when they saw the French baggage train and set about looting rather than continuing with the battle plan.

The battle dissolved into a confused melee – and then the French unleashed their field artillery. Although the cannon did relatively little damage, they had a devastating effect on the League army, forcing it to retreat back across the River Taro.

With the way clear, Charles ordered his army to hurriedly advance. He had received reports that there were reinforcements on the way to bolster the League and, still many miles from safety, he judged it better to make good his escape.

The hasty departure of the French left the Italians in possession of the French baggage train, which contained the loot of their Italian adventure. This, together with the fact that the League army remained in possession of the field of battle, allowed Francesco Gonzaga to spin the Battle of Fornovo as a victory. But in reality, he had completely failed to achieve his aim: the French suffered only minimal losses and were able to make good their escape, while the League suffered much heavier casualties and failed to stop the French retreat.

In the longer term, the Battle of Fornovo would prove catastrophic for Italy. Charles had proved that a great power, such as France, could bulldoze its way through Italy and that there was nothing the Italian city states could do to stop it. What's more, his conquest had brought home to the rest of Europe just how wealthy the Italian city states were.

They were like jewels, glinting in the Mediterranean sun, waiting for someone to claim them.

Covetous eyes, that had previously not looked south with any great interest, now began to develop an interest in the doings of the peninsula. What was more, taking the fight to Italy meant that the great powers – France, the Empire, Castile and Aragon – could contend for dominance without incurring the risks of direct, face-to-face confrontation.

The Italian Wars had begun. They would devastate the region for the next 64 years.

As for Charles, you might wonder why you've never heard of such a pivotal figure. After all, he had invaded Italy, ended the Middle Ages, started the era of cannon warfare, all while cutting a monstrous and debauched figure through European royalty.

His historical forgetting started with the French failure to hold their possessions in Italy. The Spanish landed their own army in southern Italy and eventually drove the French out. Naples became a part of the Crown of Aragon, with the Spanish kings taxing their Italian possession heavily to pay for their wars.

As for Charles, rumour had it that one of his Italian conquests gave him a parting gift: syphilis. The rumour grew up as a result of the prevalence of syphilis among French troops returning from Naples and resentment against Charles. However, he showed little actual sign of having contracted the disease, fathering four more children on Anne after his return to France. Charles's end came from a much more unlikely direction: above.

On 7 April 1498, Charles was at his palace in Amboise when, hurrying to watch a game of *jeu de paume* (real tennis), the famously short king somehow contrived to find a door that was too low for him, and struck himself a fearful blow on the head. He appeared to recover, and went on to watch the game, but after it finished, Charles collapsed. His doctors were unable to rouse him and, nine hours later, he died.

Charles was 27. He died without an heir, so the throne passed to his second cousin, Louis XII.

As for Anne, Charles's death meant she had to marry the new king. With Louis, Anne had a further four stillborn sons, although two daughters survived to adulthood, before the poor woman, her body broken down by constant pregnancies, died in 1514. She was only 36.

6

The New Ways of War

War, and its fighting, oscillates between periods when defence predominates and times when the attacker has the advantage. The First World War is the most recent example of a time when a mixture of new technologies, in particular the machine gun, and old tactics, trench fortifications, gave the defender the advantage. The Second World War provides its opposite, when tanks and aircraft gave the attacker the advantage.

The wars of the Italian city states during the 15th century had been small-scale affairs where, in general, the defender, secure behind his walls, had the advantage unless the attacker could maintain the logistics necessary for a lengthy siege.

But Charles's army did not need to lay a city under siege. With their mobile and highly effective artillery, they could quickly blast a hole in any wall that stood in their way. The speed of their advance is all the more remarkable when you bear in mind just how difficult the geography of Italy makes it for an army to advance in the face of determined resistance. Despite the general advantage of the attacking force in the Second World War, Allied progress north through Italy was painfully slow; the soft underbelly proved to be pricklier than a porcupine.

Charles's conquest of the Kingdom of Naples left the whole of Italy,[3] and indeed, the rest of Europe, in shock.

Although the peoples watching these events unfold would not necessarily have been able to put into words their sense of dread at what was happening, we, with the benefit of hindsight, can see how this war represented a dreadful harbinger of what was to come.

In Italy, during the previous century, warfare had been conducted largely by paid mercenaries led by *condottieri* whose main aim was profit. For the men who hired them, the dukes and doges of Italy, they were pieces on a huge chessboard; war was a risky but rule-bound game where everyone knew and, generally, abided by the rules.

Elsewhere in Europe, wars were generally fought by and between lords and kings whose men were tied to them by bonds of loyalty and the slowly fraying ideals of medieval chivalry. Indeed, during the roughly thousand years since the end of the Roman Empire in the West, most conflicts had been between barons asserting their independence and kings trying to bring them under their control. As such, wars were usually local and of relatively small scale. But as those thousand years came to a close, the kings of Europe were consolidating their power, concentrating it at the centre, while their previously notoriously unbiddable barons slowly found that they could no longer match the power that a king could bring to bear on them.

The new way of war was unveiled by Charles VIII during his invasion of Italy and conquest of Naples. The tax revenue that Charles could command enabled him to field an army of a size that none of the Italian city states could match, employing the new gunpowder weapons in numbers that they could not counter.

From 1494 onwards, warfare in Europe became the conflicts of the newly consolidating and still quite fluid nation states. Only nations could raise the funds necessary to fight the new wars. Only nations could afford to fight such wars and the wars themselves became broader, eventually spreading to become the pan-European conflicts characteristic of the next few centuries.

This all came as a terrible shock to the Renaissance humanists of Quattrocento Italy.[4] Its ideals prescribed that man was the measure of all things, the centre around which this sub-lunar world revolved, and that his duties lay in building, beautifying and civilising. In the Florence of the Medici during the Quattrocento, there were mock battles, mock sieges, mock jousts, all staged for the entertainment of the people of Florence. Mars was not exactly mocked but for the Renaissance humanists he was a god tamed by his love for Venus; beauty had the mastery over the god of war.

The Italian Wars started by Charles's invasion destroyed such beliefs. Mars stalked the continent, blood soaked, dogs trotting at his heels, and beauty vanished behind the smoke of the guns.

7

THE EDUCATION OF A MILITARY ENGINEER

The evidence, plain for everyone to see, that Mars stalked Italy unchecked by Venus provided the young Gabriele Tadino with all the evidence he needed to persuade his reluctant father to allow him to pursue his wish.

We know little about Gabriele's early life. According to his earliest biographer, Giovan Battista Gallizioli, the young Tadino was a healthy, robust child (and given his later life, a resilient nature was necessary for him to survive the diseases and injuries of many battlefields).

No records survive giving the name, or lifespan, of Gabriele's mother. She must have lived long enough to give birth to Gabriele and his siblings, but there's nothing about her after that.

However, we do know that, from an early age, Gabriele was fascinated by the new weapons of war. He drew plans for city defences, he made clay models, he conducted his own little war games, as boys have been doing for most of history.

In Martinengo, Dr Clemente Tadino had attempted to teach Gabriele the basics of medicine. It was generally expected that children would follow the same trade or profession as their parents. Having four sons and one daughter, Clemente undoubtedly expected the boys to become doctors too. The Tadini had practised medicine for at least two generations at this point, and medicine had served them well: they had become wealthy.

As was normal for the time, Gabriele started to learn the skills of the family business.

But the young Gabriele, although clearly intelligent, proved a reluctant medical student.

At some point, Dr Clemente decided to see if his third son's passion for making models and drawing sketches of castles and cities might be put to some use. Although we don't know the exact timing, it's likely that the French invasion, when Gabriele was in his mid teens, further encouraged him to let his son follow his interests.

It was clear, even to a doctor like Clemente, that the new arts of war were based on science in a way that made them very different to the old medieval notions of chivalry. So rather than sending Gabriele off to an old and experienced *condottiero* to be trained in fencing and riding, Clemente set about teaching his son Euclid.

It was a happy choice. Much of Gabriele's later career would be based upon his knowledge of mathematics and, in particular, his understanding of geometry. Euclid was, of course, known as the father of geometry. Having been lost in Europe for centuries, Euclid's work, and in particular his masterpiece, the *Elements*, had been reintroduced by a succession of translators from the 12th century onwards. The first Latin translation was made by Adelard of Bath around 1120. Adelard is one of those figures of whom I wish we knew more: it appears he got hold of the Arabic translation of the *Elements* while travelling in Spain and posing as a Muslim scholar. With his Anglo-Saxon name, Adelard must have been overlooked in his native Bath so soon after the Conquest, so he left for France, studying in Tours where he developed a love for astronomy and mathematics. Following a spell teaching in Laon, Adelard went east, travelling through the lands of the Crusades, which appear to have included Palestine, Greece, Syria, Anatolia and Sicily. It's likely that Adelard learned Arabic in Sicily, which by 1091 was under Norman control but where, under its Norman rulers, there flourished a polyglot civilisation that melded Norman, Byzantine and Islamic influences. As such, it was a good place to learn Arabic, a language that would obviously have facilitated Adelard's journeys in the East.

However, it's likely that the version of the *Elements* that Dr Clemente used when teaching his son was that translated by Gerard of Cremona, a version that was produced a little later than Adelard's version. Gerard was an Italian who moved to Toledo in Spain. Alfonso IV of Castile had conquered Toledo from its Muslim rulers in 1085 but the kings of Castile protected its Jewish and Muslim populations, making it a centre of learning. Having moved to Toledo, Gerard spent the rest of his life there, translating texts from Arabic into Latin, most notably Ptolemy's *Almagest* and Euclid's *Elements*.

In 1505, the Italian humanist Bartolomeo Zamberti translated the *Elements* directly from its original Greek, which had been preserved in Constantinople, but this would have been after Dr Clemente had completed his tutoring of his precocious son. However, amid the general intellectual ferment of the 16th century, it's quite likely that Gabriele obtained the new translation.

But that lay in the future.

Now, let's return to Martinengo, where Dr Clemente is teaching his son. Johannes Gutenberg had invented the printing press in 1440. Forty years later, there were printing presses busily printing books in 110 different places throughout Europe, with Italy one of the earliest adopters of the new technology. By 1480, we can assume that Dr Clemente would have had access to printed books with which to teach his son, as they had become universal throughout Europe.

Indeed, in the speed and spread of its adoption, the printing press bears comparison with the modern revolution in communications technology that we are living through.

For children like Gabriele, a time when books were always rare, hand-made, valuable heirlooms would have been as inconceivable as children today find a time when you had to go to a library to find out something. No doubt, in between drilling Euclid into Gabriele, Dr Clemente took time to expound on how easy young people had it, when they could get books on any subject just by going to a printer in a nearby town.

Euclid derived his mathematics from 23 definitions and five axioms and five common notions. Among his definitions are some that you might remember from your own mathematics classes, which shows how long lastingly influential they were: a surface has length and breadth only; a line is a breadthless length; a point has no parts. Among Euclid's axioms (which he originally called postulates) are other ideas that will be familiar from early maths classes: all right angles are equal to each other; you can draw a circle with a centre and a radius; a straight line can continue indefinitely.

As to what and how Gabriele learned, despite our sources telling us nothing beyond the fact that his father tutored him in Euclid, we can be reasonably confident of our answer. For the Renaissance in Italy was founded upon a revolution in teaching that occurred there before anywhere else, one that set the pattern for European and, later,

American education for the next four centuries. It's a curious paradox of Quattrocento Italy that while it was characterised by a huge variety of political forms, educationally it tended towards standard methods and syllabi.

During the 14th century, inspired by humanist ideals, there had been a huge expansion of education in Italy, particularly in the northern city states. Venice, Florence and other states established networks of primary and secondary schools, many of which were run by the local *comune* (the town council), although others were privately funded. In cities and towns, between 10 and 30 per cent of boys attended these schools, receiving at least a basic education at the *abbaco* (elementary) schools, which taught reading, writing, arithmetic and geometry.

At the secondary level, grammar schools espousing humanist ideals did away with much of the rote learning of medieval education, choosing to focus on classical texts and moral philosophy.

There's no indication in surviving historical records that Martinengo had an *abbaco* during this time, so it's likely that Gabriele went to Bergamo to study at an *abbaco* there. The two towns are ten miles apart and Gabriele might have lodged with the master while studying the basic curriculum at the *abbaco*. The *abbaci* were particularly used by the sons of merchants and artisans as they focussed on the more practical branches of knowledge such as arithmetic, commercial mathematics including bookkeeping, vernacular literacy with occasionally some Latin thrown in, and geometry. All of these were necessary skills for a doctor, although for Gabriele to go on to study as a doctor, he would have had to transfer to a grammar school to learn Latin, a necessary prerequisite for a university education at Bologna.

Boys usually attended an *abbaco* between the ages of eight and 13, studying for between two and four years.

In Gabriele's case, it seems that once the *abbaco* had taught him the foundational skills for learning he returned home where his father then tutored him in Euclid's geometry.

Growing up, outside the usual concerns of boys, all the talk was of what was happening in Italy, of how the French and the Spanish and the Empire were contending for power while the Italian states attempted to use these foreign powers for their own ends.

THE EDUCATION OF A MILITARY ENGINEER

In some ways, it would have been like growing up in one of those contested countries during the Cold War where the Soviets and the Americans vied for influence while trying to avoid direct confrontation. For the rulers of the Italian states, it must have been like trying to ride two horses simultaneously, horses which frequently went off in different directions.

But, unlike the Cold War, the contest in Italy soon involved direct conflict between the foreign powers. These conflicts would define the next two decades of Gabriele's life, as well as the future of Italy itself.

8

A Peach, Ripe for Plucking

There are reasons no one talks about the Italian Wars – even in Italy. For outsiders, the wars were interminable and inexplicable. Everyone seemed to fight everyone else. Alliances changed overnight. One day, Florence, Venice, Milan and the Papal States were bitter enemies, the next they were allies. Sometimes they fought the French and the Empire, sometimes they invited them in. Leagues were formed and dissolved: Cambrai, Cognac and Holy. If foreigners find it confusing, it's because it was.

As for the Italians, in general they prefer to draw a blank sheet over this whole era in their history. My mother, who is Italian, went through her entire school career with barely a mention of what happened in the country during the 16th century. In the view of later Italians, this era saw Italy become the battleground of foreign powers, a pawn and a plaything to be fought over, while her own feckless rulers bartered their inheritances for minor advantages against local rivals, paying no mind to the wolves that ravened beyond the Alps.

The Italian Wars were the presage to a long period of Italian humiliation, at least according to the 19th century nationalists who eventually reunited the country. They saw this period, and the three centuries afterwards, as a time when the Italians were ruled from abroad: by the French, the Spanish and the Austrians.

Italians know their history. For a people that had once ruled all the shores of the Mediterranean, this was felt keenly as a disgrace.

What was worse, they were being ruled by barbarians.

When Charles VIII led his army into Italy, it became immediately clear to him, and to the other northern Europeans who accompanied him, that Italy was rich. Despite the disruptions accompanying the end of the Western Roman Empire, Italy had remained more urbanised than anywhere else in Europe. Even at its second lowest point, in the 7th century, before the city's Black-Death nadir the population of Rome was still somewhere between 20,000 and 50,000.[5] But Rome was by no means the most populous city in Italy. Naples, Venice and, probably, Milan all had populations of 100,000 or more. Florence too had a larger population than Rome, while Genoa was comparable.

By comparison, most other cities in Europe were backwaters. Only Paris was comparable to the Italian cities, with about 150,000 people living there. But the concentration of large cities in Italy made the country much more urban than anywhere else in Europe.

There was, of course, one other city that outstripped all others in splendour and population at this time: Constantinople, with a population of about 200,000.[6]

But it wasn't just the number of people living in Italian cities that the French marvelled at; it was their wealth. The Italians had effectively invented banking between the 12th and 14th centuries, particularly in Lombardy. Italian bankers had underwritten the wars of many European kings, including monarchs as far away as England. Indeed, Edward III triggered the first international banking crisis when he defaulted on the massive debts he had run up to Italian banking houses to pay for the Hundred Years' War. Edward owed 1.3 million gold florins to the Bardi and Peruzzi families of Florence and when he defaulted both banking houses collapsed.

However, banking, and the money it made available to kings, clergy, nobility and merchants, was too useful to lose and the Italian banking houses bounced back. Banking, and its accompanying skills such as double-entry bookkeeping, had enabled trade to flourish in the Italian city states. Famously, Venice and Genoa had become rich on trade. Venice, indeed, was a marvel to visitors both for its obvious wealth and for the fact that it had accumulated all this money without what most medieval people assumed was the basis of wealth: land. To visitors, Venice appeared a mirage of money, floating on its lagoon. That it should be so rich without vast territories beggared belief.

What was more, this wealth was put on display. There are many factors that produced the efflorescence of art and culture that led to the Renaissance in the Italy of the 1400s but not the least important was that the cities of Italy had the money to pay the artists and architects who adorned them. Another factor, equally important, was the intense rivalry between the cities, which led to them all employing, and occasionally poaching, the best artists and architects to beautify their cities so that the visiting eye could see that Florence, or Venice, or Siena, or Milan, or whichever town or city it was, really was the most beautiful and blessed place in creation.

It's interesting to see that this attitude continues to this day in Italy. My cousin lives in a small town, Porto Garibaldi, on the Adriatic coast about 50 miles south of Venice. This is the flood plain of the River Po; rich agricultural land that bakes under the summer sun and shivers through winter fogs. It's also flatter than Holland. Since the 1960s, a ribbon of coastal development has been built between the salt water lakes around Comacchio and the sea, a string of Lidi stretching south from Porto Garibaldi. As such, unlike almost everywhere else in Italy, the area has virtually no history. As for scenery, it's great if you like flat land, salt marshes and big skies but compared with the scenic variety of most of the rest of Italy it is, quite frankly, boring. I say this with some feeling, having spent many, many summers there when I was young and having visited fairly often since to see my uncle and cousin. To be honest, if it wasn't for the fact that I have family there, I would be happy never to see the place ever again. But to my cousin, Porto Garibaldi, the Lidi and Comacchio, the flat strip of land where he has lived all his life, is really, truly the best place in the entire world. He regularly sends me updates, photos of unexpected wildlife or new public art, bulletins on how the *sindaco*, the mayor, is messing up the development of the area and general news of local goings-on.

For him, it is endlessly fascinating and he wants nothing more than to make it better: more beautiful, better known, more widely appreciated.

This same attitude shaped the Quattrocento in Italy. The artists and sculptors were employed to produce public art, art that was on show to everyone rather than being shut away for the sole appreciation of a rich collector.

But being on display, it was seen by these visitors from abroad, the French. The wealth on display in Italy was staggering. And much of it was portable. Wealth elsewhere was largely measured by land holdings. It would be difficult to pick up a piece of France and take it home with you. But gold and silver, precious jewels and rich artefacts, these were all eminently portable. When the French made their way back from Naples, their baggage train was laden down with the loot they had collected in Naples and while they lost the baggage train at the Battle of Fornovo, the memory of its wealth went back with them to France, and spread by rumour and temptation through the rest of Europe.

Italy was rich and, like a peach hanging from a tree, ripe for plucking.

As for the Italians themselves, they had not given much thought to the lands north of the Alps. Of course they traded there. Their bankers set up branches in France and England and elsewhere. But Italian dukes and doges did not get involved in the wars to the north. There was no wish to remake the Roman Empire even if they had the power to do so (in fact, they had not).

For an Italian, the citizen of the next town, even the next village, was a foreigner. But the people who lived beyond the Alps weren't just foreigners; they were *barbari*, barbarians. The Italians lived with the assumption that they were the only truly civilised people in the world; everyone else was a barbarian. Far away in the East, the Chinese felt much the same. China was the only civilised society on earth and therefore there was no point in conquering foreign lands; they could bring nothing to the Chinese table.

The Italians were of like mind. There was nothing to be gained from conquering the barbarians north of the Alps and little point in engaging with them. Money might be made from them by trade but, living amid the splendours of Quattrocento Italy, the Italians rested upon the assumption of their fundamental superiority to the other peoples of Europe.

Unfortunately for the Italians, frescoes, murals and statues were no defence against cannon. And in the 16th century, the rest of Europe descended into Italy and turned it into a battlefield.

The impotence of the Italian states in the face of this foreign interference fostered a deep sense of humiliation among Italians. This insecurity continues to fester, at a deep level, even today, with the average Italian far more likely to run down their country when talking about it to foreigners than to boost it.

But this self-denigration lies alongside an equally deep appreciation of the uniquely beautiful culture and way of life that Italians have fostered. So while Italians might mock their own pretensions to foreigners, should foreigners echo or enlarge their points, the listening Italians will be deeply hurt. It brings those lost centuries back.

9

A LIFE WITHOUT WOMEN

It was one thing for Gabriele to get his father's agreement that he should be a soldier but it was another to find the right appointment for him. Gabriele was in his mid-teens and it certainly wasn't unknown for a boy of that age to join a *compagnia di ventura* ('company of fortune'). But doing so would mean starting at the bottom of the military hierarchy as a *scudiero*, a shield-bearer and general dogsbody to one of the company's men-at-arms. It was an apprenticeship in war.

But it was a training in the old arts of war, those that had served the *condottieri* well for the previous century but which had proved inadequate in the face of the French cannon.

To learn the new arts of war, Gabriele needed a teacher. And since the new arts of war had been pioneered by the French, a Frenchman would be the best teacher. Conveniently, Clemente found just such a Frenchman not far away, in the town of Bergamo. There, a French military engineer was undertaking work on the city walls and Clemente apprenticed Gabriele to him. Unfortunately, no record has survived of this Frenchman's name, but Gabriele was clearly both happy with his teaching and an eager pupil, for he was soon engaged in his own right to help with the rebuilding of the city's fortifications. Gabriele remained in Bergamo longer than anywhere else for the rest of his life. His father sent him there to learn the new art and science of war when he was in his mid-teens and he stayed until 1508, when he was 30.

The shock of the French invasion had left every Italian city and town scrambling to improve its defences. The problem at this point was knowing what to do in order to strengthen those defences.

Bergamo was one of the cities desperately trying to solve this new problem. The city lies ten miles north of Martinengo, and it was then, and is now, a much larger town than the latter. The present-day city is enclosed by intact city walls, called the Venetian Walls. These are, deservedly, a UNESCO World Heritage Site, but these walls were built in the second half of the 16th century, so they are not the walls that the young Gabriele was sent to work upon. However, the intact walls do give a marvellous sense of the results of a half century of experimentation in creating defences for the new age of gunpowder, experiments in which Gabriele played a huge role. In fact, there are few places that give a better sense of life in the 16th century than Bergamo's Città Alta (High Town). It's called Città Alta because it is. It sits upon hills that look down over Lombardy with a dramatic backdrop of the Alps behind the city. Getting to it nowadays requires either a reasonably strenuous, but worthwhile, walk up from the Città Bassa (Low Town) or a ride on the funicular that was installed in the 19th century.

There are four gates into the city, to the east, south, west and north. The busiest entrance to the city is through Porta Sant'Agostino, a gate which lies on the east side of the Città Alta. In the 1490s, when Gabriele arrived in Bergamo to begin his military studies, the gate was also the most travelled, since Bergamo was the major western outpost of Venice and it was through this gate that Venetian troops entered the city. With the main artery running east, to Venice, Porta Sant'Agostino naturally became the most important entrance to the city.

If you look at the map, you'll see that Bergamo is much closer to Milan than it is to Venice: Milan is 30 miles west; Venice is 130 miles to the east. And indeed, Bergamo had been under the control of the dukes of Milan in the early 1400s. Venice was founded upon trade in the Mediterranean and initially its attention was turned to the sea and the acquisition of its Stato da Màr, its maritime territories. However, from 1400 onwards, the Venetians decided that they had to get involved in the power politics of northern Italy, so under successive doges the Venetians expanded their influence inland, creating their Stato da Tera to accompany the Stato da Màr.

The competition between Venice and Milan triggered a series of wars, largely within Lombardy, that ended by balancing power between Venice, Milan, Florence, the Papal States and Naples. The smaller republics and duchies, such as Ferrara, Siena, Pisa and Mantua, lost their political influence, although the inhabitants and rulers of these smaller states chafed against their marginalisation and, should one of the dominant powers weaken, often seized the chance to increase their independence.

Bergamo, however, became a faithful part of Venice's Stato da Tera when the duke of Milan signed it over to Venice in 1428, remaining part of the Republic until Napoleon conquered Italy in 1797, bringing an end to the Venetian Republic.

With Milan so close, it's not surprising that the Bergamaschi, and their Venetian sponsors, wanted to improve the city's defences.

Although we don't have much information about the work that Tadino was involved with at the end of the 15th century, it's interesting to note that the sources say he was apprenticed to a French military engineer. This was after Charles VIII's conquest of Naples, when all the Italian states were scrambling to deal with the new reality of wall-bursting cannon that could be easily towed into place. At the start of this new reality, the French, who had brought the new age of warfare with them into Italy, were clearly seen as the innovators, and hence the Venetians employed a Frenchman to work on the defences of their sentinel city.

It would not be long, however, before Italians took first place as students of the new arts of war. This was because, over the next half century, they were going to get more practice at it than anywhere else in the world.

Gabriele clearly learned quickly from his French master since he was soon directly employed by the *comune*, the Bergamese civic authorities, as a technical assistant in the rebuilding of the city walls.

Tadino spent at least ten years in Bergamo, learning everything he could from his French master and any other experienced soldier or engineer whose knowledge and experience he could draw on.

In those years, the Italian Wars really got started.

Being part of Venice's Stato da Tera, the Bergamaschi were not involved in the fighting that took place in Italy between 1494 and 1504. Bergamo was, as mentioned above, close to Tadino's home town. Gabriele was close to family. To this day, it remains a fundamental assumption of most Italians that they have the right to live, work and die in their native town. Working in Bergamo, with Martinengo a three-hour walk away, Gabriele was living the life that came most naturally to all Italians.

And yet, in 1508, he left all that behind to enlist in the Venetian army.

The question arises, why?

Yes, there were reasons in the political situation in Italy. By 1508, Venice could no longer remain apart from the conflict in Italy. The War of the League of Cambrai lasted from February 1508 to December 1516. The constant combatants were Venice, the Papal States and France, but pretty well everyone else joined in at some point. So there was plenty of work for a soldier to do, and during war there were far greater chances of advancement and enrichment. Gabriele might therefore have decided to enlist purely to further his career.

However, if Tadino chose this path for ambition's sake, he had left it late: most *condottieri* were already experienced soldiers by their early 20s. Gabriele could easily have enlisted earlier.

Tadino went to Bergamo to learn the new arts of war. But the great rebuilding of the walls of Bergamo only happened after his death. There was not 15 years of work there for him to do, nor 15 years of learning.

The most likely reason for Tadino's long stay in Bergamo was that he was happy. It was close to his family. They spoke a dialect of Italian close to that spoken by the Martinenghesi, so the conversations he heard all around rang with a familiar music. By his early 20s he had learned everything that the French military engineer could teach him and, according to the records, he was then employed by the *comune* to work on strengthening the city's defences. When the War of the League of Cambrai started in 1508, Bergamo was on the front line. Although the initial attack came from Maximilian I, the Holy Roman Emperor, the Empire had allied itself to France (this would change!) and Bergamo was dangerously close to Milan, which was held by France. The Bergamaschi would have wanted Tadino to stay put and help in the defence of the city, and there would have been sound military reason for him to do so.

All this suggests that there was another reason for Tadino to leave Bergamo.

Information about Tadino's life before 1508 is sketchy. But after he left Bergamo, there is no indication that he ever married. There is no mention of illegitimate children and nothing in the records to suggest any involvement with women whatsoever.

Of course, one possibility is that Tadino was homosexual. However, if there were any rumours about his sexuality, his enemies would certainly have branded him a sodomite and used that charge against him. He could have been asexual but everything about his life tells of a man of strong passions and a highly romantic and chivalric nature: not the temperament of a man who feels little or no sexual attraction to others.

Tadino was 30 years old when he enrolled in the Venetian army and left Bergamo, never to return.

By 30, most men of some means had married.

My belief is that Tadino was no exception. But sometime before 1508, probably not long before, his wife died. As there is no record of any child, one possibility must be that she died in childbirth which, for women, was the equivalent of warfare for men: a dangerous rite of passage to full adulthood and acceptance within the body of the city.

Given what we know of Tadino's nature, it would not be at all surprising if the death of his wife and, possibly, a child as well made him vow to remain true to their memory for the rest of his life, eschewing all others. It's the sort of vow that fits well with his nature in other areas of his life.

If that were the case, it would also explain the almost suicidal bravery that Tadino would display throughout his career as a military engineer. He fought, in whatever situation he found himself, as if he had no fear of death. By that insouciance he survived much longer than he had any right to do.

So while there is no direct evidence in the sources for my hypothesis, it does explain much about his later life: a restless, constantly moving life without any deep or long lasting contacts with women, a life of a man who flirted constantly with death.

That flirtation started in earnest when he began his career as a soldier of Venice.

10

The Italian Wars Kick into High Gear

The road to war is paved with bad intentions.

The bad intention that really kicked the Italian Wars into higher gear was the desire by one of the local players, Ludovico Sforza, the Duke of Milan, to enlist one of the big boys on his side. In a move that was both characteristic and fateful, Sforza invited Maximilian I to intervene in Italian affairs as his ally. Maximilian was the Holy Roman Emperor; in effect, the king of Germany, although Germany didn't yet exist as a nation. By asking Maximilian to get involved in Italian affairs, Ludovico was looking for another sponsor in his own ambitions. But in his pursuit of short-term advantage over his domestic rivals, Ludovico and the other players in the game of dukes and doges among the Italian states were advertising both their domestic riches and their military weakness to the powers on the other side of the Alps. What made these invitations all the more dangerous for the Italian states was that they gave the king of France and the Holy Roman Emperor an arena in which to contend without incurring the risk of directly attacking each other's territories.

Although Ludovico did not realise it, he was creating a situation similar to the long confrontation of the Cold War, where a series of proxy wars were fought between allies and dependents of the USA and the Soviet Union, generally causing carnage in the country where the fighting was going on but allowing the sponsors of the fighting to avoid direct confrontation and too much damage. Think of the Vietnam War and the Soviet occupation of Afghanistan as examples.

Over the next half century, Italy was going to be the unwilling theatre for the confrontation between the major European powers.

Charles VIII of France died in 1498. Following his withdrawal, the French had lost control of Naples but his successor, Louis XII, held to the Valois claim to the throne of Naples and, like Charles, decided to pursue that claim by invading Italy.

In 1499, the French marched into Lombardy. Ludovico, realising too late the mistakes he had made, ordered Rocca d'Arazzo, a fortified town in the west of his dukedom, to resist the French invaders. But the French artillery blasted through the walls in five hours. Louis gave orders that the town's garrison and the senior leaders of the *comune*'s administration all be executed.

Faced with such a brutally efficient enemy, Ludovico's other strongholds quickly surrendered and Ludovico himself fled, taking refuge with, yes, Maximilian, the Holy Roman Emperor. The pieces of the game that would be played out for the next half century were falling into place.

King Louis XII rode into Milan on 6 October 1499 as its new ruler. It would not last.

During the Italian Wars, Milan became notorious as the city that everybody could conquer but nobody could keep. Indeed, so often did it change hands that, if it were Thursday in a new month, you might expect a different ruler to have been installed.

Milan's defensive weakness was the result of its natural advantages. It stands between the rivers Ticino and Adda, two important tributaries of the River Po, in the great flat reaches of the Po Valley. Any army marching into or out of Italy will pass Milan, but its exposed position means that it has no natural defences. But this central situation means that Milan could never be abandoned; it occupies too important a position. What made the city even less defensible were walls that were notoriously weak and suburbs that crowded up against them, making it relatively easy for besiegers to get over or through the walls.

However, Louis did not know that. Nor did the Florentines, who decided to ask for Louis's help to overcome the pesky Pisans, who had taken the opportunity offered by Charles's invasion of Italy to free themselves from Florentine domination.

While the French used their cannon to open breaches in the walls of Pisa, Louis was looking over the Pyrenees to his other rival for control of Naples: Ferdinand II, king of Aragon. It was the Spanish who had driven the French garrisons from Naples after Charles's invasion and Louis did not want to get into another conflict with them. For his part, Ferdinand also didn't want a war with France. Secret negotiations between the two crowns resulted in the signing of the Treaty of Granada on 11 November 1500. Under the terms of the treaty, France and Spain agreed to divide the Kingdom of Naples between them, with Louis taking Naples and its surrounds while Ferdinand would have Calabria and Apulia.

When the terms of the treaty were leaked, as the signatories no doubt intended, the news came as a dreadful shock to the man who thought of himself as the ruler of Naples, Frederick, the son of King Ferdinand I, who had ruled Naples for 36 years, from 1458 to 1494, when Naples became the greatest city in western Europe. Rather than contest the landing of the French army, Frederick fell back, relying on his lieutenants to hold the fortress town of Capua.

Now, we need to take a bit of a pause because what happens next is a good example of the treacherous complexity of these wars and how figures, infamous and famous, are interweaved with them.

In Rome, Alexander VI was pope, and had been since 1493. He's better known to legend as the Borgia pope. The Borgias were a Spanish family. As such, when Rodrigo took the chair of Peter as Alexander VI, he found himself set among long-established Italian families who had little love for this Iberian interloper. It was therefore not entirely surprising that Pope Alexander sought to promote men he could trust, and only a little less surprising that most of these men were his relatives. Most notoriously, he made his son, Cesare, a cardinal when Cesare was only 18.

However, Alexander decided that a military career would provide his son with more opportunities and in 1498, the pope released his son from his, admittedly lightly held, religious vows. Despite his Spanish origins, Alexander generally had good relations with the French, seeing them as useful allies against his domestic enemies, and Cesare accompanied Louis when he entered Milan in triumph. While not a member of the French command, Cesare worked as Louis's ally, helping to pacify resistance to the French in the areas of the Papal States abutting the Kingdom of Naples.

In July, the French army, with additional detachments of mercenaries seconded to them by Cesare Borgia, reached the fortress town of

Capua. The outer bastions were breached after four days and their defenders killed. The French then began bombarding the city walls.

The defenders, fearful for their situation, began negotiations towards their surrender, but the cannon kept shooting and, on 21 July, the cannon made a breach in the walls. The attackers poured into the city, sacking it and carrying out mass rapes.

With another example of French ruthlessness fresh before them, Neapolitan resistance crumbled and Louis's army took Naples on 12 October 1501.

But as before, relations with the Spanish quickly fell apart. War broke out in southern Italy between the French and the Spanish, with the Spanish expelling the French by the end of 1503. Thereafter, although the French crown continued to claim the kingdom until the concluding treaty of the Italian Wars was signed in 1559, Naples remained under Spanish rule for the next two centuries (it then seesawed back and forth between Austrian Habsburgs and the Bourbons, had a brief interlude under Revolutionary and Napoleonic France, before becoming the Kingdom of the Two Sicilies until finally becoming part of the unified Kingdom of Italy in 1861).

11

WHY EVERYONE WAS FIGHTING EVERYONE ELSE

In 1508, Gabriele Tadino, aged 30, rode off to war. He never really returned home. Even when, many years later, old and carrying the wounds and scars of more battles than he could possibly remember, he did go back to Martinengo, he could not settle there for long, and he took his final leave of a home that he had left many years previously.

Whatever personal reasons Tadino had to take his leave in 1508, there were also wider reasons for his decision. The Italian Wars had started 14 years earlier when Charles VIII invaded Italy. As Tadino rode away from Bergamo, he and everyone else would have been horrified to learn that the wars had another 45 years to run.

Despite being 30, Gabriele had had to ask his father, Clemente, for his permission and his blessing to enlist in the Venetian army. While to us this sounds unusual, it was not so at the time: while Clemente lived, he was the head of the family. As such, he had the authority to negotiate marriages for his children – marriages were familial contracts rather than partnerships between a man and a woman. As *paterfamilias*, his blessing was also necessary for Gabriele's change of career. Of course, Gabriele could simply ride off to war. But that would be to cut his ties to his family, thus losing the circle of contacts, patrons and patronage that Clemente had built up during a long life of looking after the people of Martinengo.

This was a world, not so dissimilar from our own, where who you knew and whether they would be willing to give you a break were vitally important. So if Gabriele wanted to make use of the familial contacts in Venice, he had no recourse but to ask his father's blessing.

These family contacts were considerable. Clemente Tadino had been the doctor to Bartolomeo Colleoni, one of the greatest of the *condottieri*, who finished his career as captain-general of Venice despite not being a native of the city but rather from a small town eight miles west of Bergamo. Bartolomeo Colleoni was a child of the Stato da Tera, the inland possessions of the Republic. While Colleoni died in 1475, Clemente remained doctor to his family, thus retaining his links with the higher echelons of Venetian society.

So when Clemente decided to allow his son, Gabriele, to enlist in the Venetian army, there was little danger of him being recruited as an ordinary soldier. Even without Clemente's letters of commendation, the Venetians would have offered Gabriele a good rank, for the Republic was always on the lookout for men of talent to enlist in her service.

In the event, Gabriele was recruited as a captain of infantry, while his particular talents and skills were recognised by his being rewarded with the salary due to an engineer.

It would not be long before Gabriele was earning his wages.

The series of wars that Tadino was about to enter, which came to be called the War of the League of Cambrai, was where the Italian Wars really earned their reputation for complexity, firstly from the number of combatants and secondly from the sheer amount of treachery and double-dealing that went on.

Firstly, the number of combatants really is unusual, particularly for a war that was largely limited to Italy. Let's list them:

- Republic of Venice
- Kingdom of France
- Papal States
- Holy Roman Empire
- Spanish Empire
- Duchy of Ferrara
- Scotland
- Florence
- Navarre
- Kingdom of England
- Swiss Confederacy
- Duchy of Milan

Of these, it's true some states, such as England and Scotland, didn't play a direct part in the fighting in Italy, but they still took part in the wider areas of the conflict. A number of the secret agreements signed during the conflict called upon a neighbouring country to invade an enemy to distract its attention from the conflict in Italy. So England was frequently approached by the enemies of France suggesting that it reclaim its territories in France and thus make the French pull back from Italy. France, for its part, attempted to use Scotland as a counterweight to the English threat, inviting the Scots to invade England to distract the English from invading France.

It was rather like a diplomatic game of rollover, where everyone was trying to push the country closest to the edge off the bed.

It's also true that some of the combatants dropped in and out of the conflict during the eight years that this phase of the Italian Wars lasted; only Venice, France, the Papal States and Ferrara fought on through the whole conflict.

But what's really confusing is the way people changed sides.

Deep breath.

Pope Julius II was the instigator of the League of Cambrai but switched sides after a couple of years. The Holy Roman Empire and the Spanish Empire also switched sides, joining with Venice against France. And then, just when you think you've got everything straight, Venice also switched sides, allying herself with France and against the Papal States, the Holy Roman Empire and Spanish Empire.

Never has a series of wars demonstrated naked political self-interest so clearly.

But it's this constant switching of sides that makes the Italian Wars so difficult to follow. People who were enemies one day become allies the next, only to start fighting against each other a few months later. It's almost impossible to keep track of everything.

But one person who did keep track of it all was the man who was in the thick of the fighting from the start: the pope, Julius II.

12

THE WARRIOR POPE

There have been 266 popes since Peter. Among all those men, it's hard to think of any who were less suited to the role of being a religious and spiritual leader than Julius II. But in 16th-century Rome, this wasn't necessarily a disadvantage. For the cardinals who elected the pope, the office of the papacy was far more a political role than a religious one, and as such it was an office that was fought over with influence, threats and, simplest of all, piles and piles of cash.

After all, whatever it cost to gain the seat of Peter could be earned back again once seated upon the Apostle's chair.

While Julius was not exactly a spiritual figure, among the run of frankly dreadful popes at this time, he stands as, at least, an effective if often ruthless ruler of the Papal States and enforcer of papal authority. Julius II was a warrior far more than he was a priest. Indeed, it was widely believed that he spent more of his time as pope wearing armour than wearing clerical vestments, personally leading the soldiers of the Papal States into battle on a number of occasions.

But despite his almost total lack of interest in religious matters, Julius II would prove one of the most significant of the Renaissance popes (few of which, it is true, spent much time on their prayers).

Julius was born Giuliano della Rovere on 5 December 1443 into a family whose blood was considerably richer than its finances. However, Giuliano's uncle, Francesco della Rovere, was elected pope in 1471, becoming Sixtus IV,[7] and the possibilities for Giuliano to follow a clerical career suddenly became much brighter – and more lucrative.

Uncle Francesco made his nephew a bishop two months after taking office and a cardinal two months later. Within the next two years, Sixtus made his nephew an archbishop as well as bishop of no fewer than eight other provinces. The della Roveres were no longer poor.

Although Giuliano showed no interest in the spiritual duties of the bishoprics that funnelled him money, what he did love was art. Now, with the funds to finance his love of art, Giuliano began what would be a lifelong passion: the commissioning of works of art and the patronage of artists. This was a warrior who loved beauty and who was willing to pay for it. Such was his interest and passion for art that he could fairly be called an equal collaborator in the extraordinary artistic endeavours that marked his pontificate.

Influence in Renaissance Rome was generally tied to family connections, but when Uncle Francesco died in 1484, Giuliano avoided the fall that often accompanied the loss of such a patron. Having lobbied hard for Giovanni Battista Cibo at the enclave, Giuliano became one of the chief advisors of Pope Innocent VIII.

When Innocent died in 1492, Giuliano might reasonably have expected to be elected as the next pope. He had done well under Innocent, making a name for himself as a decisive leader and one who was more than willing to lead his men personally into battle. What's more, Giuliano was the favoured candidate for the French and their allies, the Republic of Genoa. Indeed, the rumour was that Charles VIII (the king of France who would two years later invade Italy) had invested 200,000 ducats to ensure Giuliano's election, with an additional 100,000 ducats coming from Genoa.

In the event, though, even these huge sums were insufficient to buy the papacy for Giuliano. It went, instead, to his enemy, Rodrigo Borgia, who reigned as Alexander VI.

With Alexander VI in charge, life in Rome became dangerous for Giuliano, more so when Alexander started to plan his assassination.

To save himself, Giuliano fled to France and the court of King Charles VIII. He accompanied Charles during his invasion of Italy in 1494, hoping that the French king would depose the Spanish pope and install him in his place.

When Charles's successor, Louis XII, attempted his own invasion of Italy in 1502, Giuliano was again part of the expedition, avoiding Pope Alexander's attempts to take him captive and rid himself of this troublesome rival. Although Louis's invasion was unsuccessful,

Alexander's death in 1503 opened the way for Giuliano's return to Rome. However, Giuliano failed to win the papacy at the conclave that took place in September 1503, losing to Cardinal Francesco Todeschini. Todeschini took the regnal name Pius III but he died just 26 days after being elected pope.

Since Pius III's reign was so short, all the cardinal electors were still in or near Rome, allowing for the new conclave to elect his successor to gather at once.

This time, Giuliano took no chances: he made promises to everyone he needed on his side, and employed bribery where promises were insufficient.

His efforts were successful. The conclave, which took only ten hours to elect him, was one of the shortest on record. To ensure that no future pontiff could acquire the pontificate as he had, Giuliano promptly outlawed simony (the buying of clerical office) when applied to the election of a pope.

Giuliano della Rovere was now the 216th bishop of Rome and holder of the keys of Peter. As with other popes, Giuliano would not reign under his own name but take a regnal name: Julius. There was a Julius I, a rather obscure 4th-century pontiff, but no one in Rome believed that Giuliano named himself for him, but rather for the more famous Julius associated with Rome.

As Pope Julius II, Giuliano had twin aims: to restore the Papal States and to beautify and magnify Rome.

At the start of his pontificate, that meant taking back from Venice the cities that the Republic had acquired following the death of Alexander VI. To that end, Julius set about forming the League of Cambrai with Louis XII, the king of France, Ferdinand II, the king of Spain, and Maximilian I, the Holy Roman Emperor. Publicly, the League was supposed to be a prelude to launching a grand crusade against the rising power of the Ottoman Turks. Privately, it was geared towards carving bits out of Venice's Stato da Tera and sharing these out among the members of the League.

To that end, Pope Julius personally took command of his soldiers on many occasions and, almost as often, led them into battle, clad in shining armour. Even in the 16th century, when the popes were acknowledged as temporal powers as well as spiritual leaders, Julius's fondness for battle raised many eyebrows.

These doubts were expressed most wittily in a dialogue published in 1514, shortly after Julius's death. The dialogue, *Iulius exclusus e coelis* (*Julius excluded from heaven*), is generally attributed to the Dutch humanist Erasmus, although Erasmus never acknowledged his authorship.

In the dialogue, the lately dead Pope Julius arrives at the gates of heaven with the souls of the soldiers who had died in his battles and demands entrance from St Peter. St Peter, in Catholic belief, was entrusted by Jesus with the keys to the kingdom of heaven and he is frequently depicted as the door ward of heaven.

At first, Julius attempts to open the gate of heaven with the key that unlocks his chest of money. When that fails, he calls on Peter to open the gates but Peter refuses. Julius points out that he is the pope – in fact, he still is the pope, even though he is dead, because the conclave has not yet chosen his successor. Thus he has the right to enter heaven.

When Peter continues to refuse him entry, Julius first threatens him with his soldiers and then with excommunication. When Peter does not open the gate, Julius points out that Peter did far less with his life than he has: all Peter did was go about preaching, whereas he, Julius, has restored the papacy to glory, adorning it with beautiful buildings and rich treasures, making the pope the supreme monarch on earth.

When Peter points out that Julius can only enter heaven if he is free from sin, Julius attempts to justify his sins, arguing that even if he did any of the things of which is accused, as pope he has the authority to forgive those sins and he has, so therefore he should be allowed to enter heaven.

When Peter finally loses patience with the complete lack of remorse shown by Julius, he drives the pope away from the gates. However Julius, never one to accept a reverse, ends the dialogue by considering how to make his own heaven as a base from which he could eventually launch the conquest of the real heaven.

Julius excluded from heaven became, not surprisingly, a favourite text of Martin Luther. However, while it excoriates Pope Julius in particular, he was not personally guilty of all the long litany of sins of which he is accused: in the dialogue, Julius is used as the singular identity for the collective failings of the Renaissance popes. For instance, there's no indication that Julius was a pederast, although he is assumed to be one in the dialogue.

While his deeds in the field of war acquired notoriety, they were, nonetheless, effective in achieving the aims Julius set for himself.

Having reacquired the parts of the Romagna that Venice had taken from the Papal States, Julius decided to join forces with Venice to drive the now over-mighty French from Italy, switching sides to fight against his former League partner.

In this, Julius was successful, persuading the emperor to switch sides too so that, with Venice, they fought against the French, greatly helped by detachments of Swiss mercenaries whom Julius later recruited to form the Swiss Guards that remain the pope's protectors to this day.

Having achieved many of his key political aims, Julius was free to pursue his other great passion: art. Julius loved beauty, both in itself but also as a statement of magnificence for himself and for his church. Even as a cardinal he had been a great patron of the arts. As pope, he became possibly the most important artist patron in history.

13

THE PATRON POPE

While Julius was notorious among his contemporaries for his military exploits, he left another legacy.

The art that Julius commissioned and sponsored was his most lasting memorial and one that endures to this day.

It might seem strange that such a militant man should be so concerned with beauty. But Julius saw his responsibility as ensuring the temporal security of the church while enhancing its grandeur through works of art and architecture. To that end, he formed long-lasting partnerships with three of the greatest artists of the era: the architect Donato Bramante, Michelangelo and Raphael.

By the start of the 16th century, St Peter's Basilica in Rome had fallen into considerable disrepair. This basilica had been built following the conversion of Emperor Constantine to Christianity and was completed by about 360. Having been built over the reputed tomb of St Peter himself, it soon became a major pilgrimage site while being richly endowed with treasures and relics. However, the church was outside the old walls of Rome, leaving it vulnerable to raiders, and in 846 a Saracen army did exactly that. To protect this quarter of the city, Pope Leo IV built the Leonine Wall in the 9th century.

However, in the general turbulence of the following centuries, St Peter's Basilica became gradually more and more unkempt, falling into semi-ruin during the nearly 70 years when the papacy moved to Avignon in France because Rome had become too dangerous. Following the return of the papacy, desultory plans to repair the basilica were put in place, but the architects contracted to do so reported that the building had become structurally unsound.

Of course, the old St Peter's could have been repaired. And perhaps that was what Pope Julius originally intended. But when he looked at plans that had been prepared for a previous pope, Nicholas V, for an entirely new St Peter's, Julius saw the possibility to create the greatest church on earth, to the glory of the church and the immortality of his own name. What's more, the tomb that Julius had commissioned for himself, to be built by Michelangelo, wouldn't actually fit inside the old St Peter's. He needed a new church for that.

Julius commissioned Donato Bramante, who had worked for him before, to design a new St Peter's and on 18 April 1506, Julius laid the foundation stone for the new building.

Never one to let sentiment stand in the way of glory, Julius ordered the demolition of the old St Peter's Basilica. While it may have been tottering, the old church was aglow with mosaics and frescoes, including a vast mosaic by Giotto of Jesus walking on the water and summoning Peter to come to him that covered the whole of the wall above the entrance arcade. Within the basilica Giotto had painted further frescoes of scenes from the life of Jesus set among exquisite mosaics.

Almost all of these were lost when the old St Peter's was demolished.

It's some recompense that the new St Peter's would prove to be a work of genius. But, for myself, I would have wished the old St Peter's to have been repaired and preserved.

But the fact that Pope Julius and the artists and architects around him were prepared to countenance the demolition of a building so vested with history demonstrates the extraordinary confidence they had in what they were going to build. These were men convinced of their artistic vision: they were bringing the glories of antiquity into their present-day world but making something even greater than the Romans had done.

In Rome, the shadow of the past empire lay long. Men walked daily among its ruins and lamented its lost power and prestige. But where old Rome had been the temporal power of the world, new Rome was the spiritual power and, by building a church that united the imperial past with the church's present, Julius was making that statement in stone – stone that would endure as a testament to his own glory and the grandeur of the church.

While Pope Julius laid the foundation stone for the new St Peter's, he did not live to see it completed. Nor did he learn of the controversy that the funding arrangements his successors entered into to continue building the church produced – controversy that eventually contributed to the schism of the Reformation.

Was the glory of the new church worth the deformation to the body of the church brought about by the Reformation? No. And in fact, the new church for all its grandeur stands as testament to some of the practices that broke apart the body of Christendom. Walk into Notre Dame or York Minster and you stand in a building that bears stone witness to a unified Christian vision of the world. Walk into St Peter's and you are part of a very different vision. The proponents of the Renaissance labelled the work of the Middle Ages 'Gothic' not as a compliment but as an insult: it was shorthand for the art of barbarians. The art of the Renaissance was a self-conscious return to the rediscovered principles of Classical antiquity that overlapped with the Christian vision mainly in its emphasis on humanity – it was a Christianity of the second part of the Golden Rule – thou shall love thy neighbour as thyself – with a particular emphasis on loving oneself.

Of course, the Reformers for their part stripped even this beauty away in their emphasis on the plain, unvarnished Word. There is a sober splendour to Protestant churches but none of the wild power of beauty to unlock the soul.

This uniquely Italian vision had power but not the endurance of the old barbarian art, running through to its conclusion in Mannerism and then its dissolution in the arts of the 19th century much faster than the old, less self-conscious art.

The other two artists with whom Pope Julius II is indelibly linked manifest this revolution and this short-lived apotheosis more clearly than any others: Michelangelo and Raphael.

Pope Julius met Michelangelo in 1506 and the two men, despite their fierce and often clashing temperaments, became in effect co-workers. The greatest fruit of their collaboration is the roof of the Sistine Chapel. It was not a job Michelangelo wanted. When Pope Julius first approached him, he refused, on the basis that he was primarily a sculptor (although Michelangelo proved able to turn his hand to painting, architecture and poetry too). What was worse, from Michelangelo's slightly paranoid point of view, it also seemed that he was being set up to fail by his rivals: the roof of the chapel was a huge area and to cover it with frescoes would daunt even the most confident of artists. However, Julius, never a man to take no for an answer, managed to bulldoze even Michelangelo – who was not known for his malleability – into taking on the commission.

The work took him four years – surprisingly fast for such a mammoth undertaking – and it revolutionised Western art. It's not hard to see why. Compare the frescoes of the Sistine Chapel with those, painted by Giotto, in the Scrovegni Chapel in Padua and it is clear that we are in a new world of art. Giotto achieves a balance of the human and the spiritual, placing the characters in his paintings in the cool blue of the empyrean, figures that are part of the great chain of being that stretches from the heavens, unmoved above the turning world, down to the humblest donkey. Michelangelo's figures on the other hand burst from the restraints of the ordered world, twisting and turning, positively pulsating with a life and vigour that is not drawn from some higher realm but explodes from within. The famous fresco of God creating Adam is not so much a creation as God lighting the blue touchpaper and then stepping back before the man bomb explodes in his face. It is a view of man as the measure of all things: supremely confident and overweeningly arrogant.

It's a different world.

As for Raphael, Julius was originally going to keep the paintings he commissioned from the young Raphael for himself: they were to decorate his apartment in the Vatican. The Raphael Rooms, or *Stanze* as they are called in Italian, feature large-scale frescoes by Raphael and, after his death, his pupils. These pictures are no less dramatic than Michelangelo's but there is a quality of serenity to them that is missing from the titanic figures on the chapel ceiling. This is shown perhaps most clearly in Raphael's painting of the deliverance of St Peter from prison. Here, the light of heaven, brought by the angel freeing St Peter from his chains, drives away the dark shadows of earthly existence, freeing Peter from the chains in which he is being held. It is a sublime painting that still holds something of the harmony of the medieval vision within its conception of man as the measure of all things.

Apart from his frescoes in the Stanze, Raphael also painted the best known portrait of Pope Julius. Raphael carried out the commission sometime between June 1511 and March 1512. We know this because it portrays Julius with a full beard: he grew the beard in mark of mourning for having lost the city of Bologna during the wars of the League of Cambrai. For most of his life, Julius was clean shaven.

In the portrait, Julius sits pensively upon his chair, eyes cast down: an old man lost in memory and, perhaps, regret. An old warrior reflecting on battles won and battles lost; a prelate thinking on the judgement that waits. In the portrait, Raphael humanises and personalises a man who might otherwise seem a monster of ambition and pride.

In this, Raphael epitomises the Renaissance. The great portraits of medieval art are portraits of types: the mosaics of Justinian and Theodora in the basilica of Ravenna, the great icon of Christ Pantocrator from St Catherine's Monastery on Mount Sinai, the exquisite Wilton Diptych painted in 1400. All of these are sublime but they are also impersonal. They looked through and beyond the individual to the eternal and the archetype.

The art of the Renaissance braked hard, and stopped at the individual, in all his or her unique particularity. It was the art of Aristotle rather than the art of Plato, it was the art of the here and now rather than the unchanging present. As such, it was the perfect art for a new age.

Like all new ages, it was inaugurated with hope and confidence, and then deteriorated into intrigue, disappointment and treachery. Nowhere was this more pronounced than Italy, the birthplace of the Renaissance and the arena for the first wars that the new age unleashed.

14

First Blood at Agnadello

Pope Julius had become increasingly annoyed with Venetian encroachment upon territory that he considered part of the papal patrimony. However, Venice had become a formidable military power on land and Julius knew that his own forces were not sufficient to reclaim the territories and cities that the Venetians had taken from him. The pope was not alone in his annoyance at Venetian expansion: the French and the Empire were similarly concerned.

So long as the Venetians had concentrated their efforts on their maritime empire, the Stato da Màr, her rival powers in Italy were willing to allow her a relatively free hand. But as the Venetians expanded the territory they controlled in the Stato da Tera, her Italian rivals became increasingly concerned. Chief among these rivals was Pope Julius.

But even Pope Julius required some sort of pretext before waging war on Venice. He found that pretext in the crusade. In Europe, the idea and ideals of crusading still held some power in the popular and even the political imagination. Successive popes still dreamed and preached of organising a final crusade to free the Holy Land from the domination of the Turk. So when emissaries of Pope Julius, the Kingdom of France, the Spanish and the Holy Roman empires got together in December 1508, the League that they signed up to had, as its public aim, a crusade against the Ottomans. Making a crusade against the Turks the declared aim of the League gave it a legitimacy that it would not otherwise possess.

But behind the public words, there was a private agreement: Pope Julius, King Louis, King Ferdinand and Emperor Maximilian had agreed to carve up Venice's possessions on the mainland among themselves: the agreement even set out who would get what. As a carrot to get other powers to join the League, they also offered some of Venice's maritime possessions to the Kingdom of Hungary and the Duchy of Savoy. In the event, they didn't sign up as members of the League of Cambrai.

As for the Venetians, they had begun to suspect that a conspiracy against them was brewing. In 1508, the Republic set about building up its army and it was as part of this build-up that Gabriele Tadino entered the army of Venice, employed initially as a captain of infantry and given the salary of an engineer. It was clear that, from the outset, the Republic was minded to make use of Gabriele's particular set of talents.

But first, they needed men to fight. So Gabriele marched with his company to form part of the Venetian army defending the Republic against the most formidable of its enemies: the Kingdom of France.

By 15 April 1509, the French, led by the king, Louis XII, were ready. Louis had amassed a considerable army: 2,300 lances and 20,000 infantry as well as his artillery. More than a quarter of the infantry was composed of Swiss pikemen whose service was bought by the French crown.

To face the French, the Venetians had assembled a considerable army of their own: 1,650 men-at-arms and 22,000 infantry. The infantry was somewhat diluted by including 9,000 militia, although it was bolstered by mounted 'crossbowmen' (who might wield arquebuses rather than crossbows) and *stradioti*, mercenary troops recruited from the Balkans.

The French strategy was to bring the Venetian army to battle. By contrast, the Venetians opted to pursue a strategy of delay, blocking and diversion; they aimed to defend the heartlands of the Stato da Màr by harassing and skirmishing with the French. Well aware that the French were seeking a decisive battle, part of the strategy was to lead Louis on a merry dance through the countryside, dangling the prospect of battle in front of him but then slipping away before he could bring his army to bear. Unfortunately for the Venetians, they had entrusted command of the army to cousins, both of the Orsini family, of whom one cousin agreed with the strategy, while the other, Bartolomeo d'Alviano, didn't. A divided command is generally a recipe for military disaster. It was in this case.

Disaster caught up with the Venetians on 14 May.

Harassing and skirmishing required the Venetians to remain in close enough contact with the advancing French that they could draw the French to where the Venetians wanted them to go. However, on that morning the Venetian rearguard had spread out and the French advance guard, centred on the village of Agnadello, caught up with them.

The French attacked. Bartolomeo d'Alviano, hearing the sound of the engagement, rushed back to find out what was happening. Remember, by this time armies were using artillery and guns, called arquebuses, so the sound of battle spread much further than it would have done in the days before gunpowder weapons. He arrived to find his rearguard in position behind a dry river bed, under fire from the French artillery but holding their positions.

This was the chance Bartolomeo had been waiting for. After a month of scuttling around the Italian countryside, flirting with battle, here was the chance. The forces were even: the Venetian rearguard against the French advance guard. In neither case was the main body of the army in position. But what Bartolomeo did not take account of was the fact that the main body of the French army was marching towards the battle, whereas the main body of the Venetian army was marching away from the battle. He sent a message ahead to his cousin and joint commander, Niccolò di Pitigliano, asking him to bring his forces back to join the battle. But Niccolò, mindful of the strategy that they were supposed to be avoiding engaging the French in battle, replied simply to advise cousin Bartolomeo to do so and kept on marching south.

In Agnadello, the situation for the Venetians had sharply deteriorated. Bartolomeo had attacked with his men-at-arms, pushing the Swiss mercenaries back, but then the main body of the French army, with Louis, joined the battle.

Bartolomeo's attack was surrounded and annihilated. Bartolomeo's horse was killed from under him. Undaunted, Bartolomeo continued fighting on foot but was overwhelmed and taken prisoner.

In this, he was one of the fortunate few. King Louis had given orders not to take prisoners but, as a commander of the enemy army, Bartolomeo was a valuable hostage. The ordinary soldiers were not so fortunate.

The battle turned into a rout, the French cutting down the Venetians as they fled. Although the main body of the army, marching with Niccolò di Pitigliano, survived, the Venetians still lost thousands of men, killed and wounded. When news of the disaster reached Niccolò's part of the army, it caused such dismay that many men deserted, returning to their home cities. Those who remained retreated towards Venice.

With the army opposing him having melted away, Louis was easily able to occupy the areas of Lombardy that he claimed for his own and which the secret annex of the League of Cambrai had allotted to him.

The Battle of Agnadello was a disaster for Venice. Machiavelli, writing about it in *The Prince*, said that in a single day the Venetians had 'lost what it had taken them eight hundred years' exertion to conquer'.[8]

Gabriele Tadino's first experience of battle was one of unmitigated disaster. Given that he survived the battle, it's likely that he and his company were with Niccolò di Pitigliano rather than among Bartolomeo's rearguard. However, while his first battle had shown him first hand the danger inherent in an overbold general, he seems not to have taken that as the lesson he learned from it: through the rest of his career, Gabriele would always, when the option was presented to him, decide to attack rather than to wait. For while much of the blame for the defeat was placed upon Bartolomeo, there were those who found Niccolò at fault for refusing to return. Indeed, at the start of the engagement, it had seemed that Bartolomeo would prevail: his attack brought him near to the French king himself. It was the untimely arrival of French reinforcements that doomed the Venetians.

15

THE SIEGE OF PADUA

The Venetian defeat at the Battle of Agnadello was disastrous, but some hard-headed Venetian calculations in the months afterwards stopped it from turning into a calamity.

The first step was to try to drive a wedge into the League of Cambrai. The French, the Empire, the Spanish and the pope were uneasy bedfellows, united only by their shared desire to take territory from the Venetians.

The Venetians took a careful look at what these territories were and decided that they were willing to sacrifice the land that the pope wanted and the Neapolitan ports that the Spanish wanted in order to concentrate on the defence of the Venetian heartlands and the city itself.

With their war aims satisfied, Pope Julius and King Ferdinand had both got what they desired from the League. However, neither could simply leave the League just like that – but they could make sure that they were slow to any other fights. Besides, neither party had any wish to see France and the Empire destroy Venice and carve up Lombardy between them.

With their southern flank now secure, the Venetians could turn their attention to defending the rest of the Stato da Tera.

Not wanting to be left out of the carve-up of Venetian territory, the emperor, Maximilian I, had enlisted mercenaries, the *Landsknechte* of Germany. His army had marched south into Italy and, in June 1509, they had captured the city of Padua. Padua lies just over 20 miles west of Venice: its gateway. The Venetians, if they were to hold their city, could not allow the Empire to keep Padua.

The Venetians had appointed the experienced merchant and diplomat Andrea Gritti as the *provedittore generale* of their field army. An unusual choice on the face of it as Gritti, while accomplished in the politics of the Sublime Porte, where he had acted as the Venetian *bailo*, came into the job with no military experience whatsoever. However, Gritti proved to be a worthy choice. He managed to escape from the disaster at Agnadello with the Banner of St Mark, the patron saint of the city, and rallied the Venetians. The greater part of the army had survived the battle, while the behaviour of the French was quickly turning the peasant farmers of the Stato da Tera, who had previously chafed under Venetian rule, into a dangerous partisan force.

Padua had found Venetian rule similarly stifling but, perhaps not entirely surprisingly, the Paduans found that swapping Venetian rule for a group of mercenary *Landsknechte* was not an enjoyable experience: Emperor Maximilian I was always low on money and was always late in paying his mercenaries. When payment was delayed, the *Landsknechte* extorted payments from the Paduans.

Venetian rule began not to look so bad after all.

So when, on 17 July, Andrea Gritti led a force of Venetians that included Gabriele to Padua, they found the Paduans ready to open the gates to them. The *Landsknechte* who remained in the city retreated to the fortress but soon surrendered. The Venetians had the gateway to their city back under their control.

In Padua, Gritti took measures to ensure the support of the city against the inevitable Imperial counter-attack. Some 300 people he suspected of anti-Venetian sentiment were expelled from the city. But at the same time he imposed strict discipline on the Venetian troops; anyone robbing, extorting or raping the locals was severely punished.

Gritti had quickly recognised the value of the peasant partisans and was determined that his own men should not undermine their loathing of the foreign invaders. As it was, any German or French soldiers making their way through the countryside quickly learned that they only dared move in groups. Single soldiers going foraging seldom returned.

Gritti had two months to prepare the city for the Imperial counter-attack. On 15 September, Imperial and French forces placed Padua under siege.

Gabriele Tadino was among the garrison, working with a *condottiero* named Citolo da Perugia. Although their association was short, Citolo would have a profound effect upon Gabriele's future. As part of the preparations for the siege, the engineers oversaw the building of embankments within the walls to reinforce them and enable them to better withstand artillery bombardment; the walls themselves were lowered too. In the areas where the walls would be most exposed to artillery fire, they put up new earth bastions with wooden palisades to provide firing points for the city's cannon, as well as digging new moats inside and outside the walls.

To defend the city, Gritti had reinforced the garrison. There were 14,000 infantry, 500 men-at-arms, 600 mounted crossbowmen (although recorded as crossbowmen these were just as likely to use arquebuses as crossbows) and 950 *stradiots*. Along with these professional soldiers, much of the Venetian nobility deployed to Padua too. Their presence at the siege demonstrated the commitment of La Serenissima to defend the city. To further encourage the defenders, the Signoria told them that they were being watched by the whole world.

The Venetian defenders also keenly felt the sting of their ignominious defeat at Agnadello. This was a chance to redeem the honour of Venetian arms.

However, Emperor Maximilian saw the siege as a matter of his honour too. King Louis of France had covered himself in glory at the Battle of Agnadello. This was a time when royal honour was not a hollow word but a real concept: kings still led upon the battlefield and their standing among the monarchs of Christendom rose or fell according to how they acquitted themselves in the theatre of arms. Emperor Maximilian embarked upon the siege intent on accruing similar honour to his name.

As part of the psychological preparations for the siege, Maximilian ensured that exaggerated rumours of the size of his army were spread: tales told of more than 60,000 men converging upon Padua.

In reality, the emperor's army was much smaller: roughly of the same order as the defenders. Given that a rough rule of thumb requires the attacker to have a three to one advantage over the defender, Maximilian was undermanned.

However, this was to ignore his artillery.

Cannon had decisively changed the battlefield, giving the advantage to the attacker, and Maximilian could reasonably expect his excellent artillery to wreak havoc upon the walls of Padua, opening breaches through which his army could break. However, Maximilian's army was composed of a larger group of German *Landsknechte* and a smaller contingent of French soldiers, neither of whom spoke each other's language and between whom there was at best rivalry and at worst outright conflict. It was not a recipe for coordinated action.

The siege began on 15 September.

French and German cannon started firing on the walls of Padua, looking to make breaches in the city's defences. While the defenders were preoccupied with trying to make running repairs on the walls, one group of Imperial troops managed to divert the water from the River Bacchiglione, which acted as a moat at one of the city's gates, the Porta di San Croce, and forced an entrance through the gate.

It was Citolo da Perugia, with Gabriele among the 300 infantrymen alongside him, who pushed back the Imperial assault and regained control of the gate.

With this attack repulsed, the Imperial troops began an intense bombardment of the walls, concentrating their fire on the Codalunga stretch of defences. By the end of September, the cannon had succeeded in making a significant breach in the walls there: big enough for an assault to push through.

However, the defenders did not wait idly for the attack. Knowing where the attack would aim for, Citolo and Gabriele took advantage of the lull between the breach being made and the attack being carried out to devise a daring plan. They did this despite Citolo having been injured in the leg by artillery shrapnel. Seeing his colleague act despite being injured, Gabriele would throughout his career similarly shrug off injuries and carry on.

During the night, they crept towards the breach. Under cover of the dark sky, they carefully scooped out pits from the tumbled piles of stone and pushed barrels of gunpowder into the pits. They then covered them over while ensuring that the long fuses they had laid were within reach.

They also mined the area immediately inside the breach, while setting up arquebusiers and cannon to overlook the breach from quickly erected retrenchments put up to try to turn the area into a killing zone.

At daybreak, the assault came. Five *Fähnlein* (literally 'flag' but signifying a battalion or company) of *Landsknechte*, some 7,500 men, attacked the breach in the walls. The emperor had promised 5,000 ducats as a reward to the company that successfully took the breach and opened up the city to his troops.

But as the *Landsknechte* struggled through the breach, scrambling over the tumbled masonry and rock, the arquebusiers and cannoneers placed behind the hastily thrown up retrenchments opened fire upon Citolo's order. The fire wave cut down the first rank of *Landsknechte*. The second rank bunched up behind the survivors taking cover from the Venetian fire.

That was when Citolo gave his next order.

Tapers, ready and prepared, were put to the fuses trailing through the rock dust. Spark snakes twisted among the rocks and then disappeared under ground. Those *Landsknechte* close enough to see the fire trails, knowing what was about to happen, tried to fall back, but they were held by the second wave advancing upon them.

Then the mines exploded.

Gabriele Tadino saw first-hand the devastating effect of properly prepared mines upon an advancing enemy. Three hundred *Landsknechte* were killed, another 400 injured so severely that they could take no further part in the siege.

Taking advantage of the chaos and confusion caused by the explosion of the mines, Citolo and Gabriele led a counter-attack. With the men at their command, they sallied through the breach, crossed the ditch, striking down stragglers as the *Landsknechte* fell back in dismay, and attacked the enemy cannon on the far side of the ditch, destroying seven artillery pieces before falling back in good order.

For Emperor Maximilian, the failure of the assault was devastating. Always short of money, the cost of the siege had been like tipping barrels of money over a waterfall. He had gambled everything upon a quick ending to the siege and taking Padua by assault.

When that failed, Maximilian attempted to bargain with his mercenaries, promising them the proceeds of the sack of the city should they stay. But having suffered such devastating losses, the leaders of the *Landsknechte* knew that the siege would be long and hard.

If the emperor could not pay them, they would not continue to fight on promises.

Maximilian faced another problem too: he did not have enough horses. Horses were vital for transporting the heavy, cumbersome and expensive siege cannon to and from battle and Maximilian only had enough to move half his siege train at a time. What made a decision more pressing was the memory of how difficult it had been to transport the siege cannon through the Alps in summer, when the roads were at their best. The emperor knew well how much more treacherous the roads would become once the autumn rains started in earnest. Leave things too late and he might lose half or more of his cannon. One eyewitness reported that Maximilian had brought between 60 and 80 cannon to the siege. This was a very large number of cannon and a huge investment in money: the emperor could not afford to lose them.

So, on 30 September, after a little over two weeks, Emperor Maximilian lifted the siege of Padua and withdrew with his army.

Gabriele learned a great deal from Citolo during the siege of Padua: he learned of the value of mines and how, when used at the correct moment, they could prove decisive. He learned how to defend breaches in the outer walls by the swift placement of retrenchments and how to position these to enable enfilading fire. Enfilading, or flanking, fire allows the defender to direct their weapons along the long axis of the advancing enemy. That way, it becomes easier to hit the enemy and any shot, particularly by cannon, is likely to cause many more casualties.

Approaching the breach, the attacking *Landsknechte* had no choice but to bunch together in order to get through the breach. Coming out of the breach, they began to spread, but so long as the flanking fire caught them early enough, the defenders still had an easy group of targets.

But apart from these principles of defence, Gabriele also learned from Citolo the value of a commander leading his men in person. Citolo was always in the thick of the fighting, personally leading the counter-attack that did such damage to the emperor's prized artillery.

Reckless courage in the face of the enemy was to be characteristic of Gabriele Tadino throughout the rest of his career.

16

Whispers and Gossip

Gabriele Tadino's courage and determination during the defence of Padua increased his reputation with Venice. But with greater renown came a higher profile, which did not always redound to Gabriele's benefit.

There was a considerable amount of competition among the Italian city states to recruit the best and most able *condottieri*. And there was also competition between the *condottieri* to ensure their own advancement and to do down rivals.

Condottieri hawked out their services to the various combatants in the Italian Wars based on their own track record and the number and abilities of the men they brought with them: a captain who had a track record of victories and a company of several hundred experienced soldiers could command higher wages than a less illustrious captain with fewer men.

But to recruit soldiers to their companies, *condottieri* had to display a number of qualities: they had to be reasonably successful in battle (no one wanted to fight for a captain who lost more battles than he won) and they needed to be able to pay their men. So having a contract with a state that paid promptly and according to the agreed terms was vital for the success of a *condottiero*: without his payment, he could not pay his men. Soldiers were willing to wait a while for payment from a captain they trusted, but they would not wait forever, particularly when there were other captains ready to wave ducats under their noses in return for their service.

Among the most successful and sought after of the *condottieri* plying their trade at this time was Renzo da Ceri, who came originally from Lazio in the Papal States. Indeed, Renzo had been in the pay of Pope Julius before coming over to the Venetians in 1510 (the pope considered Renzo's transfer a useful signal of his commitment to the Holy League he was intent on forming against the French, which made him willing to pay the transfer fee necessary to recruit Renzo).

Among the men who enlisted with Renzo after he took the Serenissima's coin was Gabriele Tadino. He was paid as a *lancia spezzata* (which translates as 'broken spear' but means a freelance soldier of higher rank than the common run of mercenary troops). Indeed, Tadino was sufficiently well thought of that Renzo was willing to countenance his plan of a surprise attack on Verona, so by this stage Tadino was beginning to figure among the rank of lieutenants operating just below the major *condottieri* captains.

Verona had fallen to the French. To take it back, Tadino mooted a surprise assault on Verona, one in which his men would quickly scale the walls of the city with a large number of siege ladders that he had had made. It was a bold plan, not to say foolhardy, but one that relied absolutely on the element of surprise. When a deserter betrayed his plan, Tadino wisely decided to call off the attack.

It's likely that Tadino had acquired a small band of his own men at this point, men whom it was his responsibility to pay and lead. As we will see later, these men were Bergamaschi, men from his home district who had found in Gabriele a leader whom they trusted.

Still enlisted with Renzo da Ceri in 1511, Gabriele took part in the defence of Treviso against the French in September and October of that year.

But it is clear that Gabriele was beginning to attract increasing notice from other men who were also seeking advancement, for at this point he became the target of a whispering campaign directed towards the authorities in Venice.

These accusations went as far as the Council of Ten, the second-highest tier of administrative power in the Republic, below only the Signoria and the Doge himself. That the accusations should reach the Council of Ten was particularly dangerous for Gabriele as this was the Venetian government body most concerned with rooting out espionage and dealing with anti-government plots. Although officially subordinate to the Signoria it could act on its own authority in matters relating to the security of the state.

Tadino was accused of shirking his work and not fulfilling the duties mandated of him, spreading lies against the Signoria and conspiring to desert to the enemy. These were serious charges and while there is no indication that the Council of Ten took the charges particularly seriously, the fact that Tadino was accused of such things indicates that his profile was now high enough to attract enemies willing to employ such tactics to bring him down.

While the Council of Ten did not pursue the charges, it must have been clear to Gabriele that he needed to do something to clear his name with the Venetian authorities if he wanted his career in the employment of the Republic to advance further.

So when Andrea Gritti came looking for men to help the Brescians defend their city, Gabriele Tadino must have felt that he had little choice but to volunteer for the undertaking. With his name under suspicion, he had to prove his loyalty to the Republic.

As he set off, though, it must not have seemed as if it would be a particularly hazardous task. Brescia was a rich city with excellent defences; the pope, the Spanish and the Empire would all send troops to aid in its defence or to intercept any French army bent on reconquering the city, and he himself was part of a reasonable contingent of Venetian troops, ready to man the city's defences.

Gabriele's reputation as a master of the new art of artillery and the building of defences against cannon was growing: he was the ideal man to supervise preparations against any French assault.

But what Gabriele did not expect, as did neither the Brescians nor the Venetians, was the speed of the French response. For they were dealing with a new French commander, the king's nephew, Gaston de Foix.

King Louis was facing a new and difficult situation. The Spanish, the French, the Holy Roman Empire and the pope had all come together in 1508 to form the League of Cambrai. Faced with an alliance of his erstwhile allies, Louis acted. He sacked his previous commander in Italy, Charles d'Amboise, who was 48 and a cautious and careful general, and appointed his nephew, Gaston de Foix, to take command. Gaston was only 21 and he had all the energy, impetuosity and courage of a young man in a hurry, consumed by dreams of valour and victory. In the few months he had already been in Italy, Gaston had pushed a conflict that had been chugging along at its own, fairly stately, rhythm to a new pitch of activity – and violence. The revolt of the Brescians would see Gaston de Foix raise the war to an entirely new level of speed and savagery.

Andrea Gritti had promised Venetian support to a Brescian nobleman named Luigi Avogadro. With that warrant, Avogadro had raised a reasonable number of men from among the Bresciani and, on the night of 2 and 3 February, Avogadro entered the city. Those men from the French garrison that did not make it into the castle were killed.

Soon afterwards, Gabriele arrived in Brescia with Andrea Gritti and an advance guard of soldiers to bolster the Brescians. Gritti must have been concerned that the French garrison still held out in the castle. But the castle was surrounded by the city; the garrison could expect no supplies. Besides, he knew that the castle was not heavily manned; it would not pose a threat. As such, the garrison could be left to starve at their leisure.

Besides, the revolt in Brescia had sparked similar uprisings elsewhere. Of these, the one in Bergamo was of most interest to Gabriele. But with the rumours spread against him, Gabriele could not afford to take his own small body of men, mainly composed of Bergamaschi, and go to the defence of that city. Andrea Gritti was a rising and important figure in Venetian politics: deserting his army would ensure that the shadowy figures whispering against Gabriele could claim vindication for their charges. So Gabriele stayed in Brescia.

In Bergamo, the French garrison also took refuge in the castle, waiting for a relieving force to rescue them.

In both castles, the garrisons must have expected to have to wait a long time. Gaston de Foix and the French army had spent January force-marching through dreadful winter weather to get to Bologna, which was being besieged by Spanish and papal troops. De Foix took the besiegers completely by surprise. Winter was the time when everyone was supposed to take a break and, besides, no one thought it possible to march an army with its artillery over winter-worn roads. But exhibiting the energy and decisiveness characteristic of him, de Foix pushed the French army along, with its field artillery too.

When the Spanish and papal troops besieging Bologna realised, to their astonishment, that de Foix was just a day's march away, they withdrew with some urgency rather than being forced into the battle that de Foix would force upon them. While most of the generals of the Italian Wars pursued generally cautious strategies, avoiding battle unless they were confident that the ground and numbers favoured them, de Foix had already demonstrated that, given the chance, he would always choose to attack rather than to manoeuvre or wait.

Luigi Avogadro and Andrea Gritti had timed their action carefully. Bologna was 90 miles south-east of Brescia. The independent marquisate of Mantua lay directly between the two cities, further complicating de Foix's freedom of action. Mantua was one of those small states that, like Ferrara, was trying to steer its own path through the shifting alliances of the Italian Wars while maintaining as much of its independence as possible.

Francesco Gonzago, the short, brave and libidinous[9] marquis of Mantua had, together with his wife, Isabella d'Este, overseen a cultural golden age in Mantua even amid the violence of the Italian Wars, this flowering allowed by the marquis's ability to pretend independence while tacking to the prevailing wind. Avogadro and Gritti assumed that, even should de Foix decide to march directly to Brescia when he learned of the revolt, he would have to go around the territory of the marquisate. As a general rule, none of the Italian city states were comfortable with giving leave to an army to march through their lands. Even if the army forbore war, the depredations of military logistics were such that it could take months to recover from even the peaceful passage of an army.

Given all these circumstances, Avogadro and Gritti were confident that they would not have to deal with de Foix before the spring. So Avogadro allowed most of the 20,000 men he had gathered to take the city to return to their homes in the hinterland around Brescia – most of them were not natives of the city but lived in the villages and hamlets that surrounded and fed the city. Avogadro kept enough men to maintain the blockade of the castle but allowing the considerable force he had assembled to return to their homes simplified his logistics considerably.

For his part, Gritti had brought only a small contingent of Venetians. He had sent word to the papal, Spanish and Imperial troops and expected them all to send contingents to help him hold Brescia against the eventual French counter-attack. But there was no great rush. Nothing would happen before the spring, and even then de Foix would no doubt wait for the roads to dry out so that he could more easily move his field artillery.

As a stranger in a strange city, Gabriele needed someone to show him around. A small boy volunteered to do just that. His name was Niccolò and he was 12 years old in 1512 but, being small, he would have looked younger. He was small because, for most of his life, he had not had enough to eat. He, his mother and his two siblings scraped a living in Brescia, earning whatever they might through odd jobs, cleaning and washing. As such, foreign soldiers (even someone from Bergamo, just 30 miles west of Brescia, would have counted as a foreigner to Niccolò) were a rich potential source of money and danger. Gabriele needed a guide and no one knew the byways and alleyways, where there was danger and where there were holes in the wall, better than a local street urchin. Niccolò became his guide to Brescia, as firmly attached to Tadino as the little boy's ingenuity would allow.

And it turned out that, despite Niccolò being entirely unschooled, his ingenuity was considerable. Gabriele soon learned that the boy was sharp, clever and reliable, in spite of his illiteracy. As for Niccolò, he found the older man both exotic and fatherly. By this time, Gabriele was in his early 30s: to a 12-year-old boy that was pretty well as old as the Old Cathedral. Gabriele probably used Niccolò as his guide as he learned his way around the city. Given his previous experience, Gritti no doubt tasked Gabriele with looking at ways to improve the defences of the city against the French attack when it came.

That attack, though, came far, far sooner than they could ever have expected.

17

The Sack of Brescia

18 February **1512, Brescia.**
'Niccolò, get your mother and brothers.' Gabriele Tadino glanced back down along the street towards the Gate of Saint Nazaro. 'Be quick, the French are coming.'

The little boy nodded and scampered into the hovel that was his home. Tadino stood, sword in hand, at the door as people streamed past, fleeing.

He could hear screams, and coarse shouts, and the crack of arquebus, all coming closer. Tadino wiped the rain from his face as Niccolò emerged with his mother and two younger brothers.

'This way,' said Tadino, pointing towards the centre of the city.

'Where are we going, master?' asked Niccolò as they hurried along.

'The Duomo,' said Tadino. 'You will be safe there.'

The little boy glanced back along the street. The screams were spreading wider now, moving north and east from the gate in the city's south-west corner through which the French had broken.

'Do you think so?'

Tadino did not look back. 'There's nowhere else.' He pointed at Niccolò's mother. 'Help her.'

The woman had slipped on the mud, going down on her knees. Niccolò ran to her and tried to haul her up.

'Get up, Mamma.'

In slipping, the woman had half turned. She was looking back in the direction from which the French were coming. She gasped.

'Run, Niccolò, take your brothers, run!'

'Mamma, get up!'

Tadino, seeing the expression on her face, turned.

'Niccolò, get them to the Duomo. You will be safe there.' He shifted his sword. 'I will stay here.'

'Master...'

'Go!'

Niccolò hauled his mother to her feet. 'Mamma, quick.' They started down the street. Tadino, looking round, saw the boy turn back to him. Tadino waved him on.

'Run!'

No more time to look where they were going now. Tadino turned back towards the Gate of Saint Nazaro. He gripped his sword and waited for the first of the soldiers running towards him to arrive.

There is a plaque fixed to the side of the Duomo Vecchio (the Old Cathedral) in the centre of Brescia, a town in Lombardy. It reads, in rather florid Italian:

> Here, from the bloodshed of 1512, a poor child fled, his lips torn and speech impaired. From that broken voice arose a name – Tartaglia – destined for glory in the realm of numbers.[*]

Brescia had come over to the side of Venice in January 1512. The city lies on the northern edge of the great flat valley of the River Po, the plain that lies atop Italy's boot, stretching west and east, shaped like a broad, fat 'V'. It sits just on the edge of the hills that quickly mount up towards the Alps proper, between lakes Garda and Iseo.

On 20 November 1426, Brescia had formally become part of Venice's Stato da Tera. Brescia was a considerable city, with a population of about 50,000, making it one of the larger cities in Europe. The city contributed almost a quarter of the tax revenue that Venice took from its land domains, making its defence a key priority for the Republic.

However, Brescia, along with most of the rest of Venice's Stato da Tera, had surrendered to King Louis following the disaster of the Battle

---

*Translated by the author.

of Agnadello in 1509. But French rule proved stifling and the Brescian nobility began plotting ways to remove their French overlords.

Having sent out feelers to Venice, the leading families in Brescia knew that La Serenissima would welcome them back into her fold. With the French army quartered in Bologna, at the other end of the plain of the Po, the Brescians were confident that they could expel the French garrison, reinforce their defences and call on support from Spanish and papal troops before the French could do anything.

Faced with the loss of Brescia and Bergamo, Gaston de Foix acted with astonishing energy and urgency. Despite the season, despite his men being weary from their previous forced march, despite the danger of being cut off from his main supply lines, de Foix immediately decided to attack.

Urgent negotiations with Francesco Gonzago, the marquis of Mantua, wrung from the marquis permission for the French army to march through the marquisate. That cut miles off the journey ahead. De Foix and his army left Bologna on 8 February. Summertime visitors to Italy won't know just how cold, wet and foggy winters can be in the huge flat plain of the River Po.[10] But De Foix pushed his men on, driving them north so that in only nine days they covered the 90 miles from Bologna to Brescia. Ten miles a day, in winter, with artillery, was extraordinarily rapid progress for an army at the time. The arrival of the French army on the outskirts of Brescia on 17 February was a horrible surprise for the Brescians and the small contingent of Venetian troops in the city.

Whatever ideas Tadino may have had to strengthen the city's defences were moot; now it was desperate, backs-to-the-wall defence time.

De Foix delivered a formal call to the defenders of the city to surrender the day after he arrived. It was, equally formally, refused. Although Gritti and Avogadro did not have as many men as they might have wished, the city's defences were strong and relief forces were surely on their way. They would not have to hold out for long before de Foix and the French would find themselves trapped between the anvil of the city's walls and the hammer of the approaching Spanish and papal troops.

Unfortunately for Brescia, de Foix had no intention of waiting for the relief armies to arrive. For de Foix had learned that there was a secret way into the city that led to the castle, still manned by French troops. A more cautious commander might have suspected a trap and waited, but not de Foix.

During the night of 18/19 February, de Foix personally led an assault force of his best men down the secret way into the castle. He took with him 500 men-at-arms, the heavily armoured elite of his army, along with several thousand infantry, infiltrating them into the castle, while leaving an equal number of men-at-arms outside the city walls both to lull the defenders into complacence and to guard his rear.

As the sun rose on 19 February, de Foix ordered the attack.

It had rained heavily overnight, turning the earth to mud. So rather than risk having his men slip and fall on muddy ground he ordered them to remove their shoes and go barefoot.

At the same time as the men who had infiltrated into the castle started to break out, the French attacked the Gate of St Nazaro. In both cases, the advancing men-at-arms crouched down on command so that the arquebusiers, following behind, could unleash a devastating volley of fire on the defenders.

The defenders, caught from both sides, fought desperately, the women of the city joining in with their men, throwing stones and tiles from windows and upending pans of boiling water from the rooftops.

But it was to no end. The French had breached the defences of the city and there was nothing the defenders could do to turn back their onslaught. A few managed to escape, and Andrea Gritti was taken prisoner, but most were caught up in the massacre.

The city had refused de Foix's formal offer to surrender. By the laws of war recognised at the time, this meant that Brescia lay open to three days of sack. This law was, in part, followed because it gave due recompense to the victors for the high losses that were normally consequent upon taking a defended city by storm: during the assault, the attackers usually suffered much greater losses than the defenders.

But thanks to his rapid and brilliant stroke, de Foix had taken Brescia with light losses, no more than a couple of hundred killed and wounded. In the circumstances, he could have afforded the city mercy since he had taken Brescia at far less cost than he would have reasonably expected.

However, de Foix was in no mood for clemency. Brescia's revolt had sparked insurrection throughout the territories that France had claimed from Venice following victory at Agnadello. Leading the French army in Lombardy and the Veneto, the last thing de Foix needed was to have to guard his lines of communication back to France from these fractious new subjects of the French crown. To that end, de Foix determined to teach the rebellious Brescians, and by implication all the Italians now subject to King Louis, the consequences of treachery.

De Foix gave his men their three days of sack, loot, murder and rape.

The despoliation of Brescia was among the worst of the Italian Wars. There is no exact record of the number of civilians killed, still less of how many women were raped. But the city itself was ransacked. Scholars estimate that the French stripped valuables worth three to four million ducats from the city; no fewer than 4,000 cartloads were trundled back west to France. Indeed, so many French soldiers became so rich from the city's harvest that the French army lost a good number of its best men, content to return home to enjoy their plundered treasure. Even after the sack was over, Brescia suffered further fines, while the ringleader of the plot, Luigi Avogadro, was tried and executed. Many others were sent into exile.

Such was the toll taken on Brescia by the sack and the further punishments the French inflicted that it never recovered. From being the wealthiest city in the mainland possessions of Venice, and among the 20 most populous cities in Europe, it went into a long period of relative decline, leaving it one of those middling Italian towns that visitors are delighted to stumble upon as it still seems to exist in a state frozen not long after the disaster that overtook it five centuries ago, a lovely echo of the past but a place that nobody visits for its own sake.

The other cities that had rebelled, such as Bergamo, all had the sense to surrender rather than risk the same thing happening to them. They were also punished by fines, loss of favours and the expulsion of citizens deemed untrustworthy, but at least they were spared the brutal sack that left Brescia a shadow of its old self.

For his part, Gabriele Tadino escaped relatively lightly. He was wounded in the initial attack but rather than being killed and stripped of his valuables, he was taken prisoner, a potential source of a hefty ransom. Tadino had been present for most of the key battles in the

Italian Wars but, being a prisoner of the French, he would miss its next turning point.

The richer Brescians attempted to buy their lives with whatever goods they could give; the poor sought sanctuary in the supposed safe space of the Duomo Vecchio and the city's churches and convents. Among those who fled to the Duomo Vecchio was little Niccolò and his mother and siblings. But even there, the French broke in. In the carnage, Niccolò was struck with a sword at least five times on the head and face. One of the sword slashes cut through his palate but, by some miracle, he was not immediately killed. Niccolò's mother managed to staunch the bleeding and kept her son alive through the horror of the next two days.

Niccolò slowly recovered physically but the trauma remained with him for the rest of his life. When, many years later, Niccolò began to acquire some degree of notice for his ground-breaking work in mathematics, he had acquired a surname that told what he had endured as a boy.

Niccolò Tartaglia. Niccolò the Stutterer. The stutter was the fruit of the trauma of that terrible day many years previously.

Gabriele Tadino and Niccolò Tartaglia would renew their friendship three decades later, when Gabriele had retired and Niccolò was living in Venice, his reputation and station as high as it would ever be. There, they would collaborate on Niccolò's work, including one of the most influential books on the new ways of war, *Quesiti et Inventioni Diverse*.

18

A Life like Lightning

Having taken Brescia and put down the revolt that had spread throughout French-controlled Italy, most other commanders would have taken a break. But not Gaston de Foix. He was still a man in a hurry. The commanders of the Spanish and papal troops were cut from much more cautious cloth and had no wish to enter battle with this precipitate young Frenchman. They preferred to manoeuvre cautiously and wait for a more opportune moment – ideally, the withdrawal of the French to deal with problems elsewhere. After all, Henry VIII of England had signed up as part of the Holy League on the understanding that he could use French distraction in Italy to claim back some of the territory the English had lost in France. An English invasion of France would necessitate the rapid relocation of French forces to deal with an army that, once it landed, was only a few days' march from Paris.

De Foix, however, was determined to force the matter. When the Spanish and papal troops would not come to him for the decisive battle, he decided to force battle upon them: he marched to Ravenna.

From AD 402 to 476, Ravenna had been the capital of the western half of the Roman Empire, when Rome itself had become too vulnerable to rampaging barbarians. Although no longer an Imperial capital, the city was too precious a prize that the Holy League army could give it up without a fight – even if that fight should occur on the holiest day of the Christian year, Easter Sunday itself.

The Battle of Ravenna took place on 11 April 1512, Easter Sunday. It was another extraordinary, bloody triumph for Gaston le Foix – but it was also his last.

The French army was supplemented by 5,000 German *Landsknechte* and, crucially, the forces of Alfonso d'Este, the Duke of Ferrara, with his 50 cannon. In total, the French and their allies had about 30,000 men in the field.

Against them, the Holy League forces, mainly Spanish and papal troops, had about 20,000 men, set up on the bank of the Ronco River and protected by an encircling ditch that they had quickly dug.

One of the quirks of the Italian Wars is that even field battles were fought like sieges, with assaults and artillery barrages on fixed defences. And that was how the battle began: with the infantry and men-at-arms of both sides lying flat to try to avoid the artillery bombardment.

There are few things harder for soldiers to endure than being attacked and not responding. The infantry could at least lie flat but the cavalry suffered terribly, both men and horses. The commander of the Italian troops at the battle, Fabrizio Colonna, reported afterwards that a single French cannon shot killed 30 men-at-arms: 'We beheld a wretched spectacle, pierced by dreadful screams – soldiers and horses crashing lifeless to the ground, heads and limbs hurled through the air, torn clean from their bodies.'[11]

With his cavalry being slaughtered all around him, Fabrizio Colonna sent urgent messages to the commander of the Spanish troops, Ramon de Cardona, who had ordered his infantry to lie flat so that most of the cannon shot passed over them.

Under such attack, it was impossible to keep the cavalry from trying to fight back.

'Are we all to die shamefully because of the stubbornness and malice of a damned renegade? Is this whole army to be destroyed without us killing a single one of the enemy?'[12]

With his men and his horses dying around him, and with a long-standing enmity against de Cardona, Fabrizio Colonna could not see that tactically it made sense for his men to remain behind the defensive ditch they had dug earlier. So long as the Holy League remained behind the ditch, with the river protecting their right flank, then de Foix would have to launch a probably suicidal assault against them to achieve the victory he craved.

But watching his men die became too much for Colonna. He had to act. He ordered his men on to their horses. The cavalry rode from their encampment, charging for the centre of the French lines. They were met by the French cavalry, who had also suffered from the Holy League artillery. Both sides, for the moment free of the restraint of waiting meekly for cannonball death, engaged in a fierce and frantic melee, but the Holy League were finally overwhelmed.

The fighting had meanwhile spread to the infantry, with fierce clashes breaking out all over the battlefield. The slaughter was great, for while the infantry fought, the duke of Ferrara continued to direct his artillery to enfilade the Spanish, even at the risk of hitting his French allies too.

Eventually, the Italian and Spanish forces were overwhelmed. All contemporary accounts tell of the great slaughter on both sides, but particularly among the defeated army. And the killing was not confined to the rank and file. This was a battle where the captains and generals were at almost as much risk as the rank and file. Of these, the greatest of all was Gaston de Foix himself.

The battle all but won, de Foix was watching, with his small personal entourage, when he saw that one part of the enemy army, the formation that had held the river flank and fought back the assault from de Foix's *Landsknechte*, was retreating down the river in good order, their colours still held high. For the rest of his army, there were far easier targets among the routing troops. Running men are much easier to pursue, kill and spoil than men retreating in formation, their weapons ready.

The battle was won. It was time for the survivors to enjoy the fruits of victory, most commonly done by stripping whatever valuables they could find from the dead or looting the enemy camp.

But for Gaston de Foix, the sight of some of the enemy retreating in good order told that he was settling for a shell of a victory rather than the total triumph he desired, both for his own glory and to end the resistance of the Holy League to King Louis.

De Foix had already fought in the front lines in this battle and in others. Despite his destructive use of artillery, he was still at heart a knight, raised on tales of martial heroism.

So, he charged. With about 15 of his men-at-arms, all horsed, he rode after the retreating Spanish, intent on scattering their defence and wreaking havoc as they broke.

But the Spanish infantry, seeing the cavalry charging down upon them with lances lowered, did not break. Instead, they crouched, grounded their long pikes in the earth, and waited upon the advancing French.

With the river to their left and a ditch to their right, the Spanish were in a strong position, so long as they did not break under the psychological threat of the charging cavalry. The troops of a beaten army will usually break under further threat, the instinct for personal safety overcoming the discipline that has also been broken by seeing their comrades cut down and their commanders flee. Sometimes, a captain might rally a group of broken men but, in this case, there is no report that the Spanish were being led by any notable commander: they had fought together and now they were retreating together.

Their discipline held. Their courage did not waver even as the French rode down upon them, lances levelled.

And the French broke against the Spanish pikes. Some of de Foix's men were pushed into the river or the ditch, falling from their horses as they fell. De Foix, in one of those sudden clearances that sometimes happen in battle, had his horse killed under him. With none of his men-at-arms near, the Spanish infantry started stabbing at the fallen man with their pikes. De Foix was wearing armour fit for a king. But even the best armour will not protect the wearer when he is on the ground with the enemy swarming over him.

Odet de Foix, Gaston's cousin, was nearby and saw his cousin fall. Too far away to intervene, Odet shouted to the Spanish, 'Spare him! He is our viceroy – your queen's own brother!'[13]

But amid the chaos and the blood lust, the Spaniards did not hear, or understand, what Odet was trying to tell them. The French attack beaten off, they continued their retreat, unaware that they had killed the commander of the French army.

Gaston de Foix's body was left broken and bleeding. His men counted 14 or 15 wounds on his body, most of them fatal. He was 22 years old. He had been commander of the French forces in Italy for a little over six months. In that time, he had transformed the dynamics of the war, changing it from a war of siege and attrition to one of sudden battles and swift assaults, fast marches and furious battles. If he had lived, it's possible that the Italian Wars might have had quite a different outcome.

But it was not only Gaston who died at Ravenna: while a victory for the French, they had suffered grievous losses too. The butcher's bill presented by contemporary authors varies quite widely but they all agree that the battle was notable for the number of the dead left upon the field. There were probably at least 10,000 men killed in the battle, at a rough ratio of one Frenchman for two soldiers of the Holy League.

In the aftermath of the battle, the weary and vengeful French army fell upon Ravenna, despite the city offering to surrender, subjecting the city to three days of looting and killing that left thousands of civilians dead.

Following the sack of Ravenna, the rest of the Romagna surrendered to the French. Despite the loss of their commander, it must have seemed to the French that they had won the war: they had won a decisive battle; they had put down the revolt in Brescia, leaving subject cities in no doubt as to what would happen to them should they rebel. Surely it was all done: Gaston de Foix's thunderbolt had won northern Italy for the French crown.

But it was not to be. After some wavering, King Ferdinand and Pope Julius decided to continue the fight and to send more troops north. Meanwhile, from their mountain fastnesses, the Swiss were on the march. A mix of loathing for the French and the prospect of Holy League gold brought an army 24,000 strong down from the cantons into northern Italy.

Gaston de Foix would have relished the fight, but Gaston de Foix was dead. The French left in Italy were longing to return home. It must have begun to seem that they were fighting some sort of hydra: no sooner had they cut down one army than another sprang up in its place. France itself was also under threat and King Louis had to withdraw his household troops to look to the defence of his own realm.

The bitter upshot for the French was that, by July of 1512, only four months after their apparently decisive victory at Ravenna, they had been forced completely from Italy, leaving only a few garrisons in scattered strongholds in Lombardy and Genoa.

There have been few wars in history where one side has won so many decisive battles to so little strategic effect. For the French, back in France, it must have seemed completely mystifying, as if some peculiar magic permeated the country over the Alps, a magic that rendered battles won meaningless and that allowed the defeated enemy to reap the victory.

The French were not the only ones taken by surprise by their collapse in northern Italy: the members of the Holy League were just as taken aback. Because the French collapse was so unexpected, there had been no negotiations beforehand about what to do with all the territory that was now, suddenly, falling back into the hands of the League. It will come, I think, as no surprise to readers to learn that, faced with this unexpected bonanza, the members of the Holy League soon started to argue as to who should have what.

However, what will come as a surprise to readers is the result of these disputes: in March 1513, Venice entered into a new alliance... with France.

Yes, the country that had started the Italian Wars and which had been trying to take Venetian possessions for the last five years now officially became a partner to La Serenissima.

Under the terms of this new alliance, the Venetians ceded Cremona to France but Louis agreed that they would have Brescia, Bergamo and Crema, so long as the Venetians helped him retake Milan.

There was one other significant section to the treaty: the prisoners that the French were holding were to be freed.

Gabriele Tadino had been held prisoner since the fall of Brescia. Now, after more than a year of captivity, he was a free man once again. The question was, what was he going to do with his newly regained freedom?

19

A Not-So-Romantic Interlude

April 1518, Outside the Caprioli villa, near Brescia.
'We've got her. Let's go.'

Gabriele Tadino turned round from where he was standing in the dawn dusk with his horse beside him and a charged arquebus leaning on a tree to see five men approaching. But in their midst, slim and veiled, was another, who had not been there when they had left him, half an hour earlier, as the first hint of light brightened the eastern horizon.

Now the eastern sky was streaked rose and gold, first light gilding the long strips of clouds, but in the west it was still dark and the last, brightest stars stared coldly at the approaching dawn.

Gabriele looked past the approaching figures to the villa beyond, its roof rising over the walls that guarded and protected it. Even with the wall in between, he could hear cries rising from the building, shouts and screams and then, bright and clear and silver, the first peal of the bell. The alarm bell.

He looked back to the men hurrying towards him.

'I thought this was supposed to be done in secret, Camillo?'

The man in the lead shrugged. He had delicate, fine features that belied his fierceness as a soldier and the rashness of his courage – Gabriele had seen him charge, alone, a troop of French infantry and scatter them.

'It was secret, until the Caprioli objected.'

Gabriele pointed at the slight figure behind Camillo, being guided by Camillo's cousin, Theofilo da Barco, on one side and his friend, Gasparo della Pallata, on the other. Gasparo was the grandson of the great condottiero Bartolomeo Colleoni, in whose service

A NOT-SO-ROMANTIC INTERLUDE

Gabriele's grandfather and father had passed most of their lives in Martinengo.

'I presume this Caprioli did not object?'

Camillo smiled, his eyes wide and merry. 'Object? Of course not. Francesca replied to every one of Roberto's messages.'

Gabriele looked around, theatrically. 'I do wonder, then, why your brother did not come to claim his bride himself?'

Camillo laughed. 'It brings bad fortune for the groom to see his wife before his wedding day; too often, the eager groom, seeking an early glimpse, has seen his dreamed-of love become a frog before his eyes. Let the lovers meet when they are wed!'

From behind, the shouting intensified and began to gain some order as commands were shouted out and the sound of running feet grew louder.

Gabriele looked past Camillo, to where the ladders they had used to scale the walls rose up as stark silhouettes against the rising light. As he watched, he saw the first figure appear above the lip of the wall and, looking towards them, point and call in their direction.

Gabriele sighed and turned back to Camillo. 'I told you not to leave the ladders. You might as well have painted an arrow to tell the Caprioli where you were going.'

But Camillo's smile grew only wider, his eyes glinting though there was barely light enough to see for they glittered with the fire of his spirit that loved always the bold stroke and the daring stratagem.

In truth, this was one of the reasons Gabriele loved his friend so, for boldness and courage were dear to his soul too. But as the elder by 15 years, for Camillo was but 25, Gabriele knew that it fell to him to temper the wilder excesses of his young friend's zeal.

As he watched the first of the Caprioli men climb over the wall after them, he realised that, in this case, he had failed.

Camillo pointed to the tethered horses beneath the stand of poplars where Tadino had taken up his lonely sentry duty as his young friends scaled the walls of the villa of the Capriolo family.

'It is as well, then, that we have horses and they...' he turned back towards the men who, having climbed down the ladder, were starting to run towards them, '...have only their own feet. To horse, my friends, and you, dear lady, my brother's bride-to-be.'

Tadino picked up the charged arquebus, pushed its stock into his shoulder and, turning his head slightly, blew over the pan. He had done that when he first charged the arquebus but habit meant that he blew again to make sure no grains of powder were left sticking on the outside of the pan, ready to spark into his face.

Then, he levelled the arquebus at the approaching men.

'I am the knight, Gabriele Tadino of Martinengo, and I do not miss. This is a matter of love: do not die contending with the greatest of the gods.'

There was enough light now for the approaching men to see il cavaliere standing before them, the arquebus level and steady, death waiting for whoever came on.

Tadino looked steadily down the barrel of the arquebus. None of the Caprioli men were armoured – why would they be, it was dawn? – but even had some of them been wearing armour while on guard, at this range the ball from his arquebus would punch right through all but the very finest plate.

At the sight of death waiting, the Caprioli guards slowed, then stopped, looking from one to another, waiting for an order.

They knew, Tadino knew, that there was but one shot in the arquebus. Once it was fired, there would be no time to reload; it would then be sword work.

If there had been a sergeant present, he might have ordered the men on – and, in doing so, earned the ball that nestled deep at the base of Tadino's arquebus. But there was no one yet to order the men on, to command one of them to die so that the others could rush forward and lay hands upon the escaping men.

Beside him, Tadino heard the sounds of his friends taking horse.

'It is well that you have decided not to try to thwart love, the greatest of the gods.'

With the arquebus lowered but held so that he could raise it to fire in a moment, Gabriele began to move sideways towards the horses.

As he did so, he heard the vague sound of struggle. He knew he should not look away from the men: it was his gaze as much as his arquebus that held them immobile. But as the sounds continued, he could not stop himself from looking to the side.

There, he saw the slight figure of the Caprioli girl pushing and struggling against Camillo as he tried to lift her onto a horse.

This was not what he had expected to see.

'What is it? Why does she fight you, Camillo?'

Camillo, grasping the girl more tightly, turned his bright, but now brittle smile, towards Gabriele.

'Francesca is young and this is frightening for her.'

Gabriele stared at the veiled figure that Camillo was holding.

'How young?'

'Stop them!'

At the shout, Tadino turned back. Standing on the ladder, looking out over the villa's wall, was a man whom, by his clothes and voice, Tadino knew to be one of the Caprioli's lieutenants, if not a Capriolo himself. With him on hand, the guards could no longer hide behind the lack of orders.

'Get her on the horse, Camillo, now!'

'I'm trying...'

The man started climbing down.

Tadino levelled the arquebus in his direction. This was an affair of the heart. He did not want it to end in death but neither did he want to die himself.

'She's up!'

A quick glance, and Tadino saw Camillo on the horse with the Caprioli girl held firmly before him.

Tadino looked back, sighted along the barrel, and squeezed the trigger.

Sparks and smoke splashed up from the pan, the brightness of the firing blinding Tadino for an instant. But as his sight came back, he saw, as he had hoped, the men milling around, looking to see who had fallen.

None had. He had fired deliberately to miss, but they did not know that.

The arquebus now empty, Tadino ran to his horse and vaulted up onto its saddle.

'Stop them...'

The cry came from behind but already he was turning his horse's head away, then spurring it into a gallop, following in the hoof steps of Theofilo, Gasparo, their men-at-arms and, just in front of him, Camillo and the Caprioli girl.

The shouts faded away behind them. But they did not slacken their pace; the Caprioli would soon saddle their own horses and give chase.

As rearguard, Gabriele kept looking back the way they had come. The road they were following was good and now, with the sun new risen, its light allowed them to give their horses their heads. The animals galloped with the freedom of the wind. Beneath him, Gabriele felt the smooth shift of muscle while the eager beast laid his head forward and his ears back, drumming the stone beneath his hooves.

Turning his head, Gabriele saw dust rising from the way they had come. The Caprioli were following.

'They are coming!' he shouted forward to Camillo.

Camillo, turning, grinned back to Gabriele.

'But of course they are!'

Gabriele could not help but grin back.

For ten years he had marched and ridden across Italy, fighting for Venice, first against the French and then with the French, never knowing when a cannonball might take away his leg or an arquebus leave him blind. But this, this was… fun. This was as the stories of old, of knights defending the honour of their loves, of Lancelot and Guinevere, of Tristram and Iseult, of Orlando and Angelica.

Camillo gestured ahead. 'See, the wood. There, they will not find us.'

The riders galloped in among the trees. Theofilo, in the lead, slowed the column down and then, as the trees thickened about them, he turned off the main path and led them deeper into the wood.

The trees soon closed out any view of the road. Gabriele, as the last, looked carefully down at the ground as they went but it was dry and hard, taking no mark from the horses' hooves. The Caprioli would not be able to follow them.

When they had gone about a hundred passi[14] *from the road, Theofilo brought them to a halt. They waited, silent astride their horses, eyes peering back the way they had come.*

But it was only sound that told them of the passage of the Caprioli; sight could not pass through the screen of trees. Gabriele heard the rattle of hooves, of horses still moving fast even though they had lost sight of their target. The Caprioli must think that they were riding back to Brescia and be seeking to overtake them on the road. But Camillo had other plans.

Hearing the Caprioli ride past, Gabriele turned to Camillo to congratulate him on the success of his plan. But the words died in his mouth for he saw that Camillo had his hand up, covering the girl's mouth under her veil.

Seeing Gabriele's glance, Camillo dropped his hand. He leaned forward, his head beside the girl's ear. 'She is so eager to see her lover, I did not want her to cry out thinking it be him.'

Looking carefully at the girl, still veiled, her face covered, Gabriele saw that she was even slighter than he had thought. The hands that grasped the saddle in front of her were perfect and unlined, hands that had known no labour, but they were delicate as a child's.

'She is… small.'

'Sì, she is small but she is perfect. And rich too, now il Capriolo is dead.'

Tadino stared at Camillo. 'Is that why you want her to marry Roberto? For her money? I thought this an affair of the heart.'

'It is, Gabriele, it is. But gold makes Helen fairer still.'

'You think so? I do not.' Gabriele stared at the girl, sitting still on the horse with Camillo's arm around her. 'You say she is beautiful but I have not seen her face.'

'No, no, no, my friend.' Camillo shook his head, smiling as he spoke. 'I trust not even myself, and she my own brother's love: I would not lay such temptation in front of you to imperil your soul.'

'I do not fall so easily into temptation, Camillo. Let me see her for whose sake I have risked all this night.'

Camillo's smile grew tighter but it did not fail. 'When we reach the convent, before I give her to the keeping of the sisters, then I will let you see this flower we have plucked for my brother.' He gestured. 'It is not far now.'

He was right. The convent was but an hour's ride away. But as they rode, Gabriele found that the delight that had accompanied this great adventure through the night had turned to trepidation.

He began to fear that he had fallen into his own temptation: the wish to do great deeds.

He rode behind Camillo, staring ahead as if by thought alone he could pierce the flesh of his friend and see the face of the girl he carried on his horse.

But at last they came to the convent and Theofilo, the vanguard of their small army, slid from his horse and knocked upon its gate.

Camillo looked to Gabriele as he rode up alongside him. 'Our cousin is the badessa.[15] She will keep my brother's bride-to-be safe until he can marry her.'

At those words, Gabriele heard a gasp from the slight, veiled figure, and then a muffled sound as if... as if...

The gate opened and out bustled a group of women, the ladies who went out from the convent that the sisters who lived within not be soiled by contact with the world, nor defiled by the glances and lusts of men.

Camillo slid down from the horse and, reaching up, lifted the girl off as easily as if she were a child.

Gabriele dismounted too but, as the women went to take the girl, he stopped them.

'Wait.' He walked up and, taking the girl's veil, lifted it from her face.

'Madonna santa!' The old women who had come out from the convent clucked and gestured while the one leading them struck Gabriele's hand so that he let go of the veil.

It drifted back down and covered the girl's face.

'Andiamo.' The old woman put her arm round the girl's shoulders and gently led her towards the convent gate.

Tadino stared after them until the gate closed.

Then, he turned to Camillo.

'Bastardo!'

Camillo held up his hands.

'Did I not tell you she is beautiful!'

'You did not tell me she is a child! How old is she? Twelve?'

'Er...'

'Not eleven?'

'No, not exactly eleven...'

'For goodness' sake, ten?'

A NOT-SO-ROMANTIC INTERLUDE

'The sisters will look after her until she is old enough to marry Roberto, but she can be betrothed to him now.'

'Camillo, what have you got me into?'

What Tadino had got into was a lot of trouble.

The Capriolo family were rich and even though its head had died recently, his widow, Signora Averoldo, had an equally wealthy and powerful family: Monsignor Altobello Averoldo was the papal legate to Venice.

Not surprisingly, Signora Averoldo was somewhat put out at having her daughter, her ten-year-old daughter at that, kidnapped by armed men and taken away. Going to the mayor of Brescia, she brought the case before him and the mayor forced the convent into whose keeping Camillo and his group of conspirators had placed the girl to give her up: the mayor moved the young girl into a convent of his own choosing until the case could be resolved.

From our perspective, it seems ludicrous that Camillo might think he could kidnap a rich heiress and marry her to his brother. But it wasn't quite as mad a scheme as it appears.

Firstly, marriages were not love matches but business arrangements, concluded after negotiations between the respective families. In this case, there must already have been some contact between the families. While the Capriolo/Averoldo family was clearly not going to agree immediately to a marriage, Camillo could well have decided that they were just holding out for a better deal. His plan was probably designed to put extra pressure on them so that they would agree to a deal, and the betrothal of his brother to Francesca Capriolo. That also explains her young age: while a marriage might be contracted at that age if the families were willing, it would not be consummated until she was older.

So it wasn't quite as mad a plan as it appears.

However, given that Gabriele made no attempt at a defence at his trial but threw himself upon the mercy of his judge, it seems likely that he was not clear about all the details and, in particular, the girl's age and her general unwillingness to be spirited away to a strange convent run by Camillo's relative. When the plan backfired, and it became clear that Signora Averoldo was not going to negotiate but litigate, Gabriele realised that he had put himself into a terrible situation.

Despite the protestations from their families, Camillo and Theofilo da Barco, and Gasparo della Pallata, together with a man-at-arms of Camillo and a friend of Theofilo, were hauled off to prison – as was Gabriele Tadino. His family, although well thought of, did not have the wealth of the da Barco or the della Pallata families, but even their riches and connections were not enough to save Camillo, Theofilo and Gasparo from the indignity (and some danger – prisons were noisome and unsanitary places) of confinement.

The case itself went quickly before the magistrates and their judgement was rendered with equal speed, being imposed on 23 June 1518 after Gabriele and the rest had spent a month in prison. Camillo and Theofilo da Barco were banished from the district of Verona, in which Brescia was situated, for five years, while Gasparo della Pallata and Gabriele Tadino were banished for three years. Presumably on the basis that he didn't have anyone important standing up for him, the man-at-arms was banished for ten years and Theofilo's friend Ferrazin also got three years' banishment. Should any of them break the terms of their banishment, the magistrates said:

> To Brescia with him – there shall his hand be struck off, clean from the arm, before the very house whence he stole the maid!

This was in addition to a further two years in prison should the ban be broken.

What was more, the news of the verdict was carried to the Signoria and, in response, the Venetians revoked the commissions they had given Gabriele and Camillo: the men were no longer soldiers of Venice.

Released from prison, Camillo and Theofilo fled to Ferrara. The sources are silent on what Gabriele did but his most likely course was to go with the cousins. Ferrara was under the rule of the d'Este family, who had played each side against the other during the Italian Wars, retaining their independence and their formidable artillery train.

In Ferrara, the cousins and Gabriele could only wait and hope that the intricate web of family connections, patrons and interests could act to ameliorate or overturn their convictions. After all, if Venice and

France could enter into an alliance after shedding so much of each other's blood, then there was surely hope that the well connected da Barchi and Colleoni families could find a way to soften the sentence against them.

Stuck in Ferrara, Gabriele was left to reflect on the events of the last year that had ended his service with Venice and put a sentence on his head. And it had all started so well...

20

THE DREGS OF WAR

The War of the League of Cambrai had finally dragged to a close in the final months of 1516, ending with the signing of the Treaty of Noyon in August and then the Treaty of Brussels in December.

After all the fighting, destruction and death, the treaties left the contending parties in pretty much the same positions they had been in at the start of the fighting eight years earlier.

In the peace that followed, Gabriele returned to Brescia, living in his house between Carmini and San Cristoforo. He must have renewed his friendship with Niccolò Tartaglia during his time in Brescia, as we know about this from a sentence in Tartaglia's later book in which he reminisces about his friendship with Tadino. In Brescia, Gabriele also continued and deepened his friendships with the young men he had fought alongside during the war years, including Camillo and Theofilo da Barco. His connection with the Colleoni family, the descendants of the *condottiero* Bartolomeo Colleoni, was apparently so close that many people thought him a member of the family.

Now, those connections of friendship were being put to the test. In Italy, ties of blood ran much deeper and tied much closer than ties of friendship. As he languished in Ferrara, Gabriele must have worried that the efforts being made to clear Camillo, Theofilo and Gasparo would not extend to him.

It had all seemed so much clearer when they were fighting together…

Pope Julius II died on 21 February 1513. He left Rome a building site, with the new St Peter's unfinished and unpaid for (with consequences that would be far reaching, to say the least), but the Papal States had recovered most of the territory they had lost, while the papacy had regained much of the temporal and political power it had lost.

That resumption of papal power came at a cost that would only slowly be revealed. For the Italians, the fact that the pope was both a spiritual leader and a worldly power had been something known and accepted for centuries. The papacy's assumption of temporal powers had begun relatively benignly, with popes such as Leo the Great helping to save and secure the city in the desperate years following the end of the Western Roman Empire. With the emperor now in Constantinople, the only power left in Rome was the pope and, reluctant or not, these successors of Peter had little choice but to take hold of the levers of power in the city and its surrounding districts; there was no one else. The representative of the Byzantine emperor, his exarch, claimed theoretical political control over Rome but he lived in Ravenna and, as the reach of the Byzantine emperor lessened, that control declined too, until the popes looked to new and closer protectors: the Franks.

By 1300, the Papal States had become, to all intents and purposes, independent and the pope a temporal ruler as well as a spiritual leader. However, for most Europeans, the pope's political activities were confined to squabbles with the other Italian states. The machinations among Roman families as to who would take the see of Peter when it next fell vacant were of little concern elsewhere.

However, when France led the other European powers crashing into Italy, they ran straight into the popes as political players. While this was well known to the nobility of the rest of Europe in theory, it nevertheless came as a real shock to see a successor of Peter personally leading his soldiers into battle, as in the case of Pope Julius.

The political machinations of the popes fed into the tales of returning soldiers spinning stories of Roman debauchery. The city was old, moneyed and a lot of people visited. It's not entirely surprising that alongside the spiritual consolations to be found among the ancient churches and relics, there were corporeal satisfactions on offer as well. It's not hard to imagine the scandalised, although titillated, soldiers returning home, sitting down by the fire and starting a story by saying, 'You'll never believe what I saw next to the church of St Paul...'

With Pope Julius dead, and the whiff of betrayal hanging over the League of Cambrai, the Venetians did their deal with the French. The fighting continued for the next three years with neither side able to gain a decisive advantage – a recurring theme of the Italian Wars.

During these years, Gabriele gained further experience and renown for his expertise in fortifications. After he was released from French captivity in March 1513 following the alliance between France and Venice, he was given the job of improving and reinforcing the defences of the cities and strongholds the Venetians had regained in the previous year, with particular responsibility for Crema.

Bergamo, where Gabriele had spent so much time, had fallen to the Spanish on 24 June 1513. With two well-known *condottieri*, Gabriele hatched a daring plan to reclaim the city and earn some money at the same time. All too aware of the fate that had befallen Brescia, the citizens of Bergamo had paid the Spanish a bribe, 6,000 ducats, to save their city from that fate. With his connections to Bergamo, Gabriele learned in which house the Spanish treasurer had taken up residence – holding the money with him for safekeeping.

Taking 600 men, Gabriele and the two *condottieri* rode from Crema to Bergamo. Using his intimate knowledge of the city's defences, Gabriele led a party of soldiers into the city to the house of the Spanish treasurer, where they captured him and the city's Spanish governor and liberated 6,000 Bergamaschi ducats.

It was a typical Tadino plan: forceful, brave and borderline suicidal. But it worked, and Bergamo returned to Venetian control.

In the next three years, Tadino continued to play his part in the fighting, taking roles in battles and sieges from Crema to Bergamo to Brescia to Verona. The fighting continued with only the natural pauses imposed by the seasons and the need for the combatants to replenish their armies, their stores and their treasuries. The wars that had started with Charles XIII's invasion of Italy in 1494 were still dragging on 20 years later. By that point, it must have seemed to many of the inhabitants of Italy that war was the natural state of mankind, the brief interludes of peace but passing gleams of light before the clouds massed once more. But even the most war-hardened among the *condottieri* and the *Landsknechte* would surely have been shocked to learn that the Italian Wars still had another 40 years to run.

Wars have always been the forcing ground of development. Think of the extraordinary evolution of the aeroplane during the First and Second World Wars.

The Italian Wars applied the same final filtering device to the rapidly evolving tactics, strategies and technologies of the time.

But perhaps more than anything else, they fundamentally transformed the politics and ethics of war.

When Charles VIII launched his invasion of Italy in 1494, his stated aim was to secure his claim in Italy before then embarking on crusade against the Turks to reclaim the Holy Land. The First Crusade had conquered Jerusalem in 1099, leading to the foundation of Outremer, the Crusader states. These endured for nearly 200 years, the final outpost on the mainland only falling in 1291. But crusade had become woven into the mind and martial imagination of the European knightly class – or at least some of them. Fascinating work on wills, bills and legacies has conclusively proved that the old assertion, that European noble families sent off landless younger sons to do a bit of crusading and save them the burden of providing for them, is hopelessly wrong.

In fact, crusading was very much a family affair, and largely pursued by families through generations, while other nearby noble families of equal status remained almost completely uninvolved. And far from this being a profitable operation for the families concerned, it was rather a considerable drain on their resources. What's more, it was usually the family head who undertook the peril of crusading rather than some surplus son.

In these 200 years, crusading had become the imaginative ideal for the knightly class. Even if they and their family didn't actually do any crusading, it was still something everyone acknowledged as the highest ideal for a knight.

So even when Outremer was lost, the ideal wasn't. Besides, while the mainland states were gone, the Knights Hospitaller, the surviving martial monastic order, had its base on the island of Rhodes, sitting atop the sea lanes to and from the Holy Land. And after all, the First Crusade had managed to conquer Jerusalem without any local support. The crusading ideal told that, with God's help, such a conquest would be possible again.

And it was not just knights who felt the lure of crusade. Kings too had gone on crusade, from Richard I of England to Louis IX of France. At the end of the Quattrocento, it was still the ideal that Charles VIII aspired to, while also providing him with some useful political cover for his Italian land grab.

The ideal continued to be employed as cover for naked political advantage. When Pope Julius II brought together the League of

Cambrai its public aim was to prepare for crusade against the Turks. It was only in its private codicils that its true purpose, to strip territories from Venice and split them between the Papal States, France, Spain and the Empire, was made clear.

But the first two decades of the Italian Wars increasingly revealed the mendacity and naked personal political ambition at the root of this interminable conflict. There was nothing noble about it. All this talk of crusade, of uniting against the common foe of Christendom, was just that, talk. Given a choice between claiming a city in Italy or a city in the Holy Land, it was clear that the princes of Europe would choose the prize close to home rather than the prize far away.

And in 1513, a Florentine diplomat named Niccolò Macchiavelli wrote the work that stripped the hypocrisy from European statecraft and laid bare the ambitions and calculations that lay beneath the wars that had torn apart his homeland for the last two decades. *The Prince* was probably the most important political work for a thousand years. While it was written to mimic the mirrors for princes genre of political writing, books that were in effect textbooks on how to rule, Macchiavelli's book entirely subverted the advice that had been given by previous writers. Before, rulers were enjoined to cultivate the Christian virtues, to remember humility despite their estate, to be brave, honest and true to their words: these books were, in effect, textbooks attempting to civilise and Christianise a violent and volatile nobility. Medieval romances were the other arm of the efforts to do so, offering a chivalric ideal as the object of the imagination while the mirrors for princes provided more practical advice.

The Prince turned all that upside down.

Machiavelli stated, upfront and without any attempt at disguise, that in order to secure the state and solidify his rule, a prince should be prepared to use violence and deceit, that he should be willing to liquidate whole families if they had a rival claim to the throne, that force and lies were the bedrock upon which to build a secure hold on power. Once his enemies were eliminated or cowed, then a prince might be magnanimous, but not before.

Fear, not love, was the glue that held the state together and a prince who was not feared would not reign long.

Although Macchiavelli wrote *The Prince* in 1513, it was not published during his lifetime. He knew it was incendiary but he also knew it was revolutionary, a book to ensure his name lived on far longer than he. But although *The Prince* was not officially published until after Macchiavelli died, it circulated widely in manuscript form, attracting criticism, praise and the horrified fascination of a European political class having their linen hung out for all to see.

The publication of *The Prince* was the point at which political theory turned its back on the cultivation of virtue and embraced power.

For a long time it had been clear that the old saw, the enemy of my enemy is my friend, was true, but the increasingly blatant way this was applied during the Italian Wars led to that maxim being applied in slowly wider and more surprising contexts. We have seen how the Venetians allied with the French despite their previous enmity, but soon European princes would come to look with interest upon the possibility of gaining allies beyond the bounds of Christendom, with the traditional enemy, the Turk. No greater repudiation of the old Christian crusading ideal could be imagined than for one of the great European kings to enter into an alliance with the Grand Turk, the embodiment of Islam and the forces that had conquered the Holy Land. But that was what would happen within a few years.

The old ways were dying.

But it was not just in politics that things were changing. The Italian Wars forced through immense changes in the practical art of war.

One of the many things that makes the Italian Wars so confusing is that victory seemed to bear little fruit. The French had won crushing, seemingly decisive, victories at Agnadello and Ravenna, but these did not seem to make any difference to their long-term position. Cities changed hands with dizzying rapidity, none more so than Milan, which seemed to exchange ruler every third Thursday in the month. Armies marched backwards and forwards over northern Italy, besieging cities, laying waste and retreating and, at the end, everything went back to pretty well the same situation as at the start.

This was because combatants were trying to work out how to fight war with the new technologies that were coming on stream, as well as how to pay for larger armies while supporting them in the field. The wars were forcing wholesale changes in finances, logistics and recruitment, and strategy and tactics.

The most obvious change was in the men making up the armies tramping across northern Italy. At the start of the Italian Wars, the armies were made of equal numbers of cavalrymen and infantry. By the pause in hostilities brought by the treaties of Noyon and Brussels, there were six infantrymen for every man mounted on a horse.

Even the French, who had for centuries been the epitome of chivalry (even the word comes from the French) and whose armoured knights had been the basis of French power since Charles Martel, had switched to an infantry-based army, although it took longer for the traditions of martial chivalry to die out there than anywhere else.

The other armies in the Italian Wars spent its early decades attempting to counteract, emulate and develop the example of the Swiss mercenary infantry companies. Formations of highly drilled pikemen became the dominant force on the battlefield for a short while until other nations realised that the Swiss could be defeated by the use of combined arms, using arquebusiers, pikemen and halberdiers to support and protect each other.

This great expansion in the size of armies was possible because infantrymen were much cheaper to hire and to support than cavalrymen. They came from a lower social class and their weapons, be they pike, halberd or arquebus,[16] were much cheaper than the armour and weapons required by a man-at-arms. Furthermore, training the infantry was much quicker and cheaper than the years of practice required to turn a boy into a man-at-arms.

Gunpowder weapons also improved substantially during this era. The matchlock firing mechanism had been developed in the 1480s and this allowed arquebusiers to fire from the shoulder, sighting down the barrel, instead of shooting from the hip, which had been the previous practice. The cost of gunpowder also fell precipitously, becoming 80 per cent cheaper, while its quality saw an almost as impressive improvement: this meant that not only could arquebusiers afford to train properly, but when they did shoot they were far less subject to misfires.

Arquebuses were still inaccurate, particularly at longer ranges, but the effect of volleys of gunfire from ranks of arquebusiers was becoming increasingly marked on the battlefield.

Away from the battlefield, there had been very swift improvements in fortifications and defences. Even on the battlefield, commanders realised the value of digging ditches and raising banks to protect their men, particularly the artillery and the arquebusiers, from enemy fire. When it came to protecting cities and fortresses, the dismay and despair that had greeted the violent onset of the French in 1494 had given way to rapid changes in design. The old high, thin walls were ripped down and replaced by low, thick embankments. With a sufficiently willing populace, a good thick earthwork which could absorb any number of cannonballs could be thrown up in a matter of days. Meanwhile, more permanent defences were being built that featured heavily armed bastions standing proud of the city's main walls that could direct enfilade (flanking) fire right along the length of the walls, turning any attempt to get through a breach into a slaughter.

Because cannon remained large, heavy objects, defenders found it much easier to place them in bastions, protected by thick walls of earth and rock, than to trundle them around the countryside. So as long as a city or fortress had remade its fortifications in the new style, called in the rest of Europe the *trace italienne* (the Italian plan), then they could use much heavier and more devastating cannon in defence of their city or fortress than the attackers could bring to bear against it.

The pendulum, which had swung violently towards the attackers, was beginning to swing back towards defence.

However, the initial shocks of the Italian Wars had produced a pronounced change in military psychology. During the long medieval period, all-out, pitched battles were relatively rare. Of course, we learn about the battles at Hastings, Agincourt, Tours and suchlike, but in truth the day-to-day reality of medieval warfare was small-scale raiding and drawn-out sieges. Battles were not generally sought because of their chancy and irrevocable character.

But the Italian Wars saw a lot of battles. The commanding officers, in particular Gaston le Foix but not only him, sought out the enemy with the aim of forcing him into a decisive battle and defeating him.

This was a new strand to European war-making but it was one that would become the main strand of military thinking for the next few centuries – even though the battles of the Italian Wars proved peculiarly indecisive.

But the Italian Wars were not simply the result of impersonal economic forces and changing political ideas. It was a conflict driven by ambition and the personalities of the princes driving it. Among these princes, none was more important than the king of France.

And on 1 January 1515, this all changed: King Louis XII died. On 9 October 1514, the 52-year-old Louis had married Mary Tudor, the sister of Henry VIII, who was 18. Louis had no surviving male heirs and rumour has it that, desperate to finally produce a successor, the king wore himself out with his exertions in the bedchamber while trying to impregnate his much younger bride (there were 34 years between them).

Louis's efforts failed. He died.

The new king of France was his cousin, Francis. Francis was young, 20 when he took the throne, vital, energetic and the bearer of a truly magnificent nose.

The thrones of Europe were slowly being filled by young, healthy kings, pumped full of testosterone and dreams of chivalric glory. Henry in England. Francis in France. And there was the prospect of another to come: the putative heir to Spain and the Holy Roman Empire was the 15-year-old Charles, grandson of Maximilian.

The prospect was stormy.

21

A Military Engineer Abroad

Gabriele's escapade with Camillo da Barco had left him an exile and unemployed. But while the Capriolo and Averoldo families were influential, so was the family of Camillo and his cousin, Theofilo. The da Barchi immediately began calling in favours and pulling the strings of patronage, the unseen webbing that tied – and still ties – Italian society together.

It took a while but slowly the whispers and pleas began to have an effect. The efforts of the da Barco family were helped because Camillo, known as '*il contino*' ('the little count'), was genuinely much loved in Brescia before his expulsion. Camillo's charm even worked on members of the Averoldo family: he managed to persuade Monsignor Averoldo, whose testimony had seen his and Gabriele's service to the Republic ended, to plead their case to the Signoria.

With such advocates, and with the Republic's clear-eyed sense of its own advantage, it was only a matter of time before the verdict was quashed and Camillo and his band of adventurers released from the terms of their sentence.

Thankful to Monsignor Averoldi for his intervention, Camillo and Gabriele wrote to him, saying that they were very grateful to 'the Signoria and Monsignor the Legate, ever wishing to be good servants of the Republic'.[17]

By May 1520, Gabriele Tadino was once more a soldier in good standing with La Serenissima.

And it was becoming increasingly clear that the Republic would need his services in a new sphere: the Stato da Màr.

This was the maritime empire of the Republic, the string of ports and islands that guarded, maintained and enabled the trade routes to the East that had made Venice rich.

But it was also obvious that they needed to reinforce their defences on the islands of the Stato da Màr that they still held. Of these, the chief and most important was Crete – Candia to the Venetians.

It was 1520. Gabriele Tadino was 42. He had been studying the *trace italienne*, the new style of fixed defences, for nearly 30 years. He had fought in the Italian Wars for 12 years, taking part in battles, skirmishes and raids. He had gone on reconnaissance and acted on the reports of scouts. He had taken part in sieges as both defender and besieger. He had brought down defences by the skilful direction of artillery and defied cannon by designing new defences. He had pressed his ear to the floor of a tunnel, listening for the scritch-scratch of miners beneath him, and he had led sallies from concealed ports to attack sappers digging towards the walls.

Apart from the unfortunate Averoldo affair, he had served the Signoria faithfully, the gossip raised against him by a jealous rival subsumed under his conspicuous bravery in the face of the enemy.

He had served under some of the most able *condottieri* in Italy and he had led men himself, from small companies to full battalions. The winnowing fan of war had turned him into one of the most capable, and most versatile, commanders that the Republic had at its disposal.

As such, Gabriele was too valuable a resource to be left in retirement in Brescia. He was also too valuable to allow his expertise to be claimed by a rival power. The Venetians knew all too well that if they did not employ Tadino, then somebody else would.

So, they made him an offer: the governorship of Cyprus.

The birthplace of Venus was part of the Stato da Màr and service as its governor brought responsibility, prestige and an excellent salary, plus many opportunities to enrich oneself by other means. The Venetian empire was not corrupt by the standards of its time, but presents and exchanges were accepted parts of diplomacy and trade.

It was too good an offer to refuse. But hardly had Gabriele accepted, and before he had taken ship to claim his office, when he was given an even better offer: to be superintendent of the fortifications and captain of infantry of Candia (Crete), the most vital of all Venice's remaining overseas territories.

Crete was no easy posting but, with the exception of the *bailo* in Constantinople, it was the most important post in the Stato da Màr.

Gabriele accepted.

Without knowing it, a life that had heretofore been turned to the conflicts between the European princes would henceforth change its focus to the East, to the Ottomans, and to their great sultan, Suleiman.

Gabriele Tadino embarked with the quartermaster, Sebastiano Giustinian, sailing to Capodistria on the other side of the Adriatic (modern-day Koper in Slovenia). From there they sailed on to the island of Veglia (Krk in today's Croatia), where they boarded a galley to take them to Candia.

They did not travel alone. Tadino took with him considerable reinforcements for the island's defence: 20 infantrymen, 20 sergeant arquebusiers and 30 trained arquebusiers with their weapons. The Signoria, not content with the responsibilities it had already handed to Gabriele, also appointed him superintendent of artillery on the island, responsible for all the Venetian strongholds, fortresses and cities on Crete.

So far as we know, this was the first time that Gabriele had left Italy. Serving Venice, he would have met many people from abroad but, standing on the deck of the galley as the oarsmen pulled away, Venice disappearing into the light shimmer of the lagoon, Gabriele must have known a new chapter of his life was beginning. But he can have had no inkling of just how much his life would change in the next two years.

22

How Venice Became Rich

The Venice that Tadino watched disappear into the light glimmer of its lagoon floated on those waters as a mystery and a miracle. To the other states of the Middle Ages and the Renaissance, wealth was land and land was power: it was an equation from which neither term could be removed.

But Venice was rich and, for much of its history, it had almost no land beyond the island and lagoons of the city itself, and a few isolated ports and poor islands in the east. It was powerful, but its power lay in its ships and galleys rather than its men-at-arms – indeed, being a republic, the city did not even have a king who could confer such titles on his subjects.

As such, the city exercised a peculiar hold on the European imagination: it was beautiful but untrustworthy. Stories of Venice told of the city's unearthly beauty and its unimaginable wealth, but leavened those tales with gossip about how the Venetians would sell their own mothers for a good deal on spices from Alexandria.

For Venice was a city built upon trade at a time when European nobility reckoned their worth by blood, whether that be through bloodlines or bloodshed, rather than wealth. Yes, kings and princes, dukes and marquesses, counts and barons were generally rich men, but their wealth and power was something they measured by the land they controlled – hence in part the violence expended upon getting or defending land that these men regarded as rightfully theirs. Venice, on the other hand, during its ascent to power between the 11th and 15th centuries, had little in the way of land and not that much interest in acquiring more. What it did do was secure vital ports and islands to protect its trading interests to the east.

The Venetians were traders and merchants. They sailed to the markets of the Levant and Egypt, docking in the ports at Alexandria, Tripoli (the Lebanese port, not the one in Tunisia), Beirut and Smyrna, as well as the Great City, Constantinople, before returning home to sell on the goods they had bought there. These goods were chiefly high-value, luxury items such as spices, silks, gemstones and expensive dyes (some dyes were more valuable than gold but much lighter to transport). As such, they were perfect for merchants, allowing them to make greater profits while not having to hire huge fleets to transport the goods.

With the city's wealth and power dependent upon its trade with the Muslim East, Venice avoided involvement with the Crusades. But in 1202, the Venetians decided to assist the Fourth Crusade. The crusade's strategy was sound: with the main danger to the remaining Crusader states coming from Egypt, the plan was to attack Egypt directly, thus removing the chief peril to Outremer.

Through a series of misfortunes, errors and mistakes, coupled with decision-making on the galley and the pursual of short-term ends, a crusade that was meant to culminate in the conquest of the Muslim sultanate established in Egypt by Saladin instead ended with the Catholic Crusaders conquering the Orthodox Christian capital of Constantinople, establishing in the Greek-speaking empire a short-lasting, Latin-speaking, Catholic kingdom.

And it was not just Constantinople. With the temporary shattering of Byzantine power, many of the Crusaders, looking to the main chance and abashed at returning home as conquerors of Constantinople rather than Cairo, set about establishing their own petty kingdoms in the entrails of the Byzantine Empire. These short-lived kingdoms included the despotate of Epirus, the principality of Achaea, the triarchy of Negroponte, the duchy of the Archipelago and the megaskyrate of Athens and Thebes. The Crusaders elected a new emperor, who reigned as Baldwin I. Meanwhile, the Venetians, in the negotiations that carved up the Empire, had done well for themselves, securing three-eighths of the Empire, including Crete (three-eighths is 37.5 per cent). The Venetians, in their inimitable, mercantile manner, preferred to say that they were rulers of a Quarter and Half a Quarter of the Empire of the Romans.

The conquest of Constantinople opened up undreamed-of opportunities for Venice's merchant adventurers, and led to the creation of its Stato da Màr. It's characteristic of the Republic's approach to its territories abroad that the symbol of Venice, the lion of St Mark, was carved into the gates and ports 'for the honour and profit of Venice'. To the Venetians, unlike other Europeans, the two were twins.

As masters of a Quarter and Half a Quarter of the Empire of the Romans, including three eighths of Constantinople itself, the Venetians were now in a position to close their rivals, the Pisans and particularly the Genoese, out of the trade routes to the east. But the Genoese did not go down without a fight. The conflict dragged on for nearly two centuries and only really ended because the belligerents both came to realise that they had more formidable rivals to deal with: Aragon for the Genoese and the Ottomans for the Venetians.

While their deal with the Crusaders gave Venice a Quarter and Half a Quarter of the Empire, the Republic was not much interested in its land holdings. Let the knights spend their blood on petty wars between tiny kingdoms. La Serenissima knew that the true fruit of her victory lay in securing the trade routes to Constantinople and the spice markets of Alexandria, Acre and Beirut. To that end, the Venetians bought Crete from Boniface of Montserrat for 5,000 gold ducats. They expelled pirates from Coron and Modon, two strategic ports on the south-west of the Peloponnese, and claimed the long island of Euboea, which they called Negroponte (that's the long island to the north of Athens that comes so close to the mainland that a cursory glance at the map means most people think it's connected to the mainland).

The Venetians took control of a string of further islands and ports, but it was these four, Coron and Modon, Crete and Negroponte, that formed the core of the Stato da Màr: these were the possessions that the Venetians would fight long and hard to keep.

Coron and Modon (Koroni and Modoni in modern-day Greece) lie 15 miles apart as the crow flies, 20 miles by the sea routes the Venetians took. These twin ports were the eyes of the Republic, vital dispensers of information as well as victuals. Every ship returning from the Levant was required to stop at Coron and Modon to pass on whatever intelligence they had gathered about pirates and raiders, any wars that had broken out, while updating the merchants there on the latest price of spice.

Coron and Modon were Venice's first true colonies but its most important holding was Crete. Looking at the map, it's not hard to see its significance. It sits at the base of the Aegean Sea, like a giant broken lid at the bottom of a great pot. Any traffic passing north to Constantinople has to cross the 60-mile channel between the north-western tip of Crete and the south-eastern peninsula of the Peloponnese, while ships heading east to the spice ports of the Levant have to sail along the whole length of the island. As such, it commands the two major trade routes that brought wealth to Venice: Constantinople and the Levant.

It's easy to see why the Venetians were prepared to pay big money to Boniface of Montserrat to buy the island.

But it was one thing buying Crete, it was another thing keeping it. The island is big, covering 3,218 square miles (8,336 km^2) but it's also long and thin, 150 miles across but only about 30 miles wide. What's more, there were many more Cretans than Venetians, while the geography of the island, formed from six different mountain ranges which produced isolated valleys, small fertile plains and thousands and thousands of caverns, made the island a bandit's paradise.

The Venetians were a fundamentally urban people and they established themselves in the main city, Candia (modern-day Heraklion) and the towns of Retimo and Canea. Outside these urban hubs, Venetian rule was contested and, deep in the mountains and valleys of the interior, all but non-existent. The Cretans were fiercely loyal to the Byzantine Empire. The Venetians were representatives of the hated Latin Empire and, while that did not last, the Palaiologos dynasty that overthrew the Latin emperors was unable to reconquer Crete.

Moreover, the Venetians were Catholic and the Cretans were Orthodox. While Venetian rule was relatively benign elsewhere in the Stato da Màr, despite heavy taxation, it was fierce and often brutal in Crete, the Venetians responding to both the intractable resistance of the Cretans and their own vulnerable position. The Venetians imposed a thoroughgoing apartheid system, requiring anyone in a position of power to be 'flesh of our flesh, bone of our bone'. Should any Venetian convert to Orthodoxy, then he immediately lost his possessions on the island. No Orthodox priests were allowed to enter the island from abroad and the native Orthodox church was repressed although never entirely suppressed: such an act would have inspired the Cretans to a final rebellion. Even so, the 450 years of Venetian rule saw 27 separate revolts. If it were not for feuding between the various Cretan clans, the Venetians would surely have been expelled long before they finally lost the island to the Ottomans in 1669.

23

VENICE AND THE OTTOMANS

The Venetians were the first of the European powers to pay the Ottomans serious attention. On 1 June 1416, a Venetian fleet led by captain-general Pietro Loredano met an Ottoman fleet as he approached the port of Gallipoli. Loredano signalled that he wanted to talk, but his signal was mistaken as the opening shot of a Venetian attack, and the Ottomans opened fire, raining arrows down upon the Venetian galleys.

It was the start of the first major naval battle between the Venetians and the rising power in the east, the Ottomans.

The outcome was a decisive Venetian victory. The Venetians captured six Ottoman galleys along with their crews, which in this case means the slave rowers required to propel the galleys, and nine galleots (a shorter galley, with two masts and 16 pairs of oars).

The Venetians, in an early example of the brutal pragmatism that would govern their dealings with the Ottomans for the next two centuries, quickly realised that the Ottomans had recruited Christian renegades to captain and navigate their fleet: these they put to death. Those who had been the most enthusiastic converts to the Ottoman cause were impaled on stakes, left to writhe in agony along the shore as a dreadful warning to any others thinking about taking the Ottoman coin. The slaves who had been brought in to row the galleys were freed, although most were then enlisted to row the Venetian galleys as free men. The Republic was unusual in that most of the men who pulled the oars of its galleys were free, not slaves. Indeed, through most of the history of the Republic, taking the oars was seen as an important part of the education of even the highest-born Venetian.

The savage response to the Christians working freely for the Ottomans was recognition, on the part of the Venetians, that this was where their greatest danger lay. The Ottomans were the descendants of Turkic peoples who came originally from the great open plains of central Asia. They were horse nomads, at home in the grass plains. But when they reached the sea, they encountered a new plain that was entirely outside their experience. Realising the strategic importance of naval power, the Ottomans, who were becoming an increasingly multi-ethnic empire, brought in outside knowledge to build, crew and command their ships: rowers they could obtain easily from the slave traffic that was one of the most lucrative trades in the empire.

Pietro Loredano's victory in 1416 gave Venice a long breathing space. It also gave them what would prove to be a misplaced confidence in their naval superiority. Venetian captains boasted that it required four or five Ottoman galleys to best one of their own.

This might have been true in 1416, but the odds slowly tilted more evenly as the century progressed and the Ottomans began to control longer and longer stretches of the Mediterranean shore. By 1481, the Empire controlled the whole of Asia Minor, Greece and most of the Balkans. Putting that onto a modern-day map, it would include the whole of Turkey, Greece, Bulgaria, Albania, Macedonia, Kosovo, Montenegro, and most of Bosnia, Serbia and Romania. The Ottomans controlled the whole upper right coast of the Mediterranean.

The two could hardly have been more opposed in religion, culture or political philosophy. The Christian Venetians were merchants to the core, measuring success on the scales with which they doled out the gold to buy the goods they traded. The Ottomans were nomadic adventurers, addicted to gold and glory, who measured success in land and slaves. Venice was a republic where anyone who seemed on the verge of becoming over-mighty would be cut down by the combining of enemies; the sultan ruled as an absolute ruler, his chief servants, in the army, the political class and among his own lovers, being his personal slaves, his to do with as he willed.

The Venetians had long had dealings with the mamelukes, the rulers of Egypt, but they quickly realised that the Ottomans were different: restless, energetic and addicted to war. A new sultan legitimised his rule by conquest. Failure to expand the Empire would lead to his removal.

As the coastline that the Ottomans controlled lengthened, the Venetians became increasingly aware of the vulnerability of their scattered port fortresses and islands to such a widely based land empire. To counter this, they began to devote more and more resources to understanding this new power and the men who ruled it. In 1362, Venice had sent an ambassador to congratulate Sultan Murat I on establishing his new capital in Adrianople, modern-day Edirne. Having their capital in Adrianople meant that the Turks had surrounded Constantinople, leaving it to all intents and purposes an Imperial city minus the empire required to sustain it. Byzantium was a spent force. It was clear to all but the most optimistic of the Romans that the Ottomans were the heirs to the old empire.

Venice began to expend serious money on buying influence at the Ottoman court. When an embassy went to visit the sultan, it took gifts carefully calculated to be fit for the king of the world: the richest robes, a pearl-buttoned fur coat and, a gift especially suitable for a sultan who loved to hunt, two huge hunting dogs named Falchon and Passalaqua. The dogs proved a particular hit: Sultan Murat sent a message with the returning ambassador, asking the Venetians to send him a matching bitch so that he could breed from Falchon and Passalaqua.

This response was characteristic of the particular genius of the Ottomans: they were not too proud to learn. Having come from the great Asian plains, where toughness, the endurance to ride a horse for a long day, and the ability to survive killing weather were more important to survival than an appreciation of the finer points of courtly etiquette, they nevertheless had the typical nomadic love of beauty, particularly in words. As the descendants of Osman became the rulers of an empire, they brought with them the pragmatism of their forebears: so what if they did not know how to cast a cannon, for surely someone in their vast empire would have that knowledge. And if there was something that no one within the empire knew how to do, then they would pay for someone to come to them with that knowledge. For the Ottomans quickly demonstrated that they were generous employers. What was more, those who were prepared to embrace Islam had the prospect of advancing very high within the empire.

Osman, the founder of the empire, had laid the foundations for its longevity by analysing and overcoming the fundamental weakness of nomad confederations: the rivalry between different clans that led to civil war. While retaining the various clans, Osman and his successors derived their army and the chief officers of the empire from the sultan's personal slaves. This was institutionalised through the *devshirme*, the 'child tax' the Ottomans levied on their Christian subjects.

Ottoman rulers had originally taken their slaves from prisoners of war or slaves traded into the empire. But to ensure their independence from the powerful Turkish clans, the sultans began the practice of regularly harvesting promising children from their Christian subjects in the Balkans. Ottoman officials would tour a specific region, inspecting children between the ages of seven and 20. Almost uniquely for the time, the officials were completely uninterested in the children's backgrounds or breeding. They could come from the meanest, poorest village in the empire but if, in such unpromising soil, a boy was growing of uncommon intelligence and beauty, then he would be taken.

The attitudes of the sultan's subjects to the child tax were mixed. Obviously, many parents objected to losing their children. However, refusal to give the child up would result in the torture or execution of the parents, and the child would still be taken away, so such resistance was futile. Nevertheless, many people did attempt to save their children by hiding them, bribing officials, or converting to Islam.

To minimise the opposition to the *devshirme*, Ottoman officials generally took most of the children from the poorest villages. In such areas, parents were faced with a dreadful dilemma. If their son proved able, then he would likely gain a place among the Janissaries, the sultan's elite troops, or become a member of the Imperial civil service. In either case, he would be able to provide for them and the rest of his birth family. Records suggest that many of the children pressed into the sultan's service retained links to their birth families, sending them remittances that, in the context of village poverty, would have made them immensely wealthy locally.

So some parents chose the pragmatic path and sent their sons away, hoping to reap the rewards of his service.

The boys taken were trained, converted to Islam and prepared for service to the sultan. The prospects for an intelligent, able child could be very great: most of the grand viziers of the Ottoman Empire were originally children taken through the child tax.

The Venetians put a great deal of effort into learning the inner dynamics and personalities of the Ottomans, finally even training a specialised group of interpreters, the *giovanni di lingua*, to facilitate communications with the Sublime Porte.

Just as much effort was put into learning the rules of *baksheesh*, and greasing those wheels. Ottoman officials expected to receive gifts from supplicants and ambassadors; these were not seen as bribes but tokens of appreciation and respect. One would no more approach a pasha without a suitable gift than one would today arrive at a dinner party without a bottle of wine or a bunch of flowers.

This worked both ways. Ottoman ambassadors and messengers to Venice brought presents from the Sublime Porte. The Venetians, flinty merchants that they were, received these gifts with exclamations of admiration and gratitude, and then promptly had them professionally valued so that they could be sure to return the gifts in kind and value. It would not do to be outdone in the contest of generosity when seeking a favour with an Ottoman official.

As Ottoman power grew, Venetian policy shifted. When there was a strong sultan in place, then they avoided conflict as far as was possible, even going so far as to pay 'Turkgeld' to forestall attacks and the border raiding that the Ottomans used to soften up their next targets. But when a sultan seemed weak, or there were rival claimants to the throne during the bloody fratricidal strife that followed the death of the reigning sultan, then the Venetians would do whatever they could to muddy the waters of succession by supporting rival claimants to the throne as well as making fleeting alliances with some of the rival Turkic tribes that threatened the Ottomans from the east and north.

On 3 February 1451, a new sultan came to the throne, Mehmed II. During his education, Mehmed had learned of the civil war that had raged when his grandfather, the first Mehmed, took the throne, when for eight years the first Mehmed had struggled against his three brothers for the right to rule.

Mehmed was determined this would not happen to him. So, the day after his father died, Mehmed had his younger half-brother strangled while the boy's mother was congratulating him on his accession to the throne. Having disposed of all his rivals, Mehmed then promulgated the Law of Fratricide in his *Kanūnnāme*, the Imperial law code:

> And to whichever of my sons the sultanate may come, it is fitting to execute his brothers for the sake of the order of the world. The majority of the ulema have also sanctioned this. Let action be taken accordingly.[18]

To the Venetians, it was clear that Mehmed was bent on continuing the conquests made by his grandfather. It was not only the Venetians who saw what was coming. Constantine, the emperor of Constantinople, saw it too. While the empire was much truncated, the city itself endured, surrounded to east and west by the Turks but safe behind walls that had repelled almost all efforts to take the city for the last thousand years. In fact, the only people to have successfully conquered Constantinople would soon find themselves the recipient of a desperate letter from Constantine. The emperor needed friends and he needed them fast. To that end, he wrote to the Republic, telling them what they already knew, of the preparations being made by Mehmed, and, swallowing a bitter pill, asking for their help: 'There is no doubt that this time the city will succumb if no one comes to the aid of the Greeks and the courageous help of the Venetians would be a great prize.'[19]

In response to this plea, the Venetians vacillated. Merchants though they were, they were not immune to Constantine's appeal, nor to the call to defend the city that had figured so greatly in Venice's history and its dreams. But they were realists: in the face of the immense forces that Mehmed was amassing, they could not act alone. So they passed on the desperate plea to the pope and the other Christian princes, calling on them to put aside their differences and unite in the defence of the bulwark of Christendom.

Of course, that plea came to nothing. The pope wanted to dispatch five galleys to Constantinople but expected the Venetians to pay for them on credit. The Venetians, nursing bitter memories of previous papal defaults, refused to supply the necessary credit.

While Venice and the Christian kingdoms dithered, the Ottomans tightened the noose around the city on the Golden Horn. But trapped within that horn were Venetians too, the merchants, sailors and soldiers who plied the centuries-old trade route between the two cities, and the *bailo*, the chief Venetian diplomat to the city and the emperor.

Faced with the choice of slipping out of the city in their fast galleys while they still could, or staying to man the defences of the city, the Venetians stayed. The only exception was a crew of Venetian sailors who managed to escape the blockade around the city by pretending to be Turks and sailed out across the Sea of Marmara to the Dardanelles to keep watch for the longed-for relief force.

After keeping watch for three weeks, the Venetians realised that no help was coming.

They could return home – or they could go back to Constantinople and take part in its final defence. As true Venetians, they voted – and they decided to return.

The Venetians in the city fought to the end alongside the Greeks, all distinctions of faith and enmities of history forgotten in Constantinople's final travails.

The city that had stood for 1,100 years fell on 29 May 1453.

Some Venetians managed to escape, sailing away in their galleys, returning to Venice to bring the news the Republic expected but feared. As the ships arrived, announcing the news to the waiting, silent crowd, 'there were great and desperate wailings, cries and groans, everyone beating the palms of their hands, beating their breasts with their fists, tearing their hair and their faces, for the death of a father, a son or a brother – or for their property'.[20]

Having taken a short while to get over the shock, the Venetians sent an embassy to Mehmed, in his new capital, to offer him their compliments on his success and to ask for their accustomed trading rights to be respected and renewed. Mehmed, equally pragmatic, accepted the gifts the embassy brought and gave the Venetians excellent terms.

From the accession of Mehmed, the interest the Republic took in understanding the nature and personality of the sultan deepened, becoming virtually an obsession. The *bailo* in Constantinople under the Ottomans was the most important and best paid in the Venetian diplomatic service but it was also the most difficult. Both sides protested their good faith, keen on accruing the greatest profit possible from their uneasy commerce. Nonetheless, the Venetians knew all too well that the Grand Turk was committed to their eventual destruction, while the sultan was equally well aware that, should he give any sign of weakness, then the Venetians would exploit that weakness to its full.

But there was one area in which the relationship was not that between equals: the Venetians knew that, should the Grand Turk decide, then he could stop the trade upon which their wealth depended and, with slightly more effort, take the islands that constituted the Stato da Màr. For the Grand Turk, the relationship could perhaps best be likened to a great shark swimming serenely through the sea, attended by a pilot fish that swims alongside the great predator, picking up scraps leftover from its meals, cleaning parasites from the great fish and scaring away predators by its proximity to the shark.

The relationship, and the need on the part of both sides to gain information, exert influence and influence policy, led to the early development of the whole panoply of spying and covert operations: the invention of codes and cyphers, the employment of agents, the turning of officials, the deliberate spreading of misinformation, as well as 'wetwork' that went from torture to targeted assassinations.

It was a cold war conducted with punctilious politeness and a hard nose for the costs involved. The conflict was made more difficult for the Venetians through the machinations of their Italian rivals. The Genoese and the Florentines, in particular, were keen to displace the Venetians as the favoured merchant nation of the Sublime Porte, and the Grand Turk was careful to keep representatives of both republics in Constantinople, both to remind the Venetians that there were other players in the game but also so that the Genoese and Florentine diplomats could pass on information they had acquired to discomfit their Italian rival.

As it became more and more uncomfortably aware of the scope of Mehmed's ambitions, the Signoria was forced to contemplate what it had tried to avoid: war. The sultan that history has nicknamed 'the Conqueror' was determined to do just that.

So the Venetians fought. Alone, despite the promises of other Christian princes and the rhetoric of the popes, they fought without help for 16 long years... and were utterly defeated.

Exhausted and nearing bankruptcy, the Venetians sent their most experienced diplomat to the Sublime Porte to negotiate the best peace possible.

The Republic lost Negroponte, one of its key bases in the Stato da Màr. It lost most of its forts and bases on the Peloponnese and, to regain its trading rights in Constantinople, the Venetians agreed to pay 10,000 ducats a year for the privilege, on top of the hundred thousand ducats the sultan required in a one-off payment to end the war. A new *bailo* sailed to Constantinople to resume diplomatic relations with the Sublime Porte under these new terms, taking with him the artist Gentile Bellini, who was part of the peace treaty: under its terms, Bellini would paint his famous portrait of Sultan Mehmed.

On 3 May 1481, Mehmed died. Sixteen days later, the news reached Venice. In response, church bells rang, Masses of thanksgiving were offered up and over the city's waterways rang the cry, 'The great eagle is dead!'

Mehmed's successor, Bayezid II, was a gentler soul, more concerned with religion than conquest, although on a practical level, he was also working with an empire that had exhausted its treasury in Mehmed's endless wars.

For just under 31 years, the Venetians were able to get on with business. Bayezid even let them off paying the annual tribute they had negotiated with his father. Meanwhile, business with the Mameluks, the rulers of Egypt, boomed as the Republic reaped the benefit of Europe's inexhaustible appetite for the spices and luxury goods of the East, which they bought in Alexandria and shipped to Europe.

But while Venice grew richer on its near monopoly with trade in the Mediterranean, the Mediterranean, the sea at the heart of the world, was diminishing before the Great Ocean. Classical authors distinguished between the Mediterranean, whose boundaries they knew, and the Great Ocean that flowed limitless and unknown beyond the Pillars of Hercules. But over the last half century sailors from a land that clung to the margins of the world, Portugal, had begun exploring the vast unknown. What they discovered would, in the end, cut off the taps of gold and spice that fed the wealth of Venice.

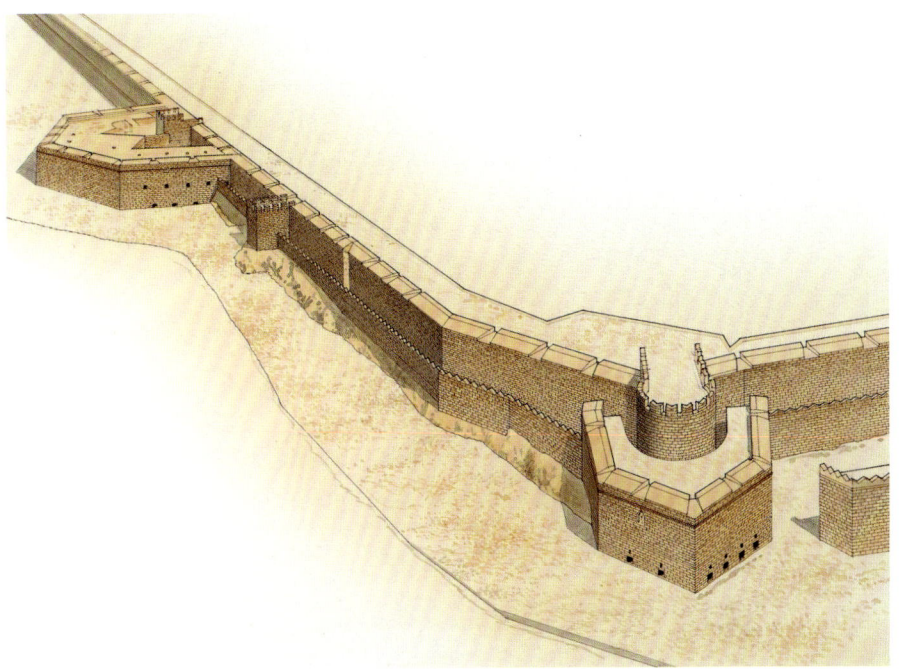

The freestanding bastion protecting the post of Auvergne allowed the Knights to pour enfilading fire along the length of the curtain wall and the moat. (Brian Delf © Osprey Publishing)

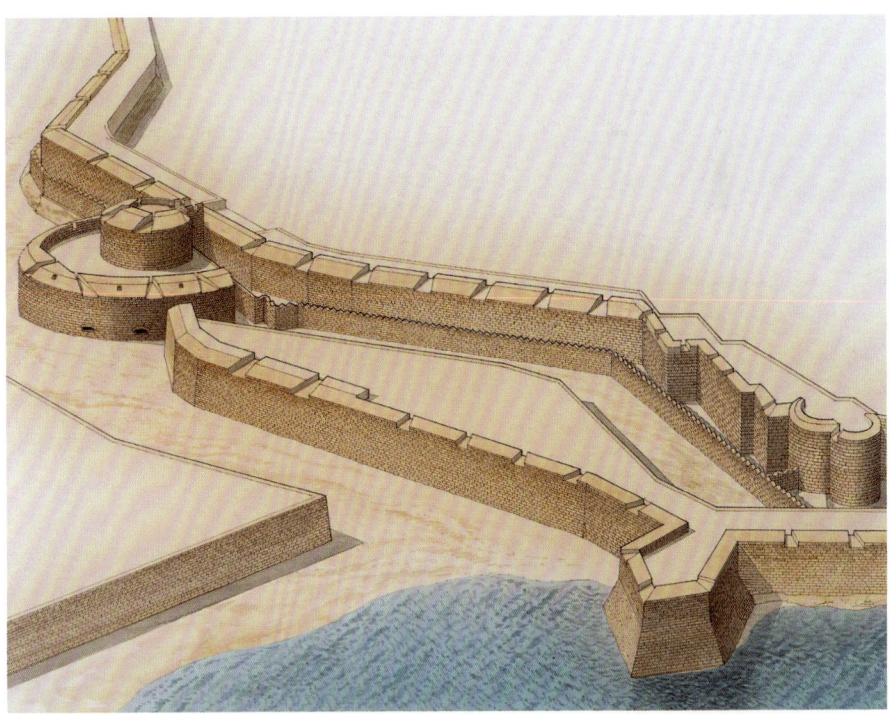

The post of Italy was protected by the substantial *tenaille* in front of the curtain. The inner face of the *tenaille* shows the width of the original moat. (Brian Delf © Osprey Publishing)

The defences of the post of England in 1480 and 1522. Note how narrow the original moat was. (Brian Delf © Osprey Publishing)

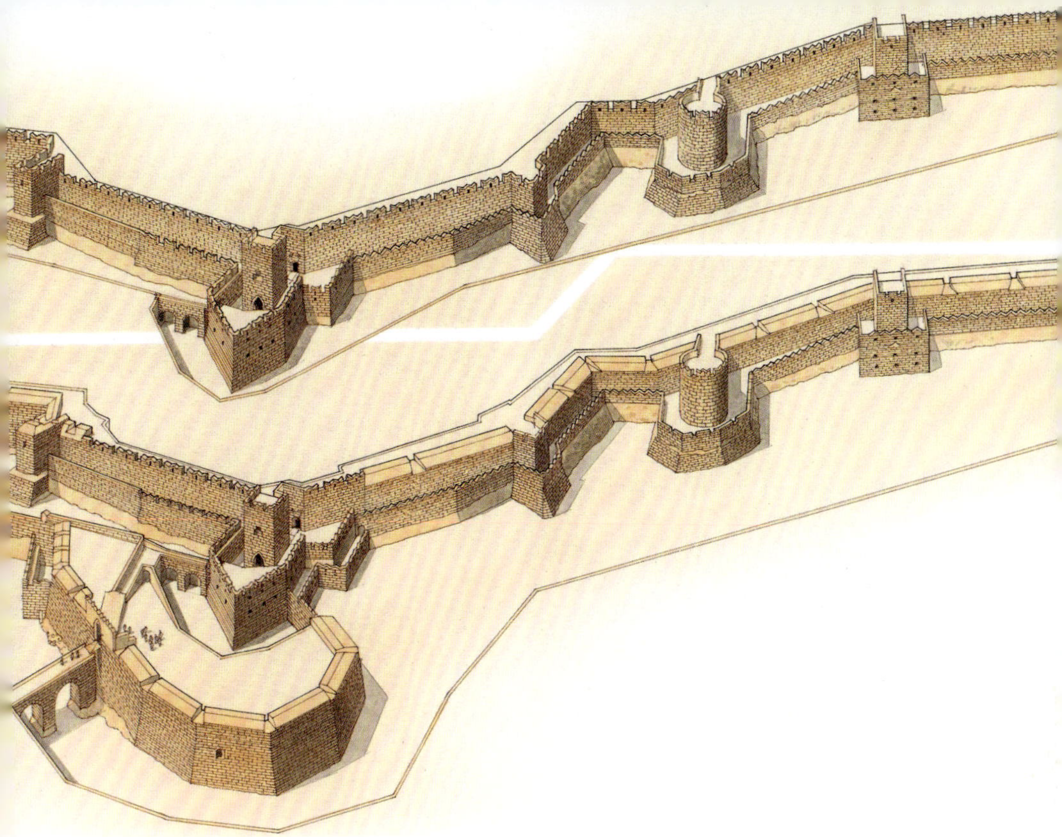

The upgraded defences for the post of Provence follow the same theme: a widening of the moat, thickening of the walls and the building of a bastion. (Brian Delf © Osprey Publishing)

The negotiations between Suleiman and the Knights Hospitaller lasted for 16 days and included three face-to-face meetings between the sultan and the Grand Master. (Getty Images)

There are few paintings of the siege in Ottoman sources. This one depicts well the distinctive uniform and head dress worn by Suleiman's Janissaries. (Getty Images)

Francis I, king from 1515 to 1547, was the first Renaissance ruler of France. (Getty Images)

Charles V, king of Spain and Holy Roman Emperor, ruled over the world's first truly trans-oceanic empire. (Getty Images)

This famous portrait of Suleiman is attributed to Titian and his workshop. (Getty Images)

Titian and his busy workshop were also responsible for this portrait of Gabriele Tadino, painted in 1538. (Alamy)

Looking at portraits of Charles VIII, it's clear that the pile-up of genetic defects that result from royal inbreeding affected his development. (Getty Images)

This painting of the Battle of Pavia does a good job of showing the crucial importance of the walls around the Visconti Park. (Getty Images)

If Gaston de Foix had not rashly charged a group of retreating Spanish soldiers, the Italian Wars might have ended very differently. (Getty Images)

The garish uniforms of the soldiers of the 16th century, such as the *Landsknechte* shown here, helped establish who was friend and who enemy amid the chaos and swirling smoke. (Getty Images)

European visitors to the Sublime Porte were always impressed by the discipline and silence that surrounded the sultan – very different from European courts. (Getty Images)

It was not only German *Landsknechte* who wore multi-coloured outfits; if anything, Italian *condottieri* were even more eye catching. (Getty Images)

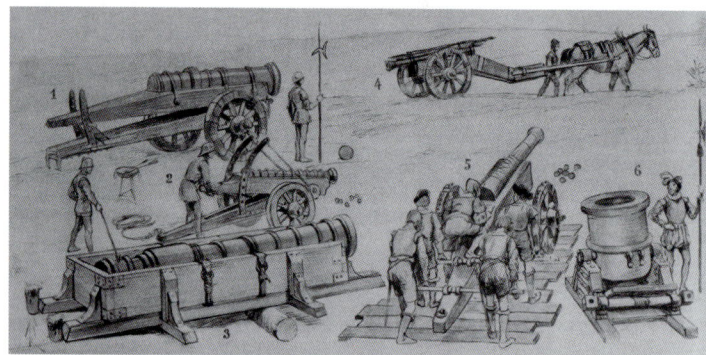

The names, design, barrel lengths and bore of cannon were far from standardised during the Italian Wars. (Getty Images)

It was not only the infantry who wore striking outfits; the artillerymen did too, making for spectacular, if increasingly lethal, battles. (Getty Images)

24

THE WORLD GETS BIGGER

Dreams are sweetest just before they end and then, in their ending, as we wake to the day, we chase after them and lose them in the waking.

The dream of wealth that had made Venice a city floating on water was to be broken by water. But not the calm waters of the Venetian lagoon; rather, the grey waves of the ocean.

The Portuguese, stuck on the edge of the world, had invented a new type of ocean-going ship, able to cope with the rigours of the Atlantic. Sailors manning these sturdy caravels, rigged with both lateen and square sails, were slowly exploring south, charting the coast of Africa in conjunction with a group of navigators, astronomers and scientists that the Portuguese kings had gathered in Lisbon, dedicated to exploring the world, finding a new route to the east around Africa and making contact with Prester John, the legendary Christian king in the East.

In 1488, Bartolomeu Dias rounded the Cape of Good Hope, proving that there really was a sea route to the Indian Ocean. The Portuguese had gradually pushed south down the African coast, marking the terminal point of each exploration by planting stone columns on prominent headlands. But their progress stalled at the Skeleton Coast, the bleak and unforgiving strand of Namibia, where desert falls directly into sea.

Portuguese sailors trying to push south faced the counter-current of the South Atlantic Gyre, a constant flow of water pushing them back north. To counteract the current, they had to rely on the winds, but in these latitudes, which came to be known as the Doldrums, winds were fickle, light and often fell away to flat calm.

Faced with these unpromising sailing conditions, Bartolomeu Dias did something extraordinary. Rather than continuing trying to inch his way south along the coast, Dias turned the rudder and sailed west, directly out into the uncharted ocean. He was gambling that, away from the coast, the winds would pick up and the current slacken off.

The gamble paid off. Dias sailed south into increasing cold and winds from the west, which grew stronger and stronger. Only after sailing south for weeks did he turn east again, riding the unending swell of the great southern ocean, where the winds play their ceaseless game of chase unimpeded by any break of land.

On 4 February 1488, after 33 days sailing the open ocean, the lookout's cry went out.

'Land!'

The expedition of two caravels had reached the southern tip of Africa. They had found the ocean route to the East. All the treasures of the Indies were there, lying ahead of them, if the Portuguese simply had the courage to claim them.

For by sailing directly to the Indies, the Portuguese knew that they could deal directly with the producers of the spices that the Venetians sold on to Europe, cutting out all the middlemen along the way who asked for their own slice of the spice pie.

Although the Signoria did not know it yet, 4 February 1488 signalled the end of Venice as a great trading power. Its decline was not immediate – it would take a century or so for the spice trade to be redirected around the Cape of Good Hope – but Dias's exploration began the age of European discovery. With the opening up of the world to ocean-going ships, the Mediterranean went from being the centre of the world to a land-locked irrelevance, a large lake with some pretty cities dotting its coast.

In time, the Venetians came to realise this, trading on the beauty of their city and its ability to entrance visitors. But Venice would never again be the power it had been.

In July 1501, the Signoria received the report of its envoy, which it had sent west, to the court of the Portuguese kings, to investigate some disturbing rumours that had reached the city about Portuguese discoveries. The news was shattering.

> At the receipt of this news, the whole city... was dumbfounded and the wisest thought it the worst news ever heard. They understood that Venice had ascended to such fame and wealth

only through trading by sea, by means of which a large quantity of spices were brought in, which foreigners came from everywhere to buy. From their presence and the trade [Venice] acquired great benefits. Now from this new route the spices of India will be transported to Lisbon, where Hungarians, Germans, the Flemish and the French will look to buy, being able to get them at a better price. Because the spices that come to Venice pass through Syria and the sultan's lands, paying exorbitant taxes at every stage of the way, when they get to Venice the prices have increased so much that something originally worth a ducat costs a ducat seventy or even two. From these obstacles, via the sea route, it will come about that Portugal can give much lower prices.[21]

Some relief came to the Republic, however, during the reign of Selim, Bayezid's son, from 1512 to 1520. Although Selim was known, with some justification, as Selim the Grim, and during his reign it became a popular curse to wish someone to be his grand vizier, so many of these officials did he execute, Selim's focus lay east and south. He pushed back the rising power of Safavid Iran and then, in a masterpiece of campaigning, overthrew the Mameluke Sultanate, adding Egypt, the Levant, and the holy cities of Mecca and Medina as well as much of the Arabian peninsula, to the Ottoman Empire. By the end of his reign, Selim had expanded the empire by 70 per cent.

Selim had made use of Mehmed's law of fratricide to remove his various half-brothers at the start of his reign. But when it came to his own successor, he did the blood work on his son's behalf, removing all the potential rivals to his ablest son, Suleiman. That left Suleiman a clear run when his father died suddenly and unexpectedly at the age of 49, probably from disease although death at such a relatively young age inevitably raised suspicions of poison. However, with all his potential rivals dead, Suleiman had no need to make such a risky move against his father, a man who had ruthlessly quashed all previous challenges to his rule. Since all Suleiman had to do was wait for the throne to come to him, death by natural causes remains the likeliest reason for Selim's death.

Suleiman's accession to the throne of the Ottoman Empire meant that the great kingdoms in Europe were all ruled by young, energetic, able and ambitious men: Francis I, king of France, born on

12 September 1494, king from 1 January 1515; Henry VIII, king of England, born 28 June 1491, king from 22 April 1509; Charles V, king of Spain and Holy Roman Emperor, born 24 February 1500, king of Spain from 14 March 1516 and Holy Roman Emperor from 28 June 1519; and Suleiman I, sultan of the Ottoman Empire, born 6 November 1494, sultan from 30 September 1520.

Contemporary observers, seeing this conjunction of rival kings, were soon predicting that these four princes would contend for mastery of the stage of history during the next few decades – and they were right.

Henry VIII, stuck on his island in the ocean, would have the least effect on events in the Mediterranean. But Charles, Francis and Suleiman became the key players, with each seeking to play the other off against their more pressing rival.

For Francis, with his kingdom surrounded on all sides by the realm of his great rival, who ruled both Spain, the Low Countries and what we would today call Germany, was acutely aware that he needed a counterweight and plausible threat to pull Charles's attentions away from him.

Suleiman, who was born just 55 days after Francis, was that counterweight and threat. The rival Spanish kingdoms of Castile and Aragon had united through the marriage of Ferdinand and Isabella. Inheriting their kingdoms, Charles also acquired the excellent Aragonese navy. With Genoa in decline, and the Balearic Islands and the whole eastern coast of Spain in his possession, Charles had the ships to turn the western half of the Mediterranean into a Spanish lake, just as the eastern half was falling more completely under the control of the Ottomans.

Look at a map of the Mediterranean. Unlike the great oceans, it's delineated by land, cradled by Europe, North Africa and the Levant, with Italy's boot drawn back to kick Sicily into the goal. What's also obvious from the map is the narrowness of the channels that separate the Mediterranean from the connecting bodies of water: the Strait of Gibraltar is less than nine miles wide at its narrowest point, while the Bosporus, which connects the Black Sea to the Mediterranean via the Sea of Marmara, is even narrower, less than half a mile wide in places.

Indeed, it's now clear that about five million years ago a vast flood broke through the spit of land that cut off the deep dry desert of the

Mediterranean basin from the ocean. In a few years, the whole basin flooded in what scientists now call the Zanchean flood.

The geography of that flood still dominates the Mediterranean. It is still a sea split into two halves, with Sicily all but cutting the sea in half and Malta rising from the waves at a crucial point so that it dominates the strait that separates Sicily from North Africa.

The Ottomans were the descendants of nomads, the horsemen of the great Eurasian steppe. But for Suleiman to claim the destiny that he believed was his, he would have to become master of a new plain: the flat waters of the Mediterranean.

The horse warriors would have to become sea warriors.

But to do that, they would need to remove the nest of pirates and raiders that sat across the sea lanes from Constantinople to the Levant, the home of the sworn enemies of Islam and the last Crusaders: Rhodes, the base of the Order of Knights of the Hospital of St John of Jerusalem, the Knights Hospitaller.

25

SULEIMAN

'This Sultan is wealthy in revenue, in men and their obedience.'[22]

On 7 November 1520, the Signoria selected one of its most experienced and able diplomats to convey the congratulations of the Republic to the new sultan of the Sublime Porte. The diplomat's name was Marco Minio. He set sail with a rich inventory of gifts for Suleiman and anyone else of influence in his court, as well as strict instructions to gather all the information he could about the new man sitting on the throne of Osman. As source for this information, Minio was pumping Venice's resident *bailo* for all that he knew, as well as gathering all other knowledge that he could find.

Venice was the world's first information state: having realised that they could not defeat the Ottomans, the Venetians swiftly realised that their prosperity and their security depended upon having the best and most accurate information about the reigning sultan, his plans, ambitions and abilities, as well as the capacity of his empire to meet those plans and ambitions.

Minio did his work well. When he left Constantinople to take up his new post as governor of Candia – the previous governor, as we shall hear, had left his post without the permission of the Signoria – Minio dispatched his secretary back to Venice with his report.

It made for chastening reading.

According to Minio, the sultan's annual income was three million gold ducats. The tax the sultan levied on his Christian and Jewish subjects, the *jizya* mandated by Islamic law, brought him 1,200,000 ducats annually. The balance of the sultan's annual income derived from a tax on sheep, which brought in 800,000 ducats a year, another 800,000 from a tax on mines, with the remainder coming from taxes on the production of salt and other businesses.

But gold was not the basis of Suleiman's power. That power lay in people. Suleiman had lots of them. More than the Signoria could easily comprehend. As Minio explained, all the sultan's subject peoples were required to supply a certain number of soldiers – the precise number adjusted to account for the wealth and population of each area – for each of the sultan's campaigns. The bill for these men had to be footed by the people sending them. They were added to the sultan's own personal army, the Janissaries.

And it wasn't just men for his army that the sultan could requisition. Minio's report told the Signoria that Suleiman was beefing up his shipyards in Constantinople and Gallipoli. Should he require more men to man his galleys, the surrounding districts were required to supply him with one in ten men, while the tackle and ropes required for the galleys could be requisitioned too. These men would be expected to be part of the fighting contingent on the galleys; the rowers were slaves, and there was never any shortage of them in the sultan's realm.

Minio also gave the Signoria a pen portrait of Suleiman himself, based on the audience he had with the sultan.

To gain admittance, Minio had been taken through the halls of the sultan's palace, going from the public halls inwards, each hall more private and more guarded than the one before, passing through serene gardens where peacocks and other exotic birds and animals paraded, until he came finally to the anteroom of the audience hall.

What particularly struck Minio, beyond even the splendour and wealth of the buildings and decorations, was the quiet and the decorum of the sultan's servants and ministers. Minio had previously been the Venetian ambassador to the pope; he was familiar with the splendour of Renaissance Rome. But while there was nothing in the sultan's palace to match the beauty of Raphael's paintings or the magnificence of the Sistine Chapel, the behaviour of the people in the two courts could not have been more different. Rome was a cacophony; people talked, walked about and called out, even during Masses; it gave the impression of market and public piazza and courthouse and theatre.

The sultan's palace was completely different. As Minio approached the centre, he was struck most of all by the quiet and stillness of the place. The slaves did their work in silence, scurrying about in soft slippers that made no sound. The dignitaries and officials whom Minio passed, with sentries standing guard at each new gate, conducted their business in whispers, while the soldiers stood in impassive, unmoving silence, lining the walls of the halls and guarding each door.

It was as if the cacophony of the world was excluded from the sultan's presence, for as he drew closer to Suleiman, it became quieter and quieter.

Then, entering the hall of audience, silent and impassive chamberlains took hold of Minio's arms, one on each elbow, and accompanied him across the great hall. His feet made no sound upon the thick carpets – of course, he had been required to remove his shoes before entering the hall, that no filth of the outside world be taken into the sultan's presence. Standing around the hall like statues, they were so still and quiet, were many of the greatest and most powerful men of the empire. Yet they made no sound but simply followed Minio's progress with their eyes.

Reaching Suleiman, who was sitting upon a magnificently embroidered cushion of the richest cloth, Minio prostrated himself three times.

The audience was short but Minio reported that the sultan's temperament was melancholic, proud, impulsive and generous. Because Suleiman stayed sitting throughout their interview, Minio could not say how tall he was but the spotless white turban he wore lent his gaze a hooded cast.

From other sources, Minio learned that Suleiman had a strong bow arm and was able to fire an arrow further than anyone else at his court – although he added that he did not know if this pre-eminence was due to the sultan's ability or a reluctance on the part of any of his servants to outdo their master in a sporting contest. He also learned that, in common with previous Ottoman sultans, Suleiman had trained in a particular craft; in his case, gold and silver smithing.

Unable to learn more from the sultan himself, Minio cultivated contacts with Suleiman's officials. This was, as Minio realised, not a one-way process: they were trying to draw information from him just as much as he was trying to draw it from them. For instance, in one conversation, the deputy vizier asked him about the character of the pope, the size of his armies and how much revenue he accrued from the church. In the delicate dance of truth and untruth, Minio exaggerated the numbers while trying to keep his disinformation plausible. The deputy vizier also asked Minio for information about

Francis I, the Most Christian King, and Charles V, the Holy Roman Emperor – although he never referred to Charles as an emperor. So far as Suleiman was concerned, the world could be home to but one emperor, and he was it.

Henry VIII was asked after but dismissed as a king too concerned with matters of the bedroom.

The deputy vizier also blandly asked, as if it were a matter of no import at all, after the relations between Venice and those two rival Christian states, France and the Empire. Minio dissembled, seeking to present their relations as cordial while knowing that the sultan's officials knew all too well of the recent wars between all three.

Just as blandly, but the blandness did not hide the threat, the vizier wanted Minio's recommendation for the quickest and easiest route between Constantinople and Rome. By implication, the sultan's mind was turning to the conquest of the first Rome, for his grandfather had taken the second Rome.

Moving on from veiled threats against Rome, the official asked Minio, whom he knew had previously been an ambassador to the papal court, if the pope would come to the aid of Hungary should the sultan choose to attack that country.

Minio assured him that the pope would, although he presumably made those assurances with his fingers crossed; he knew the pope had neither the men nor the money to help the Hungarians should Suleiman choose to attack them.

Throughout the interview, the deputy vizier played on variations of a theme: the disunity of Christendom, where many kings fought each other, compared to the unity of Islam, where all answered to the command of the sultan. As he pointed out to Minio, the sultan had very many Christian subjects, too many for him to count, whereas the Christian kings – well, they had no Muslim subjects.

Islam was united and expanding; Christendom fractious, at war with itself and retreating.

It was the will of God that one should prevail and the other fail, and it was not hard to see where God's will lay.

As for the will of the sultan, it was tantamount to God's will. During his stay in Constantinople, Minio learned of an incident where Suleiman, growing displeased with the performance of one of his pashas, decided that the man should be put to death. Rather than having to go through the rigmarole of bringing a case in law, or of trying to overcome the defiance of an overmighty baron, it was all over within a day. The sultan sent a messenger to the pasha's palace, telling the man that Suleiman had decreed he should die. The pasha, rather than trying to escape, made his farewells to his family and went away with the messenger, his household following the condemned man, weeping but doing nothing to obstruct the will of the sultan.

To Minio, accustomed as he was to the arguments, rivalries and disagreements of Venice, and witness to similar fractious decision-making in Rome, this acquiescence to the point of death to Suleiman's will seemed well-nigh miraculous. So far as he could see, and as he reported, the whole Ottoman Empire, with its vast resources of manpower, finances and raw materials, was geared simply towards accomplishing the will of the sultan.

Minio concluded his report with his recommendations. It was clear to him that the Grand Turk could, if he wished, completely cut off Venice's trade with the East, draining away the money that was the life blood of the republic. Therefore, it was in the Serenissima's vital interest not to antagonise the sultan but to placate him. The best way to do this was give him such intelligence as was possible without undermining the Republic's own interests, and to put whatever obstacles they could in the way of the pope's efforts to raise a crusade against the Turks. But, at the same time, it was vital that Venice should proclaim that it was ready to join the crusade against the Turk, that, indeed, there was nothing the Republic more fervently wished for than the expulsion of the Turks from Constantinople and the liberation of the Holy Land.

But although the Signoria certainly did wish for the Turks to be expelled from Constantinople and for the Holy Land to be under Christian rule once more, it knew well the difference between fantasy and possibility. That the Turks might be driven from Constantinople was sheer fantasy. That the pope might assemble sufficient forces to attempt a new crusade was unlikely but possible, for still the princes of Christendom paid lip service, and even heart service, to the crusading ideal.

Therefore, this possibility had to be strangled, tied down with objections, requests for clarification and, most destructively, the refusal to provide transport to any crusading army on credit.

That was the substance of the report that Marco Minio sent to Venice following his visit to Constantinople.[23]

By the time the report arrived, it would have been accompanied by another vital piece of information: the target of Suleiman's first campaign.

Suleiman's father had turned much of the Mediterranean's southern shore into Ottoman territory. He had suppressed the only possible eastern rival to the Ottomans, the Safavid kingdom that occupied most of modern-day Iran. The rivalry between the Ottomans and the Safavids was the more intense because the Turks were Sunni Muslims, generally accommodating towards their Christian and Jewish subjects but fiercely intolerant of Shia Safavids. For their part, the Safavids sponsored undercover missionary operations into Ottoman territory, seeking to turn Sunni Muslims Shia.

But Selim's military victories against the Safavids had, for the time being, cooled their missionary ardour.

That left the west as the vector for Suleiman to explore, the arena in which he would seek the conquest to legitimise his rule.

The question was, where?

By the end of 1520, it had become clear that the sultan's target would be Hungary and its fortress city, Belgrade. Mehmed had tried to conquer Belgrade and failed. Suleiman intended to succeed where his forebear, the man who wore the title 'Conqueror', had failed and, by implication, outdo the Conqueror. For Suleiman took his role as *ghazi*, holy warrior for Islam, seriously: he intended to expand the boundaries of the Dar al-Islam, the house of submission, and push back the frontiers of the Dar al-Harb, the house of war.

Belgrade sits on the River Danube. Conquering the city would open up the Danube river valley, giving the Ottoman armies a clear path to Budapest and then Vienna.

The Hungarians, realising that they were going to be Suleiman's target, sent out urgent requests for aid and assistance – and were roundly ignored. The Venetians, of course, had decided to avoid confrontation with the Sublime Porte, but the Hungarians might have hoped for more from the pope, the king of Poland or the Holy Roman Emperor. The pope, Leo X, had pleaded with the Christian princes to put aside their conflicts and unite in a crusade against the Turk that would reclaim Constantinople. The plea was met with polite expressions of interest, along the lines of, 'Of course I will take up the Cross so long as King... does so too,' coupled with a complete disinclination to follow through.

Charles, the Holy Roman Emperor, was preoccupied with the growing religious disorder in his German domains, where a monk named Martin Luther had an increasing following and was issuing denunciations of the papacy that were becoming more and more inflammatory. In an effort to resolve these differences, Charles convened the Diet of Worms on 28 January 1521. The assembly went on to May of that year and ended with the condemnation of Luther; it was the start of the Reformation as an active and growing rupture in the body of Western Christendom.

On 6 February 1521, soon after the Diet of Worms had convened, Suleiman made his formal exit from Constantinople as the reigning sultan riding to war. The sultan's departure to war was a piece of political theatre, expressly designed to overawe the enemies of the empire.

The column was led by 6,000 cavalry, resplendent in spotless velvet and silk, each horseman armed with bow, short sword and shield. The Janissaries, the sultan's personal slave soldiers, marched behind them, wearing their distinctive hats, a crown of gold cloth from which leapt a high white tail that trailed down the back of the head, with a spoon attached to the hat band.[24] The Janissaries marched in silence – in contrast to when they went into battle, when they were accompanied by drums, bells and cymbals. They also marched in perfect order, again underscoring their discipline when compared with most European armies of the time.

Once the Janissaries had left Constantinople, the sultan's pashas and generals followed, each riding upon the most splendid thoroughbred horse and attended by their own retinue of slaves and officials. These highest dignitaries of the empire processed in front of the sultan himself.

Suleiman rode forth on the most magnificent horse that could be found within the empire, clad in a silk robe and wearing a turban bearing a plume of diamonds. Suleiman had been trained for this since childhood: there were few better horsemen within the Empire.

Three pages rode behind Suleiman carrying a coffer, a cloak and a water-bottle – symbols of the nomadic past of the Ottoman emperors. Then, as the rearguard, there followed the eunuchs who were the sultan's personal slaves and an honour guard recruited from the sons of the most prominent Ottoman families.

The discipline of the army on the march was exemplary: anyone found guilty of rape or theft could expect summary execution. The army broke camp at dawn and marched until noon, pitching a new camp in a suitable area chosen by the army's scouts. The camp itself was arranged in a strict hierarchy, with the sultan's tent, well-nigh as luxurious as his palace, in the centre, surrounded by the tents of his pashas; around these, the Janissaries and imperial troops camped. The regional troops levied along the way camped further out.

The camp was broken down and put up again after each march: an everyday example of the organisation and logistics that made the Ottoman army the most formidable in the world.

The same could not be said for the Hungarian army.

John Hunyadi had led the Hungarians to a famous victory against Sultan Mehmed in 1456, buying Hungary 60 years of peace. But the Hungarian nobility had squandered that breathing space, fighting petty wars against each other while treating the peasantry so abominably that they actually managed to spark a revolt in 1514. After initial success, the revolt was put down with great savagery. To make sure the peasants didn't get ideas above their station again, the Hungarian Diet passed an act on 19 November 1514 that stated that

> the recent rebellion... against the whole nobility, led by a robber chief, has for all days to come put the stain of faithlessness on the peasants, and they have thereby utterly forfeited their liberty and become subjects to their landlords in unconditional and perpetual servitude. The peasant has no sort of right over his master's land save bare compensation for his labour and such other rewards he may obtain. Every species of property belongs to the landlords, and the peasant has no right to invoke justice against a noble.[25]

Faced with such a draconian law, and a nobility all too willing to enforce it (a preamble to the above act had exempted the nobility from all taxes, meaning that the peasantry was being squeezed even more than before), it was not surprising that the Hungarian peasantry might look to the Ottomans as preferable masters: they could hardly be worse.

Into this poisonous mix came young King Louis. Born weeks premature, baby Louis was kept alive by putting him in the bodies of freshly slaughtered animals, their warmth acting as a primitive incubator for the tiny child.

Louis survived but there was little he could do to curb the excesses of the nobility, particularly since he took the throne when he was only 14.

Suleiman's army made slow but steady progress. Given the size of the force, the slow pace was not surprising: 10,000 wagons take a long time to get going and a long time to stop. In support, Suleiman ordered ships from his fleet to sail up the Danube.

While on campaign, Suleiman kept a diary, a terse record of the events of the day in which he always referred to himself in the third person. One entry reads:

> On July 7 came news of the capture of Šabac; a hundred heads of the soldiers of the garrison, who had been unable to escape across the Sava [the river on which the fortress stood], were brought to the camp. The next day, those heads were stuck on pikes alongside the road to the camp, and Ahmed Pasha was granted an audience to kiss the Sultan's hand. Suleiman visited the city and ordered the building of a new bastion and a surrounding moat; he also commanded that a bridge should be thrown across the river so that the army might cross to the northern bank... He sat in a shed nearby to encourage the men working on the bridge by his presence. The pashas, armed with rods, also encouraged them to work hard.[26]

Suleiman's advance guard had already placed Belgrade under attack and, at the end of July, the sultan arrived in person. The main Ottoman cannon were with his army and they immediately began to blast the city walls.

Impatient, and aware that the autumn rains might arrive early leaving his army dangerously exposed, Suleiman ordered an assault on the city on 2 August. His diary entry for that night reads, 'Assault; moat is filled with corpses; five or six hundred men are lost.'[27]

A week later, the Turks attacked again and this time the defenders were forced from the city walls, retreating to the fortress. There, they held out for three more weeks but, with no hope of relief, they surrendered.

Belgrade had held out against Mehmed the Conqueror. Its fall signalled that there was a new Ottoman conqueror on the march.

The question was where he would turn to next.

26

THE OTHER EMPEROR

The Sublime Porte ran its own network of informers in Europe but its information-gathering abilities were supplemented by the great majority of the sultan's personal slaves and advisers being from Greek, Balkan, Slavic and Albanian stock. Some accounts state that there were Greek- and Slavic-speaking circles at the sultan's court.

Among the information the sultan most assiduously sought was knowledge of the rivalries between the princes of Christendom and, in particular, the relations between Charles V and Francis I, the kings respectively of Spain and France. Charles became king of Spain on 14 March 1516; at that point, Francis had been king of France for a year.

On 12 February 1519, Maximilian, the Holy Roman Emperor, died. Now, the Empire was not like Spain or France: the next in line did not simply become king on the death of his predecessor. The Holy Roman Empire, which roughly maps onto today's Germany, was thought of as the successor to the Roman Empire, giving the emperor a prestige unmatched by other European sovereigns, even if he often could not match them in power.

The Empire was an elective monarchy: the new emperor was chosen by the votes of seven prince-electors – the archbishops of Mainz, Trier and Cologne, the king of Bohemia, the count palatine of the Rhine, the duke of Saxony and the margrave of Brandenburg.

Upon the news of Maximilian's death, both Francis and Charles put themselves forward as the next emperor. The best way to ensure election was to buy it and both Charles and Francis poured huge amounts of money into their election campaigns. Gifts and gold flowed along the Rhine and the prince-electors, enjoying the largesse their temporary position brought them, dragged out the process.

THE OTHER EMPEROR

But, in the end, Charles outspent Francis, largely by taking out huge loans and, on 28 June 1519, he was proclaimed Holy Roman Emperor by the prince-electors.

In Constantinople, the election of a new Holy Roman Emperor did not go down well. So far as Suleiman was concerned, he was the rightful successor to the Roman Empire. Mehmed had conquered Constantinople, new Rome, whose rulers always styled themselves as emperors of the Roman Empire. Mehmed had taken that title by right of conquest and his heirs held it still, their right to the title demonstrated by the expansion of their empire. The so-called Holy Roman Empire was, in reality, a collection of small, relatively independent kingdoms which paid lip service to their overking but which each largely went their own way.[28] In comparison, Suleiman's writ ran over a far larger area and within the empire his wish was law. What was more, by the definition of an emperor accepted by both Suleiman and Charles, there could only be a single emperor, although there might be many kings. One God, one empire, one emperor – and then many kings and princes under the emperor. For Suleiman to acknowledge Charles as the Holy Roman Emperor would be for him to devalue his own status as emperor. So, it's notable that in all their correspondence and dealings, Suleiman never once addressed Charles as 'Emperor' but always called him 'King of Spain'.[29] That, Suleiman could accept. But emperor? Never.

While Charles might style himself 'Emperor', Francis was a plain and simple king. In Constantinople, the sultan and his advisers were well aware that Charles's acquisition of the Empire left France almost entirely surrounded. Francis would be looking for allies against Charles, whose possessions now included Spain, the Empire, the Low Countries and Spain's territories in the New World. With Francis not setting himself up as an alternative emperor, and the time-worn adage that 'the enemy of my enemy is my friend', channels of communication began to gradually open up between Constantinople and Paris, tentative feelers marking the first tentative contacts between the 'Most Christian King' and the 'Amir al-Mu'minin'. At this point in their reigns, neither could openly admit to being in contact, let alone contemplating cooperation, but both could already see that it might be in their interest to do so in future.

But that was a question for later. As the armies of Suleiman consolidated their hold on Belgrade, a new question drew alarmed contemplation from the princes and dukes of Christendom: who would next receive the attention of Suleiman?

Emboldened by his success against Hungary, Suleiman chose to make no secret of this. Indeed, he wrote a letter to announce his intentions.

10 September 1521, from Belgrade

Suleiman the sultan, by the grace of God, king of kings, sovereign of sovereigns, most high emperor of Byzantium and Trebizond, very powerful king of Persia, of Arabia, of Syria, and of Egypt, supreme lord of Europe, and of Asia, prince of Mecca and Aleppo, lord of Jerusalem, and ruler of the universal sea, to Philip de L'Isle Adam, Grand Master of the island of Rhodes, greetings.

I congratulate you upon your new dignity, and upon your arrival within your territories. I trust that you will rule there prosperously, and with even more glory than your predecessors. I also mean to cultivate your favour; rejoice with me, as a very dear friend, that following in the footsteps of my father, who conquered Persia, Jerusalem, Arabia, and Egypt, I have captured the most powerful of fortresses, Belgrade, during the late autumn; after which, having offered battle to the Kuffar, which they had not the courage to accept, I took many other beautiful and well-fortified cities, and destroyed most of their inhabitants either by sword or fire, the remainder being reduced to slavery. Now after sending my numerous and victorious army into their winter quarters, I myself shall return in triumph to my court in Constantinople.[30]

The man to whom Suleiman addressed this letter, written from the shattered remains of Belgrade, had been elected Grand Master of the Order of Knights of the Hospital of St John of Jerusalem on 22 January 1521. The Knights Hospitaller were the survivors of the two great orders of crusading monastic orders, their brethren and rivals, the Knights Templar, having been suppressed by Philip the Fair, king of France, in 1312. The Knights Hospitaller had survived the destruction of Outremer by taking Rhodes and turning the island into a base on which they nurtured their aim of leading a new crusade to take back the Holy Land while continuing to harass and raid the Muslim realms of the Levant.

Rhodes is set in the southern reaches of the Aegean Sea, just 11 miles (18km) away from Anatolia (modern-day Turkey). It sits squarely astride the sea route linking Constantinople to the Levant and, as such, it offered unrivalled opportunities for the Knights to operate as sea-based pirates and raiders, a sort galley-driven version of the Vikings. The Knights, of course, framed their operations in terms of crusade, as part of the long war to reclaim the Holy Land, but it's perhaps not so surprising that a lot of the people they dealt with saw them as pirates, pure and simple, raiding merchant ships and pilgrim vessels, plundering merchandise and taking slaves.

Philippe Villiers de L'Isle Adam was 56 when he was elected Grand Master. The runner-up in the election, Andrea d'Amaral, he made his chancellor, a decision that he would come to regret.

As for Suleiman's letter, de L'Isle Adam saw it not as a proposal of friendship but as a veiled threat. He wrote back tersely while at the same time he dispatched a letter to his king, Francis, warning him of the threat and asking for his help.

The diplomatic dance continued, with the letters slowly being stripped of their diplomatic niceties, until finally, on 10 June 1522, Suleiman made his intentions clear. The Knights, whose intelligence service was second only to that of Venice, had learned over the winter of 1521/22 that the arsenals and shipyards of Constantinople and Gallipoli were hard at work constructing ships and laying in stores, while during the spring the men necessary for an invasion army were slowly assembled. The Knights knew what was coming but the sultan's letter made clear that they were about to face the full strength of the Ottoman Empire.

> The Sultan Suleiman to Villiers de L'Isle Adam, Grand Master of Rhodes, to his Knights, and to the people at large. Your monstrous injuries against my most afflicted people have aroused my pity and indignation. I command you, therefore, instantly to surrender the island and fortress of Rhodes, and I give you gracious permission to depart in safety with the most precious of your effects; or if you desire to remain under my government, I shall not require of you any tribute, or do aught in diminution of your liberties, or against

your religion. If you are wise, you will prefer friendship and peace to a cruel war, since, if you are conquered, you will have to undergo all the miseries as are usually inflicted by those that are victorious, from which you will be protected neither by your own forces, nor by external aid, nor by the strength of your fortifications which I will overthrow to their foundations. If, therefore, you prefer my friendship to war, there shall be neither fraud nor stratagem used against you, I swear this by the God of heaven, the Creator of the earth, by the four Evangelists, by the four thousand Prophets, who have descended from heaven, chief amongst whom stands Muhammed, most worthy to be worshipped; by the shades of my grandfather and father, and by my own sacred, august, and imperial head.[31]

The Grand Master did not reply. But, reading the letter, he must have rued the accuracy of the sultan's information, for by now he knew as well as Suleiman that no help would be forthcoming from the princes of Christendom: the Knights were on their own.[32]

27

The Last Knight of Christendom

It turned out that the Knights were not quite on their own.

By the spring of 1522, it was clear that Suleiman was preparing his forces for an attack on Rhodes. The Grand Master sent envoys to the pope, the kings of France and England, and to the Holy Roman Emperor, but the messages were sent more in hope than in expectation, vain wishes that shame might drive the Christian kings to put aside their differences and come to the aid of the Knights.

More practically, de L'Isle Adam also set about making preparations for siege. The defences of the city were strengthened and the new bastion that protected the section of the city walls defended by the Knights of Auvergne was completed. The dry moat that separated the city walls from the counterscarp[33] was dug deeper and cleared of any cover. The Knights who manned priories throughout Europe were recalled to Rhodes, arriving in dribs and drabs through the spring and early summer; never enough, even though all the Knights were highly trained and proficient soldiers.

Two fast galleys were set to patrol the Gulf of Goköva, the strait separating the mainland from the island of Kos. The Ottoman fleet, sailing from Constantinople, would have to pass through the gulf on its way to Rhodes.

Everything that could be harvested on the island was brought into the city (Rhodes the island shares its name with Rhodes the city). The city's suburbs, which before had been covered with gardens and villas, were razed.

To ensure that Rhodes had sufficient supplies to withstand a siege, the Grand Master dispatched one of his most trusted Knights, the Italian Antonio Bosio, to Candia to load up with gunpowder, victuals and wine (both a medical necessity and far safer to drink than water during a long siege). Fra' Antonio also took with him gold sufficient to recruit 500 men to bolster the city's garrison.

Bosio had no difficulty buying up the supplies – Candia was of course part of Venice's Stato da Màr and trade was its lifeblood – but it was a different matter when it came to recruiting soldiers.

The Duke of Candia, Paolantonio Emiliano, refused to grant permission to Fra' Antonio to recruit soldiers in his dominion. Venice had recently signed a treaty with the Sublime Porte and the duke had no intention of breaking its terms: La Serenissima intended to sail serenely past this dispute between the sultan and the Knights.

Fra' Antonio, displaying the ingenuity he would show throughout the long siege, publicly agreed and then set about recruiting five hundred mercenaries, passing them off as sailors and merchants so that they could come aboard his little fleet of ships.

Communication between Candia (Crete) and Rhodes was always good. They stood across the access straits to the Aegean Sea and both were natural stops for ships sailing east or west. The Knights had surely heard about the new superintendent of fortification and artillery who had arrived on Candia two years earlier; they had probably already sought his advice on how best to strengthen the fortifications of Rhodes.

Now, recruiting on Candia, Fra' Antonio went to see Gabriele Tadino, first to ask his advice but secondly to ask for his help. For during his stay on Candia, he had seen for himself how Gabriele had strengthened the defences, and learned from the Knights' agents on the island the respect in which Tadino was held.

Fra' Antonio laid out before Tadino the situation in which the Knights found themselves: they faced the entire might of the Ottoman Empire. They could expect no help from the princes of Christendom. Gabriele's own employer, the Republic of Venice, which could have provided considerable aid from Candia, wanted no part of such a hopeless fight. The Knights had resolved to fight to the end in defence of Christendom, even though Christendom wanted no part of them. The likely outcome was death.

Would Gabriele like to join them?

Of course, he said, 'Yes.'

Gabriele Tadino's nickname in Brescia had been '*il cavaliere*', 'the knight'. His exploits told of an almost suicidal bravery while his involvement in the mad scheme to kidnap an heiress for love spoke of a romantic streak in his soul that the Italian Wars, with their pragmatic treachery, could not extinguish. Being asked to risk his life – and in all probability lose it too – in defence of Christendom while those tasked with defending the religion he believed in turned away could only appeal to a boy who had grown up on tales of Crusaders and brave *condottieri*, before those self-same princes who now refused to defend Christendom had invaded his homeland and made it a theatre of perpetual war.

Gabriele Tadino could not turn down such an appeal.

But, unfortunately, he was bound, by word and contract, to the service of Venice. He was not a free man. He could not just sail off to Rhodes with Fra' Antonio. Gabriele asked Fra' Antonio to return to Candia with a letter from the Grand Master, asking the governor of Candia if he would release Gabriele to the service of the Religion (the Knights Hospitaller's own name for their order) for the duration of the siege. Such an appeal, Gabriele thought, might find a ready audience.

So Fra' Antonio sailed back to Rhodes with the provisions and five hundred mercenaries disguised as sailors, and the intention to return to Candia as quickly as possible with a letter from the Grand Master asking the Duke of Candia, Paolantonio Emiliano, to second Tadino to Rhodes for the duration of the approaching siege.

However, when Fra' Antonio arrived on Rhodes, he learned that the first Ottoman transports had already landed on the island, while the famous Ottoman corsair Kurtoğlu Muslihiddin Reis had started a blockade of the island in an attempt to stop any further supplies or reinforcements reaching it. Fra' Antonio's testimony to the Grand Master, however, convinced de L'Isle Adam that the risk of Fra' Antonio running the blockade was worth it, should he manage to return to Rhodes with Tadino.

After all, Fra' Antonio had averred to the Grand Master that Gabriele was a military engineer unmatched in all Europe, conversant with the new ways of war and able to bring mathematical precision and the experience gleaned from 14 years of war to bear on the defence of Rhodes. Fra' Antonio presented his case to the Grand Master and the council of senior Knights, who agreed that he should return to Candia carrying a letter from the Grand Master to the duke of Candia, asking him to release Gabriele into the service of the Religion.

Running the blockade proved easier than Fra' Antonio might have expected. It turned out that Kurtoğlu, although appointed admiral of the Ottoman navy, could not easily shake off his corsair past and, whenever a likely vessel went past, he tended to set off in pursuit of plunder and slaves, leaving the blockade unblocked.

However, while Kurtoğlu's blockade proved straightforward to evade, the duke of Candia's objections, even when presented with public letters from the Grand Master, proved harder to shift. The duke first tried to delay, suggesting that the request had to be relayed to the Signoria in Venice. When Bosio insisted upon a decision, pointing out that waiting for a messenger to travel to and from Venice, not to mention the delay while the Signoria debated the question, would mean that the siege would likely be over before a decision was made, the duke fell back upon the treaty that Venice had signed with the Sublime Porte. Under its terms, he could not permit Venice, nor any of its ships, soldiers or engineers, to fight against the Turks.

Permission was refused.

However, when Fra' Antonio, deflated and despairing, came to Gabriele to tell him of the duke's decision, he was completely unprepared for Tadino's response.

Gabriele told Fra' Antonio that he would leave Candia in secret and come with him to Rhodes.

The Knight pointed out to Tadino what that would mean. He would have explicitly and knowingly gone against the direct orders of the duke of Candia. He would have disobeyed the terms of the treaty the Republic had signed with the Sublime Porte.

As such, he would certainly be stripped of his position as superintendent of the fortifications of Candia. His generous salary would stop. Whatever possessions he left in Candia would be forfeit. He would turn the duke of Candia into an enemy and the Republic into foreign territory, for the Signoria would certainly declare him a renegade for endangering its treaty with the Sublime Porte.

All that Gabriele Tadino had worked for would be lost. The state for which he had risked his life over and over again would regard him as a traitor.

Did he really want to give all that up in order to go and die as one of the defenders of Rhodes?

Fra' Antonio later reported that, to these questions, Gabriele replied that, should he die, then they would all be moot.[34] But should he succeed, and aid the Knights in the successful defence of Rhodes, then the service of God and the honour he would accrue from his part in such a venture would greatly outdo any material loss he might suffer.

The service of Tadino secured, the question remained as to how Fra' Antonio was going to get him to Rhodes. The duke of Candia, suspicious of his intentions, had men keeping watch on the Knights' brigantine, so Tadino could not simply board it and sail away with Fra' Antonio.

To allay the duke's suspicions, Fra' Antonio publicly sailed from the harbour in his brigantine while Gabriele remained, just as publicly, in Candia. However, once out of sight of the port lookouts, Fra' Antonio brought his ship back in to land, mooring it in a secluded bay under cover of a hollow rock, and waited there for two days.

The duke of Candia, satisfied that Fra' Antonio had truly sailed back to Rhodes, allowed the watch to lapse and the men he had set to keep tabs on Gabriele to return to their own affairs. That was the cue Gabriele had been waiting for. With two friends and comrades, Giorgio di Conversano and Beneto Scaramosa, Gabriele crept from his house in the middle of the night and made his way to the bay where Fra' Antonio was waiting for them.

With Tadino on board, Fra' Antonio immediately set sail, hoping to make quick time back to Rhodes.

But no sooner had they set sail than the wind turned violently against them. The brigantines of the Mediterranean were light galleys, rigged with two lateen sails and between eight and 12 pairs of oars. They were light, fast and completely unsuited to sailing in bad weather. Fra' Antonio had no choice but to bring his ship back to the safety of the little bay he had been sheltering in for the last two days, and hope that the wind would drop before the duke discovered that Tadino had absconded.

It didn't.

They were stuck on a lee shore, praying for the wind to change.

As the sun rose, the wind continued to pin them to the shore, while the duke of Candia, expecting to find Tadino attending him as was his wont, sent servants to check what was delaying the engineer, only to hear that there was no sign of Tadino, nor of his two friends, Giorgio di Conversano and Beneto Scaramosa.

Realising what that meant, the duke ordered all Tadino's possessions confiscated and issued a proclamation promising a rich reward to anyone who found and returned Tadino to his court. The duke also realised that, since Tadino had only left during the night, Bosio's ship must still be in the vicinity of Crete. So he at once dispatched his fastest galleys with orders to chase down and capture Bosio's ship and bring Tadino back.

With many more rowers, the duke's galleys were able to make headway against the contrary wind, and they were soon scouring the coast, looking for the fleeing brigantine.

What they didn't know was that the brigantine wasn't fleeing at all, but was hiding in a little cove a short way up the coast. But Bosio and Tadino, knowing that the duke would send his hunting ships after them, did what they could to make the brigantine less conspicuous to seaborne lookouts: they dismasted the ship, reducing its profile, and dragged it ashore, so that the rocks hid most of its hull, while they concealed the oars among the rocks, all in the effort to make the ship look less like a fast-sailing brigantine and more like a small merchant vessel pulled up onto the beach while its crew made repairs.

The ruse worked. Several galleys sailed right past the brigantine, some crew even shouting out to them to ask if they had seen one of the Knights' brigantines sailing past.

At last, when night fell, the wind finally changed. Fra' Antonio and his crew remasted the ship, shipped the oars and, together, they pushed it back into the water.

Its oars cutting through the dark water, pulling streaks of phosphorescence under the dome of stars, the ship rowed away from Candia and out on the open sea. Fra' Antonio unfurled its sails and the wind, now friendly, carried them east to Rhodes.

28

A Short History of the Knights Hospitaller

The Order of Knights of the Hospital of St John of Jerusalem began as a hospital before any knights were involved, at least in a fighting capacity.

The Hospital of St John was just that, a hospital and infirmary dedicated to the care of sick and ailing pilgrims who had come to Jerusalem. The hospital was situated on the site of the monastery of St John the Baptist. It predated the conquest of Jerusalem, having been established in 1023 to replace the previous pilgrims' hospital that had been destroyed by the caliph Al-Hakim in 1005.

In 1080, Gerard, a lay Benedictine brother, was given charge of the Hospital of St John. When Jerusalem was besieged in 1099 by the soldiers of the First Crusade, the Fatimid governor of the city, Iftikhar al-Dawla, expelled all the Christians in the city. However, he allowed Gerard and a handful of other brothers to stay at the hospital so that they could care for the sick and injured.

Following Jerusalem's fall to the Crusaders, Gerard and the Hospital of St John tended to the Crusaders injured in the fighting, and a number of them decided to join the order and care for other sick and injured pilgrims. In gratitude for his work, Godfrey of Bouillon, the new ruler of Jerusalem, gave additional benefices to Gerard and the brothers of St John so that the Hospital soon outstripped its parent organisation. To regularise the situation, the Hospital was recognised as an independent religious order on 15 February 1113, when Pope Paschal II issued a papal bull, *Pie postulatio voluntatis*, putting the new order under his protection, which freed it from the control of the patriarch of Jerusalem, giving it the right to elect its Grand Master without outside interference, and requiring of its brothers the vows to poverty, chastity and obedience.

By the end of the century, the Hospital had grown to such an extent that it could treat 1,000 patients, which it did for free, admitting everyone without regard for religion or nationality.

But as part of its remit to care for pilgrims, and with a large number of trained military men among its brothers, the Hospital of St John soon began providing armed escorts for parties of pilgrims making the difficult and dangerous journey from Jerusalem to the port of Jaffa. The change from a medical order to a military/medical one was gradual but it became formalised under the second Grand Master of the order, Raymond of Puys, who was elected in 1121. It was Raymond who organised the order into knights, men-at-arms and chaplains so that it became the Order of Knights of the Hospital of St John of Jerusalem, or the Knights Hospitaller.

While Outremer, the Crusader kingdoms, endured, the Knights Hospitaller and the other order of militant monks, the Knights Templar, provided crucial military protection to the kingdoms. There were never enough men so both orders became masters of military architecture, creating fortresses that a handful of men could hold against a besieging army in the thousands. The Knights Hospitaller were responsible for turning the Krak des Chevaliers into a well-nigh impregnable fortress, but they built many other fortresses and strongholds too. This institutional expertise in defence would come in useful in the future.

Following the fall of Acre in 1291, the Knights Hospitaller lost their last base in the Holy Land. Their rival military order, the Knights Templar (whose full name was as long as the Hospitallers: 'The Poor Fellow-Soldiers of Christ and of the Temple of Solomon') found itself in a similar position, expelled from the Holy Land and left with no home base.

However, neither order had lost all their possessions.

Both the Hospitallers and the Templars had considerable holdings throughout Europe. These commanderies, as they were called, raised money to support the overall mission of the orders. The Hospitallers divided their commanderies around Europe into different *langues* (literally, 'tongues'), which roughly matched onto linguistic and national boundaries in Europe. There were seven original *langues*:

Auvergne, Provence, France, Italy, England (including Scotland and Ireland), Germany (including the Holy Roman Empire, Poland, Hungary and Scandinavia) and Aragon. Aragon was later divided, adding an eighth *langue*, that of Castile, Leon and Portugal.

The *langues* themselves were divided into priories, with a prior given command of the priory and its associated territory. The priories controlled the commanderies, the basic units of Hospitaller territory, from which they derived the order's income through rents, taxes, customs dues and direct production.

The priories provided secure retirement positions for older Knights as well as acting as recruiting centres for young men interested in joining the order.

While we think of the Knights Hospitaller as very much a military order, it's worth remembering that they were founded as a medical order and even when they broadened into a military order, they retained their commitment to healing alongside their interest in killing: when founding a new priory, the first building the Knights built was a hospital. There was a large hospital in Rhodes and it, like all their other hospitals, provided free medical treatment for whoever needed it, although the rich were invited to donate money to the order.

To enter the Knights Hospitaller was to leave the largely parochial world of medieval Europe and to go into something much larger and all-encompassing. As such, it's no coincidence that the Knights' own name for their order, the name they used among themselves, was the Religion. Just that. The Order of Knights of the Hospital of St John of Jerusalem was their Religion.

But their Religion faced an existential question of its continued purpose following the Knights' expulsion from Acre. They had been founded to care for and protect pilgrims to the Holy Land – and now they were no longer in the Holy Land. As such, what was the point of their continued existence?

The Religion decided to dedicate itself to continuing the crusade so that, some day, they would reconquer the Holy Land. To do so, the Grand Master Guillaume de Villaret decided that they needed a base. But this would not merely be a physical location; it also had to be the Religion's sovereign territory, in which it would not be beholden to the good will of any earthly king. The Religion had first retreated to Cyprus but there it became caught up in local politics. Guillaume de

Villaret identified the island of Rhodes as a more suitable base and, after four years of campaigning and under the rule of Guillaume's successor, Foulques de Villaret, the Religion captured the city of Rhodes.

Now the Religion had its home. Based upon an island, the Knights became consummate sailors and sea warriors, their galleys famous, or notorious, throughout the eastern Mediterranean.

The fate of the Templars highlighted the wisdom of Guillaume's decision to find a sovereign base for the Religion. The Templars, while interested in doing likewise, had not yet done so when King Philip the Fair of France, heavily in debt to the order, decided to clear his debt by destroying the Templars. The pope, Clement V, had moved the papacy from Rome to Avignon in France, leaving him highly exposed to pressure from Philip. Clement proved signally incapable of resisting that pressure, and he condemned and suppressed the order.

Philip got his money. The Grand Master, Jacques de Molay, who had confessed under terrible torture to blasphemy and heresy only to recant his confession, was executed by burning on 18 March 1314. A contemporary witness, Geoffroi de Paris, reported that de Molay, at the stake, declared before all present that he was innocent of the crimes of which he had been accused and called on God to avenge him on those who were condemning him unjustly.

When both Pope Clement and King Philip died within a year of Jacques de Molay, these last words were remembered as calling on those who had unjustly condemned de Molay to join him before God's judgement seat within the year.

The Religion, secure on Rhodes, could not be dealt with in such manner. They continued to harass and raid Muslim possessions throughout the Levant, earning a thoroughly deserved reputation for piracy among the Muslim populations of the region. Indeed, the Knights were seen by their enemies in a very similar fashion to the way the Christian kingdoms came to regard the Barbary pirates of North Africa.

On Rhodes, the Knights were organised in a manner that matched their international order, with the Knights from each country living in quarters, an *auberge*, with compatriots who spoke the same language. Each *langue* was also responsible for the defence of a particular section of the walls of Rhodes. The Grand Master lived in his palace, while the various *auberges* of the *langues* lined the Street of the Knights in Rhodes.

Of course, with the Knights organised according to languages, this raises the question of how they communicated with each other. Within each *langue* there was obviously no problem but when giving commands and information across *langues*, or from the Grand Master down to the particular *langues*, the Religion had to develop efficient methods of communication.

At the highest level of the Religion, this was Latin. The Grand Master and the senior Knights were all fluent in Latin. Most of them were multilingual too, speaking at least one other language along with Latin and their native tongue. Indeed, facility with language was encouraged and for many of the Knights who came from multi-ethnic areas of Europe it was a normal part of their education.

The one exception, showing that some stereotypes have deep roots, was the *langue* of England. The English Knights were notorious for their heavy accents, frequent recourse to interpreters and their few words during debates.

There was a strong French presence among the Knights, making French the *de facto* language of much of the Religion. However, there was another language which served to bridge linguistic barriers, both between the different *langues* and when the Knights had to deal with the many peoples whom they encountered on their travels or who called in to the port at Rhodes.

This was what scholars now call Sabir. It was the *lingua franca* of the eastern Mediterranean, particularly of the trading ports frequented by Italian merchants. Sabir was a pidgin language, with simplified grammar, that drew chiefly from Italian, in particular the Venetian and Genoese dialects, Provençal, Catalan, French, Greek and Arabic. The language was never codified and it's recorded in few written documents, being very much a language of instant communication, but the Knights used it both among themselves and when dealing with other people, particularly the Rhodians, as relatively few of the Knights spoke Greek.

In 1480, Mehmed, the conqueror of Constantinople, dispatched an expedition to conquer Rhodes and finally rid his empire of this nest of pirates so near its heart. The siege failed. The prestige of the Knights grew and some much-needed funds and recruitment were funnelled east.

However, the Knights were well aware of the way that war was changing, and in the first decades of the 16th century they embarked on a programme to strengthen and modernise their defences. Recruiting Italian military engineers, including Basilio della Scuola, a Vicenzan engineer, the Religion set about rebuilding the defences of Rhodes.

Starting from the walls, they raised and thickened the medieval walls, making them some 40 feet deep. Elsewhere in Europe military engineers were lowering walls but this was not practical in Rhodes, since lowering the walls would have given the artillery of a besieger, set upon the counterscarp, a height advantage, allowing them to fire down upon defenders.

The towers, which before had been freestanding, were built into the walls so that they could not be knocked down by artillery fire.

Into the walls protecting the *terre plein*, the flat walkway on top of the walls, the Religion cut splayed gunports, the first such embrasures to be constructed. This is where the interior opened out to allow the cannon to be moved to fire at different targets through the narrow, and hard to hit, gunport. The moat, which had originally been quite narrow, was hugely widened. In some places, the old counterscarp was left in place and the new moat dug out behind it, creating a freestanding *tenaille* (a long, thick wall set into the moat) to provide further protection for the city walls against cannon fire.

The Religion also built freestanding bastions in front of the walls at key points to provide enfilading fire support along the walls that they were protecting. These bastions would prove their worth during the siege.

The improvements illustrate the changing thoughts about the most effective defences. The bastion protecting the wall assigned to the *langue* of Italy was built round, and this proved less effective than the angular bastions protecting the *langues* of England, Provence and Auvergne.

This was the city that Gabriele Tadino was sailing to Rhodes to defend. Its defences were among the strongest in the world, but defences were only as good as the men manning them. The coming days would test their mettle to the fullest.

29

How to Get into a Besieged City

As his brigantine approached Rhodes with July drawing to its close, Fra' Antonio saw that the city was already being invested by the Turks. Galleys patrolled the coast, searching for blockade runners. His own little ship was swift but, in a flat race, it could not outrun a fully oared war galley.

Rather than risk losing his valuable passenger, Fra' Antonio, using his intimate knowledge of the bays and coves of the island, sailed into a secluded and sheltered bay behind the Ottoman lines, a place where the patrolling galleys could not observe his boat. There, he waited for dark.

However, Fra' Antonio knew that the sentries set on the port of Rhodes would not permit him entry during the night: only with first light would they admit his ship, for to allow a ship to enter during the night might be to allow a disguised Ottoman ship into the harbour where it could unship its crew, sailors and rowers alike, and storm the Fort of St Nicholas, the tower that protected and defended the harbour.

His plan was to carefully slip out of the bay in the last hours before dawn when the moon had set and then, in the darkest part of the night, make his way along the coast so that the ship could be standing to at the harbour entrance at first light.

But in the meantime, Fra' Antonio decided to make use of the early part of the night to gather some intelligence on the enemy. As the preferred emissary of the Grand Masters, Fra' Antonio had been given that position for his intelligence, his ability to interpret the intention behind his masters' orders and his command of the languages of the Mediterranean – including Turkish. Putting aside his Knights' tunic, embroidered with the cross of the order, Fra' Antonio slipped ashore and made his way to the nearest Ottoman camp, passing through the sentries and taking his place by the communal cooking pot.

There, Fra' Antonio learned that the initial Turkish landing had taken place on 26 June when a fleet of 400 ships commanded by Suleiman's brother-in-law, Çoban Mustafa Pasha ('Pasha' was actually a title), had landed to the north of the city, establishing initial lines and securing chains of supply while they waited upon the sultan's arrival. Çoban Mustafa Pasha, the Serdar-ı Ekrem, the vizier in charge of the operation to take Rhodes, exemplified the meritocracy at the heart of Suleiman's entourage. Çoban Mustafa Pasha was a Serb, recruited as a boy through the *devshirme*, the Ottoman child tax, and placed among the Janissaries where he excelled, rising through the ranks while gaining sufficient political and military experience to be appointed vizier by Sultan Bayezid. As vizier, Çoban Mustafa Pasha was sufficiently exalted to marry a daughter of Sultan Selim; when Suleiman came to the throne he became an intimate part of the ruling family. Not bad at all for a shepherd boy from the Balkans.

Fra' Antonio also learned that the sultan, Suleiman himself, was coming, marching across country to shorten the sea journey.[35]

Suleiman's personal presence meant that his commanders could accept no result other than victory: the sultan's prestige, and their own survival, depended upon them delivering that victory.

To that end, Çoban Mustafa Pasha and the other Ottoman commanders had assembled a huge siege force. Contemporary Christian accounts claim this army was a quarter of a million strong. This was an overestimate, but the Ottomans had probably landed a hundred thousand men on the island. Among them, Fra' Antonio learned, were many miners and sappers, recruited from the mountainous Balkans. Alongside the normal supplies necessary for an army, the Ottomans had also transported from the mainland many hundreds of spades, picks, shovels, mine supports, buckets and everything else needed to undermine the walls of a city. Although the Knights did not know it yet, Suleiman had his own sources of intelligence within the city, sources that had conveyed to him how the city's fortifications had been remodelled in the new style. Such defences could not easily be stormed, nor battered down, even with the formidable Ottoman artillery. To effectively open breaches in the city walls, the Turks were banking on tunnelling under the walls, planting mines and blowing them up.

Hearing this, Fra' Antonio stifled a smile. So long as he could safely deliver Gabriele Tadino to the city, then the Religion would have a counter to the plans of the Grand Turk. For Tadino was a master of war underground, a maestro of the new ways of war.

Having gleaned as much information as he could, Fra' Antonio slipped away from the Ottoman camp and made his way back to his ship, where his crew and Gabriele were waiting for him.

When the moon slid down into the black water, Fra' Antonio gave the order to slip the mooring ropes. Oars, set in greased locks so that they would not squeak, dipped into the black and pulled the boat into the open sea. The rowers were experienced and free; they needed no drum to set their rhythm. Given the missions that Fra' Antonio was sent on, he could not risk having slaves among his rowers, for it would be all too easy for one of them to give away their position when, like this night, they were trying to slip quietly through the screen of enemy patrol vessels.

Oars dipping into the black sea with not a break of foam, the ship moved quietly through the night under the innumerable stars. On the stern, Fra' Antonio looked to larboard, judging their position by the black silhouette of the land against the backdrop of the stars, and the yellow glows of campfires. By their number, he had confirmation of the size of the sultan's army – even though the sultan had not arrived in person.

The ship slipped, silent as sleep, past the patrols set by the corsair admiral, Kurtoğlu Muslihiddin Reis, until Fra' Antonio saw, dark against the backdrop of fires, the tower of the Fort of St Nicholas, set as a finger in the sea to guard the entrance to the galley port. To the south, the fort also guarded the entrance to the merchants' harbour but Fra' Antonio knew that way was blocked, for the Knights had drawn a heavy chain across the harbour mouth. The galley harbour was also blocked by the hulls of ships sunk as artificial reefs across the harbour mouth, save only for a narrow channel between them.

As the eastern horizon began to lighten, Fra' Antonio set his lookouts to watch for any sign of patrolling galleys, while he began to signal to the sentries in the Fort of St Nicholas.

Rhodes city lies at the eastern tip of the island of Rhodes. Even before the sun has risen over the horizon, the sea lightens. The sentries saw the waiting brigantine and, once Fra' Antonio had given the necessary signals, they lowered the chain and waved him to come into the harbour.

Gabriele Tadino arrived in Rhodes, the stronghold of the Knights Hospitaller, on 22 July.

For Fra' Philippe Villiers de L'Isle Adam, Gabriele Tadino's arrival was a sliver of hope in an otherwise bleak prospect. The gratitude and the esteem the Knights felt for Tadino was demonstrated by their promising to pay him an annual salary of 1,200 ducats as well as the promise that as soon as a priory became vacant it would be given to him. (This meant that Gabriele would be allocated the income from one of the Religion's commanderies, as well as the title that accompanied it. The appointment was eventually made in the spring of 1525, when Gabriele Tadino was made the Prior of Barletta, a title he wore proudly thereafter.) The two friends who had accompanied Tadino to Rhodes, Giorgio di Conversano and Beneto Scaramosa, were also rewarded with salaries of 150 ducats.

If the Knights were pleased to have Tadino join them, it's clear that Gabriele reciprocated their regard, for he petitioned the Grand Master for permission to join the Order of the Knights of the Hospital of St John of Jerusalem. On 1 August, his plea was granted. Tadino became a full-fledged knight of the Religion and was immediately promoted to the rank of Grand Cross, which put him in the second tier of commanders, below only the Grand Master himself. Tadino's acceptance by the order is further evidence that he really was not married, and that the silence on this matter is not simply a consequence of lack of evidence: as a married man, he would not have been eligible to join the Religion as the brethren took vows of chastity, poverty and obedience.

As Grand Cross, Gabriele was given particular authority to command and, if necessary, alter the fortifications to better withstand the Turkish assault. For now, with the sultan on the island in person, the attacks were rising to a crescendo. Although the Knights did not know it, Çoban Mustafa Pasha, the officer in charge of the Ottoman operation, had promised Suleiman that it would take between two and four weeks to capture the city.

It was a promise that would come to haunt the pasha.

Suleiman landed on Rhodes on 28 July along with his Janissaries. Now the besieging army had the personnel to tighten the siege. Suleiman's headquarters were established in the village of Megasandra, four miles south of the city and near present-day Kallithea. So that he might better observe his pashas' conduct of the war, Suleiman also established a battle headquarters on a hill, called San Stefano, which was a mile from the city walls.

Suleiman's choices of targets in the first two years of his reign were highly significant. He had already taken Belgrade, which his illustrious forebear, Mehmed the Conqueror, had failed to conquer in 1456. In 1480, Mehmed had similarly failed to conquer Rhodes. Suleiman had corrected Mehmed's first failure. Now, on Rhodes, he was set to correct the second.

The implication was clear. If he should outdo Mehmed in both these enterprises right at the start of his reign, he would have proved himself a greater conqueror than Mehmed.

It was Gabriele Tadino's job to stop him.

Arriving in Rhodes, Tadino found the city as prepared for siege as it could be. The Religion had called in every knight that could reach Rhodes; it had between 500 and 700 fully armed and trained knights for the defence. To this, the Grand Master had added about four or five thousand men-at-arms, plus a local militia, paid mercenaries and the sailors from the Knights' fleet: probably not more than 7,000 men in total.

The Knights had laid in supplies of food and ammunition that they calculated could sustain them for a year. They were well aware that Rhodes' position so close to the Ottoman mainland meant that the Turks could easily supply even the vast army they had assembled. But their hope lay in two areas: the first was that, should they hold out long enough, then their defiance would prick the consciences of the Christian kings, shaming them into putting aside their differences and sending a relief force. The other hope lay in the turning of the year. Summer was the season for war. But once the weather turned, and autumn started drawing down to winter, then the Ottomans normally returned to Constantinople: the difficulties of supplying an army increased exponentially through the bad weather of winter. In addition, the longer an army remained encamped the greater the risk of a devastating outbreak of disease. The senior commanders of the Religion placed little hope in relief coming from Christian kings, but much more in the advent of General Winter.

As for the fortifications that Tadino set about inspecting upon his arrival, these had been completely overhauled since the Knights' successful defence of the city in 1480. Then, medieval defences had prevailed (just!) against medieval cannon. But the Grand Masters knew well the changes in artillery – the Knights' own cannon were among the best in the world – and they realised that their defences had to change to cope with this.

Medieval fortifications essentially replicated armour: they were strong, hard and thin. Fine for coping with stones lobbed by trebuchet but incapable of withstanding the far greater kinetic energy of a fired cannonball, particularly when it was made of iron.

The Italian Wars had demonstrated that against such weapons, the principle was not reflection but absorption. Plate armour deflected or defied arrows and swords and the same principle had applied to medieval fortifications. But in this new world of war, the shock of cannon had to be absorbed rather than deflected: it was defence by cushion! In the Italian Wars, considerable success had been achieved with simple earth banks. Cannonballs simply buried themselves in the earth, the bank closing over the shot as if it had never landed. This worked well in places where there was much earth to shovel but on Rhodes, where thin soil covered limestone bedrock, that was not an option. The walls had to be made of stone.

So the existing walls were broadened.

If you visit Rhodes today, the old medieval city comes almost as a surprise, for it squats, low and all but invisible save for the palace of the Grand Master, until you are almost on top of it. Then, there it is.

Imagine a terrapin, sitting in a pit. That's how the city appears. The head is the Grand Master's palace, which stands proud of the surrounding ground, peering around like the terrapin raising its head to see out of the pit.

The pit itself is the moat that surrounds the city. While moat is the correct term, for those of us who have grown up with the image of castles sitting in a serene lake – Bodiam Castle in Sussex is the classic example – the word 'moat' probably conjures up the wrong idea. The moat surrounding Rhodes is dry, and deeper and wider than you would imagine. If you walk around the walls today – it takes about an hour – you will find silent testimonials to the siege of 1522 in the shape of the round, stone cannonballs left lying in the moat.

The counterscarp, the far side of the moat, that is the side furthest from the wall, is sheer, sliced straight down through the limestone. The width of the moat varies but in places it's 75 yards wide (70 metres): a bare, unforgiving landscape deliberately engineered to make it a killing ground for any attackers attempting to cross it.

Covering two of the main sections of the walls, the areas protected by the Knights of Aragon and England, you will see long, thick walls set into the moat, like sandbanks rising in the middle of a river. These are called *tenaille*, a word which derives from the Latin *tenaculum* (prongs) because in many cases they resemble the end of a pair of pincers (although not particularly with the *tenailles* of Rhodes). They were built as a protection to particularly vulnerable sections of the main curtain wall, literally stone curtains raised in front of the curtain designed to block and absorb all the enemy artillery fire directed against that section of the curtain wall.

The empty space between the *tenaille* and the curtain wall could be reached from hidden postern gates, giving the defenders a sheltered place to muster before attempting a sally against the attackers. The *tenailles* were set between protruding bastions which had gun ports set into their sides that could send enfilading fire down the whole lengths of the *tenailles*, both in front and behind them.

The *tenailles* were constructed simply by leaving the old wall of the moat in place and then digging around it. This indicates just how much the moat was widened.

The bastions themselves had been completely rebuilt since the siege of 1480 in an attempt to deal with the new methods of war. Medieval bastions were generally rounded, with tall, high walls. The new bastions had been made much broader, and the same applied to the whole curtain wall. This was done to make the defences better able to withstand prolonged artillery bombardment. The walls and the bastions also now had wide flat walkways on top of them to make it easier to manoeuvre cannon from one section of the defences to another. These wide walkways were called *terre pleins* (literally 'filled earth'). The cannon were protected by embrasures on the *terre plein*, allowing their crews to target the enemy while being reasonably well protected themselves.

The bastions were remade as massive, low, squat fortifications with flat faces in a polygonal arrangement. Gun ports were built into the bastions at all levels, but most of those ports were actually directed laterally so that the gunners could direct enfilading fire down the length of the moat. Each bastion was designed to be able to send enfilading fire down the whole length of the curtain wall, and the *tenaille* if there was one, that it protected. Some of the gun ports were at ground level, so that the gunners could take out any attackers attempting to shelter in the shadow of the wall.

The bastions had been rebuilt with these new designs because the old curved bastions left dead areas in which attackers could shelter, working at undermining the walls there. The new design meant that everywhere along the defences should be exposed to the fire of the Religion's guns.

The bastions had integrated internal chimneys to vent the gun smoke from the artillerists and arquebusiers operating from their firing points within them. Even when the cannon or arquebus protrudes from its embrasure, it produces huge amounts of smoke. Without the chimneys, the gun crews would be blinded and possibly even incapacitated.

To support the bastions, and to try ensure that the moat remained a killing ground, the Knights also built blockhouses and *caponiers* to give cannoneers and arquebusiers further embrasures from which to direct enfilading fire along the moat. A *caponier* was a covered over passage, which could be a trench or raised up, from which fire could be directed.

The Knights also built *fausse braye* along much of the curtain wall. Most of the technical terms for these defences come from French or Italian, which can make it difficult to picture what they're referring to. In the case of *fausse braye*, we might call them outworks in English. This was essentially a second low wall in front of the main curtain wall, set a short distance in front of the main wall, which served to provide concentric fortifications.

Most of these improvements to the defences were made under the direction of Italian military engineers during the 42 years between the two sieges. We know the names of two of these: Basilio della Scuola, from Vicenza, and Matteo Giuenio, a Sicilian.

Now a third Italian military engineer was on hand to put their improvements to work, while trying to come up with on-the-spot counters to the Ottoman plan of attack.

30

War Underground

The Ottoman barrage began in earnest on 1 August 1522, coincidentally the same day that Gabriele Tadino was taken into the Religion. The barrage was intended to weaken, break and open the city's defences.

Jacques de Bourbon, a French Hospitaller who later wrote an eyewitness account of the siege, recorded that the Ottomans began the siege with 80 cannon, although that number was slowly whittled away through counter-battery fire, accidents, and wear and tear to 40 pieces. Judging by de Bourbon's testimony, and taking into account the mute witness of the stone cannonballs that still lie in the moat around Rhodes, the majority of these cannon were wide-bore weapons that fired stone shot at comparatively lower velocities. These were still dangerous, but it appears that the *tenailles* and the reinforced walls coped well with this type of shot. More dangerous, and much more damaging, were the narrow bore cannon that shot smaller, denser and harder iron cannonballs at much greater velocities. These balls had the kinetic energy to shatter stone and they were the Turks' most potent wall-busting weapons.

To protect their own cannon from counter-battery fire, the Ottomans made mantlets, portable screens made from wood, and piled up banked earth as temporary embrasures. These mantlets gave the Turkish gunners some valuable protection but, in the initial stages of the siege, the Knights' artillerists had far better protection and they used this to inflict considerable damage on the Turkish artillery.

On 1 August, the Ottomans began their bombardment by concentrating their fire on the post of Germany. The attack succeeded in breaking down the tower of the Church of St John, which was a useful observation post, but the Knights' counter-fire was vigorous and effective; after ten days, the Turkish commanders were forced to move their artillery elsewhere. They decided to concentrate their attack upon the sections of walls between the posts of Auvergne, Aragon and England.

While the Knights kept up their counter-fire, they noted that the Turks were also building long earthworks along the lip of the counterscarp. The labourers working on the earthworks were horribly exposed to the Knights' fire, and very many were killed and wounded, but the Ottomans simply replaced the dead and wounded with new slaves and kept on building.

The earthworks were clearly an important part of the Ottoman strategy to take the city and the Knights realised that it was vital that they glean some information about its purpose. To that end, a Rhodian named Basil Carapazio, who was fluent in Turkish, volunteered to take on the information-gathering mission. With some friends, Carapazio loaded a small boat with fish and crept out of the harbour, evading the blockade and sailing up the coast to a small bay behind the main Ottoman lines. Pulling up on the beach, Carapazio pretended to be a fisherman selling fresh fish and three Ottoman soldiers fell for the story, coming out to the boat to select fish for their supper.

Carapazio and his friends attempted to subdue them but one fought back so hard they had to kill him. They tied up the two surviving prisoners and rowed back into the harbour at Rhodes, evading the blockade again. Under interrogation, the two prisoners talked: the earthworks were intended to make mottes, mounds of rock higher than the walls and bastions of the defenders, so that the Ottoman artillery could fire down upon the bastions and walls, clearing the *terre pleins* of defenders.

Even before the earthworks were completed, the Turks were using them as cover for their arquebusiers. Although the arquebus was not a terribly accurate weapon, the range from which they were firing was not long and the fortifications of Rhodes today provide mute witness of the accuracy of the Ottoman fire: look at many of the more important and exposed window slits and embrasures and you will see that they are peppered with little pits, the marks left by the arquebus balls that just missed the intended mark of the open gap. We know that some of the shots hit their marks in the window slits and embrasures from injury reports among the Knights.

Once the earthworks were completed – the work took a few weeks because of the Knights' vigorous defence – the Ottomans could scour the *terre pleins* on top of the walls, bastions and *tenailles*. In response, the

Knights, and in particular their own teams of labourers, had to struggle under Turkish fire to make or move mantlets to protect the defenders.

But this battle was merely a part, and a small part, of the wider struggle. For while the artillery played a large part in the siege of Rhodes, it would not prove as crucial as it had in earlier sieges, for already the lessons of the gunpowder age were being learned and the defenders were learning how to respond to the advantages that had first accrued to the attackers using cannon.

Gabriele Tadino would play a large part in the artillery battle, particularly as the siege dragged on, but his key contribution lay not on the *tenailles* and *terre pleins* of Rhodes, but underground. For the key conflict in the siege played out in tunnels, mines and trenches around and under the walls of the city.

That the war should go underground was in no way unique to the siege of Rhodes. In fact, mining and counter-mining has continued into the modern age. Starting at 3.10am on 7 June 1917, the British set off a series of mines under the Messines Ridge on the Western Front that produced the largest non-nuclear explosion in history. General Sir Charles Harington, the Second Army Chief of Staff, briefed the press on the eve of the explosion, telling them, 'Gentlemen, I don't know whether we are going to make history tomorrow, but at any rate we shall change geography.'[36] They did.

But in essence the miners of the Great War were doing nothing different from the miners and sappers during the siege of Rhodes – or the men who had first developed the technique during the Middle Ages. The first miners dug tunnels under vulnerable points of the curtain wall of a besieged castle, digging out a space under a tower, for instance. To stop the tower collapsing on their heads as they dug, they braced the tunnel with wooden supports. In the early Middle Ages, miners did not have gunpowder, so to collapse the tower they would pile combustible material in the end chamber under it, set this alight and crawl back out of the tunnel as quickly as possible while the fire ate through the wooden supports. The burning wood weakened and then, when the tunnel was no longer supported against the weight of the earth above, it collapsed, bringing down the tower with it.

The adoption of gunpowder made mining much more effective. It was difficult to supply enough oxygen to a chamber at the end of a one-way tunnel to ensure that the wooden supports burnt through. Furthermore, the extent of the collapse depended upon the size of the chamber the miners had dug under the wall or the tower.

With explosives, you didn't need a big chamber for effective results. Exploding gunpowder had this way of making the hole bigger – much bigger. The corresponding collapse was therefore also bigger.

Exploding mines were possibly first used during the siege of Pisa in 1409, the charges set by an unnamed Florentine. Another Florentine, the architect Filippo Brunelleschi, appears to have known about the technique. However, the first definitive record of explosive mining took place in 1495, when yet another Italian, the military engineer Francesco di Giorgio Martini, employed mines to bring down the walls of Castel Nuovo in Naples.

It was a difficult art. The size of the charge planted depended on the result the attacker wanted to achieve: a smaller charge would crumple the wall, leaving a mound of rubble for the attackers to climb over; a larger charge could create a complete breach in the wall. Perhaps the most difficult task was the correct positioning of the charge under the fortifications. Miners were digging in the dark with only very primitive instruments to judge how far they had dug and the direction in which they were digging. The tunnel itself was normally dug straight towards the enemy fortifications, crossing under the moat in the shortest distance, but before the tunnel reached the target the miners had to dig the tunnel into zigzags. The zigzags were there to stop a massive blowback when the mine was set; the miners wanted the energy of the explosion to go up, into the fortifications, rather than back along the tunnel. To ensure that the mine went off, the military engineer in charge of the mining also had to lay two fuses.

It was a specialised and difficult job, and very few people knew how to do it well. This meant that military engineers with this sort of knowledge were in high demand. The Ottomans were always keen to enlist the best technical support and were more than happy to pay a premium to attract foreign engineers to their cause. Urban, a Hungarian master gunner, had offered his services to Emperor Constantine XI in Constantinople but when Constantine was unable to offer him the money he thought he was due, Urban went to the Ottomans. Mehmed had no problem meeting Urban's payment demands and the Hungarian cast for Mehmed the giant cannon that breached the walls of the city. Unfortunately for Urban, he did not have the chance to enjoy his pay as he was killed during the siege when one of his cannon exploded.

In response, defenders started to site castles and strongholds on ground which was harder to dig. But the chief defence was the time, effort and expertise required to dig the mines necessary to compromise the defences of a properly constructed stronghold. Few kings could muster the resources necessary, generally preferring other options. Besides, it was the sort of tactic which found no favour among Europe's military class. Even the brute bombardment of artillery was preferable to skulking through the earth, in the dark, with the ever-present risk of being buried alive.

Suleiman, however, had both the resources and the men to bring down the walls of Rhodes from below. As part of the preparations for the expedition, his pashas had recruited extensively among the miners of the Balkans. So they had the knowledge to start mining and, with the almost unlimited human resources that the Ottomans had at their disposal, they had the men to do the spade and pick work.

The miners started digging, while up in the blue air, the cannon and arquebus ground away at the walls and kept the Knights occupied. Mining was the chief plank of the Ottoman strategy for conquering Rhodes. If the cannon could open a breach and that be taken quickly, all well and good. But their spies were effective: they knew that the fortifications had been upgraded to counter cannon.

Recent work has uncovered another reason why the Ottomans came equipped to dig. The Rhodes of the Knights was built upon a much older city. The Colossus of Rhodes was, after all, one of the Seven Wonders of the Ancient World. There was a classical city there many centuries before the Knights arrived on Rhodes, and it spread much wider than the city of the Knights.

During the course of the siege, the Turks exploded no fewer than 12 mines under the walls and bastions of the city. Many, many more were detected, diverted and destroyed by the defenders. In the past, attackers had contented themselves with one or two mines. The Ottoman attack on Rhodes was of an entirely different order.

Historians have struggled to understand how this was possible. Rhodes is built on limestone. This is not a particularly hard rock, but it is rock nevertheless. Even with the manpower at the sultan's disposal, digging this number of attack tunnels represented an effort that beggared belief – save for the fact that we knew it to be true.

> Contemporary sources suggest the Turks dug about fifty mines under the walls. To excavate through solid rock that many would have been a prodigious task. Half a century later and with improved knowledge, they would only be able to drive about three shafts under the solid rock of the defences of Malta.[37]

Then, in 1993, Professor Athanassios Migos proposed a brilliantly elegant solution to this problem, based upon the ancient archaeology of Rhodes. Professor Migos noticed that the marks of rebuilding on the walls and bastions of Rhodes left clear traces of where the Ottomans had set their mines. The rebuilt sections of the walls were spread regularly around the curtain. The Rhodes of the Knights was built atop the Rhodes of antiquity. The ancient city had streets laid out in a grid pattern by the School of Hippodamus. What is more, underneath the streets of the old city, the ancient Greeks had dug conduits to channel water to the city and remove sewage. Cisterns and tunnels also ran under the foundations of the old houses. When constructing the new city, the old city had been built over but, crucially, the conduits and tunnels of ancient Rhodes were still there, lying under the fortress of the Religion. What's more, as ancient Rhodes spread wider than the Rhodes of the Religion, some of the culverts went past the moat and out into the surrounding country.

If they did not already know of this, the Knights would certainly have become aware of this network of tunnels under their city when they set about deepening and widening the moat following the siege of 1480. It's still possible to see some of the culverts as they bore under the *tenailles*.

But if the Knights knew of this, so did Suleiman. The Turks might have discovered the tunnel system during the failed siege of 1480. Even if they did not realise its significance then, their highly effective spy network must have relayed the information back to the Sublime Porte sometime before the siege of 1522. For it is clear that the Ottomans came with the plan to make the mining operation the main focus of their attack upon Rhodes.

Luckily, the Knights' spying operation was just as good as that of the Ottomans, and they learned of this too. They must have been dismayed, for their main efforts had gone into strengthening their walls and defences, not into blocking and defending against mines. This was the reason that they so earnestly pursued Gabriele Tadino, for he was one of that very small band of military engineers who had the knowledge to counter the Turkish mining operation, while also being a member of the even smaller group of people who relished the challenge of facing the might of the Ottoman Empire, even at the risk of his own life.

Gabriele took up the challenge with gusto. He set about creating a network of connected counter-tunnels under the city. In the end, these stretched around the entire active perimeter of the walls, from the tower of St George to the tower of Italy. Tadino must have made use of the existing network of tunnels and culverts, connecting and opening up blocked tunnels as well as blocking and filling tunnels that would have given the Turkish miners access to the city. With the large network of tunnels under the city, this enterprise must have taken up most of the time and resources to start with: Tadino realised that the city was sitting on top of a honeycomb and, as far as possible, he had to seal it.

But with so many tunnels giving access into the city, filling and sealing the tunnels was not the end of the job. The Turks had brought large numbers of experienced miners to Rhodes to exploit these tunnels. Where they found one blocked, they simply had to dig it out again. This was much easier than cutting a fresh tunnel through the limestone bedrock. Suleiman's resources meant that they could be clearing many tunnels simultaneously, as well as sometimes cutting new tunnels, perhaps particularly to make new interconnections between the grid of the tunnels under the moat.

Tadino's task was to find them and stop them.

First, the finding. That was the most difficult task. There were so many avenues of approach and, being underground, there was of course no way to see which way the Turks were coming.

But if the miners could not be seen, they might, perhaps, be heard. One of the first things Gabriele did upon arriving on the island was to set about training men, and sometimes boys, to be his 'ears'.

Tadino had designed various listening devices to detect the direction and distance of mining. It's difficult to mine quietly, particularly when trying to cut and move limestone. There's the strike of pick-axes, the scrape of shovels, and the grinding of wheelbarrow wheels trundling the spoil back down the tunnels. Sound is vibration.

While Tadino could not hear the work of the Ottoman miners through the limestone, he could feel it. Sometimes, if the miners were close enough, a hand placed upon the rock could feel the strike/scrape rhythm as picks and shovels worked to break and move the rock.

But more sensitive still were the devices that Tadino invented to detect the distance and direction of the Turkish miners. The most famous of these was a small, tightly strung drum which had little bells attached, via pivots, to sensors on the skin. Holding these tambours tight against the various surfaces of the counter-tunnels enabled the drums to pick up the vibrations, transmitted through the limestone rock, of the Ottoman miners.

Imagine yourself, sitting in a tunnel, lit only by the dim light of lanterns and candles guttering in hastily carved out sconces in the wall, holding the tambour tight against the rock, rotating it to bring the drum into tighter contact with the stone. Holding it there, holding your finger to your lips to call for silence and stillness from the men around you, then, slowly, moving it down the wall of the tunnel, to the floor, then up the other wall.

The bells start to sound, a sudden, bright silver sound cutting through the silent ochre light of the tunnel. The 'ear' grinds the tambour tighter against the rock. The men around, their faces ghost white from the limestone dust, look at the drum with eyes set dark into their white faces.

The 'ear' moves the tambour, shifting up and down the tunnel, searching for where the sound begins and where it ends.

With these devices, and others such as tight drums set into the tunnel floor with pebbles on the skin, or bowls of water, Tadino and the men he had trained were able to detect the approach of Turkish miners at ranges of up to 50 yards.

Then it was a matter of stopping them.

This was desperate, dangerous work. One way to stop the Ottoman miners was to set a counter-mine by digging close to the Turkish tunnel, setting a charge there and blowing it, sealing the miners into their tunnel tomb. But of course, the closer the miners got, the greater the risk that the Turks would detect Tadino's men and set their own counter-mine.

Even more desperate were those occasions when tunnellers bored into each other's tunnels. Then, it became a matter of hand-to-hand fighting, in semi-darkness, with the roof and walls pressing down upon the combatants. This was the most brutal sort of fighting, where there was no room for quarter, or finesse. It was close-up fighting, where daggers and clubs were more effective than swords or halberds, for the limited space made it impossible to wield larger weapons.

In the tunnel battles of the First World War, British miners had taken to using spiked knuckle dusters as the most effective weapons for this sort of close-quarters fighting. We don't know if the miners under Rhodes used similar weapons, but in the annals of warfare, similar conditions have tended to produce similar weapons.

But there were times when, despite the best efforts of his men, Tadino could not counter the Turkish miners before they had set their mine in place. To protect the walls and bastions from the effects of the mine exploding, Tadino developed a new technique, drilling vent holes in the walls down towards the mine so that when the explosion came, the energy from the explosion could dissipate up through the vent holes rather than bringing down the fortifications. This technique proved very effective on a number of occasions, allowing blasts that were big enough to shake the whole town to occur without serious damage to the defences.

Fra' Antonio Bosio, the Knight who had recruited Tadino to the cause of the Religion in the first place, wrote a later account of the siege. His testimony of Gabriele's role in countering the activity of the Turkish miners is fascinating:

> Because their captains were certain that a very great number of Turks would be slaughtered during the assault, knowing very well that our knights and soldiers were very able; before making the assault, as their principal hope was to capture the city, they used mines which elsewhere we have described. They were intent for many days in digging mines in such a way that, of the six sides of the city, in a very short time, five sides were mined under. Some say that the Turks dug fifty-four mines, others say forty-five, while others say only thirty-eight mines were dug. Most of them were ineffective because of counter-mines dug by the industrious and most vigilant Fra Fabritio Tadino Martinengo. He had excavated underground a trench which encircled the Bastion of Auvergne, and on one side ran towards the walls of the Langue of Germany, on the other as far as the Bastion of England. He had another dug

from the Bastion of Cosquino, as far as the Bastion built by the Grand Master Fra Fabritio del Carretto at the Bastion of Italy. Thus most of the mines of the enemy came up against these counter-mines and were broken up when they were intercepted. Great diligence was used to pinpoint them. A large number of barbers' poles with little bells inside and very well covered drums were used continuously to listen for and more easily to pinpoint the Turkish mines. They were used in the most dangerous places. As a result many mines were discovered and successfully intercepted.[38]

In this enterprise, Tadino made great use of the labourers and slaves that the Knights had on the island to carry out the manual work of digging, constructing and repairing fortifications. These men were among the most vital of their resources during the siege but they were constant targets for the Turkish gunners, as indeed was true for the Ottoman labourers and slaves, who were killed in large numbers by the Religion's artillery and gunners.

The Knights themselves did little of this manual work. As armoured and trained fighting men, they were too valuable a resource to spend their energy on spade work. But there were also barriers of prestige to their doing such labour. The Knights prided themselves on being an aristocratic order. Indeed, in later centuries, to become a Knight a postulant had to prove noble blood on both sides of his heritage for at least eight generations before he would be admitted to the order. Such a blood divide was not yet apparent in Rhodes – else the Grand Master could not have admitted Gabriele to the Religion – but some of the divisions were already present, played out in the divide between fully pledged Knights of the order and the sergeants-at-arms, who were equally active in the defence of Rhodes but because of their less exalted inheritance were generally not admitted as full brothers of the Religion.

Tadino was not interested in these niceties. He was on Rhodes to add his knowledge to the Knights and to defend Christendom – a task that the princes of Europe were conspicuously failing to do.

31

WAR OVERGROUND

While Gabriele spent much time and effort on countering the Turkish mining attacks, that was by no means the only area where he contributed. His efforts were also crucial in the Knights' response to the sustained artillery barrage unleashed by the Ottomans.

The Knights were quite certain that what they were facing was unprecedented in history. Jacques de Bourbon, a French Knight who wrote an account of the siege, gave voice to their thoughts.

> I believe verily that since the creation of the world such artillery and so great quantity was never bent and laid before any town as hath been against Rhodes at this siege. Wherefore it is no marvel if the walls been and have been be... fell down and if there be brakes and clefts in many places.[39]

By the middle of August, the Turks had moved almost all their heavy, wall-breaking artillery to concentrate on the sections of walls between the posts of England and Aragon, where the earthworks the Turkish engineers had raised along the lip of the counterscarp rose a good 12 feet over the Knights' defences, enabling them to shoot down on the defenders while providing their own gunners with much better cover.

Meanwhile, sappers were gradually digging trenches across the moat towards the walls. This was particularly dangerous work as the defenders were able to shoot down upon the sappers. However, the Ottomans provided the sappers with screens to help conceal and protect them, while the sappers for their own protection dug deep and fast so that the trenches could provide them with cover. Through the first weeks of August, these trenches slowly advanced across the moat, moving like slow-motion earthquake cracks towards the walls they hoped to break.

The artillery bombardment was slowly cracking the walls. Even though the Knights' labourers struggled to repair breaches made during the day in the following night, it was impossible to restore the walls faster than they were being broken down. By the third week of August, the Turkish artillery had succeeded in making breaches in the walls of the posts of Aragon and England. The attacks on the post of England were particularly intense and many of the English Knights were killed or wounded.

As the sappers inched the trenches closer, and the artillery gnawed away at the walls, it became clear to the defenders that an assault would be coming in the next week or two. Rather than just wait passively for that assault to come, the Grand Master agreed to the suggestion, put before him by Gabriele Tadino, that he should lead a sally to kill, destroy and disrupt the Turkish efforts. On 19 August, Tadino led 200 armed Knights, mounted on the horses they had kept safe in stables deep within the city, on a sally out of the city. They used one of the postern gates that enabled the defenders to slip through the wall undetected and rode out upon the startled Turkish sappers and soldiers in the moat.

That Gabriele managed to persuade the Grand Master to let him lead this sortie indicates the force of his personality: he was far too valuable a man to risk on such a venture so he must have overridden de L'Isle Adam's objections. Throughout his life, Tadino led his men from the front. In the underground war, he personally listened to the tinkle of the bells of his tambour; he set the counter-mines and detonated them. In the war above ground, he rode on this first sally against the over-confident Turks. The Knights, moving fast on their horses, rode down the helpless sappers before the Ottoman commanders could call up reinforcements, retiring back behind the safety of the walls before sufficient arquebusiers had been called to the sector to turn it into a killing zone.

Encouraged by their initial success, the Knights essayed further sorties on 20, 22 and 24 August. But the Turks, coming to expect these sorties, established arquebus pickets who were better able to return fire on the Knights: losses began to exceed the gains and after the sortie on 24 August, the Grand Master called a halt to any further attempts to push the Turks back. Given the respective strengths of the forces, de L'Isle Adam could not afford to lose any more through such sorties.

The Knights had resorted to sorties because the Turks were pushing the trenches closer to the walls, while the constant bombardment was beginning to breach them. As the month drew towards its close, it must have become clear to them that they could expect a general assault sometime soon in September.

On the same day as the final sortie, 24 August, the Knights received unexpected but welcome reinforcements when Fra' Emeric Depreaux ran the blockade and brought his ship into harbour with supplies and a few extra knights recruited to help the defence. While the supplies and personnel were welcome, they were not enough to change the balance for the defenders. But the fact that yet another ship had managed to successfully run the blockade did change the balance of Suleiman's mind concerning his admiral, Kurtoğlu Muslihiddin Reis. No one doubted the effectiveness of the corsair, but the steady stream of blockade runners finally convinced Suleiman that Kurtoğlu's piratical instincts were distracting him from the tedious work of blockade patrolling.

His patience exhausted, Suleiman ordered that Kurtoğlu be bastinadoed on the bridge of his own ship. This was a punishment expressly designed to be both extraordinarily painful and exquisitely humiliating.

Kurtoğlu was marched onto his bridge, tied up and then laid on the ground with his bare feet sticking up in the air, tied to a horizontal pole. For the admiral of the Ottoman fleet, there could be no more humiliating position, particularly since his crew and the crew of many of the ships of his fleet were watching.

Then, as the drums announced the admiral's punishment, a man stepped forward, clad in the baggy trousers and loose shirt of an Ottoman sailor, with a red hat on his head. In his hand, he held a springy wooden cane.

The drums stopped. The men, watching, collectively held their breath.

The cane whipped through the air, its passing loud enough for the men near to hear it, and struck Kurtoğlu on the soles of his feet.

The admiral, a tough and experienced sailor, bit back the pain on the first stroke, and the second, and the third.

But by the tenth, he was screaming.

By the twentieth, his screams had turned into a constant sobbing plea for the punishment to stop.

When the punishment did finally end, Kurtoğlu had to be lifted up and carried below: he could not stand. It would be many days before he could.

Thereafter his ships did not go chasing off after pirate prizes but stayed on station.

However, the only way the siege was going to be settled at sea was if a relief force sailed to Rhodes. Failing that, its resolution would come on land.

Tadino's contribution to the defence was not confined underground: he was crucial in organising the defences where the Ottoman artillery made breaches in the walls. In these areas, he arranged for guns to be set up on either side of the breach to ensure enfilading fire against any Ottoman troops trying to get through the breach. Should any Turks make it alive through the breach, they then found themselves facing new defences in the shape of hastily constructed but still formidable retrenchments – essentially, a low wall enclosing the breach behind which the defenders could shelter while firing upon the Turks. He also fortified the houses nearest the breach, turning them into strongpoints well stocked with ammunition, giving the defenders rallying points.

At the end of August, Gabriele Tadino took a brief break from his duties to write a letter. Although he had left Candia against the express orders of the Venetian governor, Gabriele clearly hoped that he might win back the favour of the Signoria if he kept the Republic informed about the siege – after all, intelligence gathering was the thread that tied all Venice's activities together. So Gabriele wrote to a prominent Venetian official stationed on Candia, Girolamo Cornaro, a member of the important and influential Cornaro family. Girolamo was related to Giorgio Cornaro, Procurator of St Mark, after the Doge one of the most powerful officials in the Republic. Gabriele addressed the letter to Hiernonimo (Girolamo in the Venetian dialect) but included Zorzi (Giorgio in Venetian) Cornaro in the salutation in the clear hope that Girolamo would forward the letter to his more influential relative.

My lord.
   On the first day of August, I was given the habit with Grand Cross, and in this Sacred Council, His Most Reverend Grace

granted me the general command of this campaign, which is proceeding very vigorously.

So that Your Lordship may know, since then we have been attacked from all sides by extremely heavy artillery, extensive mining operations, trenches, and threats to fill the moat with earth and wood. Nevertheless, we have responded boldly to all their efforts – to their bombardments, mines, and trenches – and with the help of Our Lord God, I hope we will continue to prevail with courage.

It is true that the siege is massive, both by land and by sea.

I beg Your Lordship to excuse me if I have not written earlier. Rhodes, August 27, 1522.

Postscript:

Zorzi da Conversano [Tadino's friend, Giorgio di Conversano, who escaped with him from Candia] was wounded in the moat by an arquebus shot, which passed through his arm and thigh. Nevertheless, I hope his injuries are not serious. But before he was wounded, I had ordered him to climb against the enemy with around 50 men.

And on another day, I ordered Messer Beneto [Beneto Scaramosa, the other friend who left Candia with Gabriele] to do the same, so that in those two assaults, more than 200 Turks were killed, and many more wounded.

The enemy is bombarding the moat with their arquebusiers and is also advancing. They have given us a lot of trouble, yet whatever they damage during the day, we repair by night.

As Your Lordship will hear from the bearer of this letter, the enemy is proceeding in a manner never seen before. They began nearly a mile away from Rhodes and are advancing by bringing the earth forward as cover – it is something unbelievable to one who has not seen it.

There is not a single hour in which they sleep or rest, for they work continuously, by day and by night, with such a number of people that they cannot be counted.

And since they are now at the moat, we expect an assault at any hour. But unless we are abandoned, we will undoubtedly be victorious.

I hope their mines will come to nothing. Indeed, with God's help, today or tomorrow I plan to discover one of their mines and blow it up from the inside, because I have made preparations.

My lord, one more postscript:

For four days I have been constantly attending to a mine made by the Turks against us. And today, at the 20th hour [i.e. around 4pm], I discovered it, and I burned and drowned the miners and their crew. It was a remarkable event and brought the greatest joy to the entire city, as the bearer of this letter will tell you.

Rhodes, August 27, 1522, at the 23rd hour [i.e. around 7pm].[40]

In his memoir of the siege, Jacques de Bourbon wrote about the measures Tadino undertook to protect the city.

> The captayne Gabryell Martyningo prompt diligent & expert to give remedies to the needful places forthwith made to make the traverses upon the wall where as the breach was with good repairs & gonnes small and great which were set in the said traverses. The which only shot not at the breaches but to… the trenches & made great murder of enemies as well at the assaults that they made as every day. And besides the traverses the said captain made to lay small artillery as arquebuses & hangonnes upon certain houses within the town that stood open against the breach with good repairs. And from those places great slaughter of turks was made at the assaults.[41]

Mustafa Pasha had promised the fall of Rhodes in 15 days, 30 at most. By the beginning of September, the siege was well past even the later date. Pressure was growing on the Ottoman commanders to provide the victory they had promised to their sultan. While the artillery was slowly breaking down the wall in various places, the Knights' defence was too vigorous to allow the Ottomans to cross the death ground of the moat and enter the city.

But then, on 4 September, Mustafa Pasha caught a break.

Tadino's ears had detected a mine under the wall of Provence and he detonated a counter-mine, burying the unfortunate miners.

However, this may have been a diversion, for later on the same day another mine that had gone undetected exploded under the bastion of England. The explosion was big enough to shake the city and it opened up a 36-foot gap in the bastion. Otttoman troops had been waiting in the trenches in the moat and, when the rubble settled, they went over the top and into the breach, setting their banners flying above the bastion.

The dazed English Knights, those who had survived the initial blast, picked themselves up and counter-attacked with pike and sword while gunners fired down into the breach.

Learning of the breach and the desperate fighting taking place there, Gabriele Tadino and the Grand Master, with his standard bearer, Henry Mansell, rushed to the breach. Mansell was carrying the banner of the Crucifixion which had been given to the Knights following their successful defence of Rhodes 42 years earlier.

Although de L'Isle Adam was 58 he fought as a man half his age, rallying the defenders.

Mustafa Pasha, desperate to present the victory he had promised to Suleiman, had led the attack in person. However, when the Turkish troops began to retreat, he was carried helplessly back from the breach, tumbling into the moat. There, he berated his men, striking them with the flat of his sword and ordering them back into the attack.

The fighting went on for two hours before Mustafa Pasha realised that he could no longer force his men forward and the Ottomans retired, leaving their dead behind.

The Knights had defended the city but they too had taken casualties, including the Grand Master's standard bearer, Henry Mansell.

Further assaults and mines followed a few days later on 9, 11, 13, 14, 18, 20 and 22 September. The defenders fought off all the attacks, but it was becoming steadily more dangerous to pursue the retreating Turks out into the moat because the Ottomans had cut gun ports along the lip of the counterscarp and manned them with arquebusiers who shot down the Knights if they attempted to follow the routing Turks.

In between these relentless assaults, on 19 September, the defenders had confirmation of their darkest fears: there were spies within the city, passing on information to the Turks. A Jewish doctor named Apella Renato, who had done great service in the hospital, was discovered in the act of a firing a crossbow from the ramparts. The bolt had a message wrapped around the shaft with information addressed to one of the Turkish pashas.

Under questioning, which involved torture, the doctor admitted that he had been sending information to the Turks throughout the siege and that he had been recruited to the service of the Sublime Porte during the reign of Suleiman's father, Selim. Having confessed, Dr Renato was executed.

Given the history of the Jews on Rhodes, it was perhaps not so surprising that Dr Renato had betrayed the Religion. During the 1480 siege, the sizeable Jewish community in Rhodes had played a full, and brave, part in the defence of the city, a part that was acknowledged in its aftermath. However, some years later, the Grand Master, Pierre d'Aubusson, who had led the defence and gained great fame, renown and a cardinal's hat as a result of his conduct, fell victim to increasing paranoia in his old age and, looking around for someone to blame, settled upon the usual scapegoats: the city's Jews.

The Jewish population were forced to convert or leave. But those who chose to leave were not allowed to take their children with them: they were held and baptised as Christians. Dr Renato remained in Rhodes by accepting baptism and pretending to be Christian, but the bitter taste of d'Aubusson's betrayal must have made it easy for him to accept the offer of Selim's agents that he spy for the Turks.

The unmasking of a genuine spy increased the suspicions that were growing among the defenders. Under the conditions of a siege, when the hoped-for relief does not come, it becomes all too easy to shift blame onto suspected spies within your own camp. Now they had found one, it became even easier to believe that there were others.

But before a further spy search could begin in earnest, the Knights realised that the Turks were building towards an all-out assault. The sequence of attacks they had faced already had all been on particular parts of the defences, which meant that the Grand Master could rush his reserve to wherever they were needed. However, should the Turks mount a general assault, attacking all along the defences, then there was a strong chance that they would be able to simply overwhelm the defenders by sheer numbers.

On 23 September, the defenders' lookouts started to report large movements of men throughout the Turkish lines. The movements continued throughout the night, the sounds carrying over the walls of the city to the waiting, watching men.

On the Ottoman side, Mustafa Pasha had promised his sultan that the morrow would see the fall of the city. So that he could see the end, the pasha had made a viewing platform for Suleiman to watch the action. Just after dawn, having said the *fajr* (dawn prayer), Suleiman ascended to the platform and waited.

The Ottoman guns opened the attack with a massive bombardment. But rather than trying to cause new breaches in the wall, this bombardment was designed to create a smoke screen to conceal the attackers as they advanced upon the breaches the guns had already made.

Under the cover of the smoke, the Janissaries marched forward. Suleiman's generals did not lack for courage: Bali Agha, the commander of the Janissaries, led the attack in person. The Janissaries swarmed onto the bastion of Aragon, sweeping aside the defenders and planting their banners on the roof and walls.

All along the defences, the Turks drove forward, pushing the defenders back from the breaches and climbing up onto the *terre plein*, the wide platform on top of the curtain wall. The attacking troops pushed forwards, reaching the retrenchments that Tadino had constructed as fall backs behind the breached walls. There the fighting, which elsewhere was conducted at the range of arquebus shot, became hand to hand, the heavily armoured Knights wading into the lightly armoured Janissaries. The Grand Master, with the banner of the Resurrection carried by a new standard bearer, went to wherever the fighting was hardest and the arrival of the sacred banner of the Religion gave new heart to the defenders, helping to push back the onslaught.

But to push the attack back in one place seemed only to allow it to advance somewhere else. The Knights might well have been overwhelmed if the Rhodians had not joined in the defence, with the men fighting with whatever weapons they could find while the women brought supplies of powder and shot to the front, helped to move the cannon to where they were most needed, supplied water and food, and helped the wounded to the hospital.

The sources tell of one unnamed local woman who had taken as a lover one of the Knights, an Englishman. This was, of course, against the vows of the order but it wouldn't have been the first time this vow was broken. They had been lovers long enough to have children together. But during the desperate struggle, the Knight was killed. His lover, seeing his body and believing that the city was lost, succumbed to despair. Rather than see her children taken as slaves, she killed them. Then, taking what items of her lover's armour fitted, she put them on and, a fury of despair, went seeking death. So appalled were the Turks by her advent of this harpy that they fell back, the grief-stricken woman cutting down those who fell as they fled. But such fury could only end one way, and the woman was, in the end, herself killed.

The bastion of Aragon, which the Janissaries had captured at the start of the attack, had to be retaken and Jacques de Bourbon was given that mission. Using one of Tadino's tunnels, de Bourbon and his squad entered the bastion from below and made their way up, killing the Turks they found along the way. However, when they reached the top, they found almost all the Janissaries there dead, cut down by the enfilading fire from the flanks.

They ripped down the Ottoman banners flying from the bastion. The tide was retreating.

The fighting went on for six hours but, at the end of those desperate, bloody hours, the attack was beaten back. Despite the imprecations and threats of the Ottoman commanders, the troops could not be persuaded to mount a new assault but ran for safety, the dogs of war, Phobos and Deimos, nipping at their heels as they ran. The exhausted defenders made no move to pursue them.

Watching from his viewing platform, Suleiman had a clear view of the day's proceedings, of the initial success, of the way the attack had been held, the wavering back and forth through the thickest of the fighting and then the final breaking of the attack.

Mustafa Pasha had promised him the city in two weeks, a month at most. Suleiman himself had been on the island for seven and a half weeks. His forces had arrived on the island on 26 June.

Suleiman was not a happy sultan.

His wrath fell upon Mustafa, the pasha who had promised him a swift and sure victory. No matter that Mustafa was his brother-in-law; Suleiman ordered his execution. So far, Suleiman had been notably more merciful than his father, but such failure demanded vengeance. However, the other pashas, in a notable show of solidarity, united to plead mercy for Mustafa. Suleiman's order was to hang Mustafa on the top of the counterscarp that all might see his fall, but they pointed out to the sultan that the Knights would take encouragement from such evidence of discord in the Turkish camp. This argument struck home and Suleiman commuted the sentence he had handed down on Mustafa. But the pasha was stripped of his command, control of the siege passing to another officer, Ahmed.

Mustafa was allowed to live but on the understanding that he would lead from the front and lay down his life if necessary to exhort his soldiers to follow him.

However, even one of the once-great pashas leading them on could not persuade the Turkish soldiers to commit to fresh assaults against the bastions where so many of them had died.

While the defenders had lost fewer men in that desperate defence, they were far less able to absorb those losses. The fighting had been particularly acute in front of the post of England and, by the end of September, almost all the English Knights were either dead or wounded, so that a Knight from another post had to take command of their sector.

32

AN EYE FOR AN ARQUEBUS

On the last day of August 1522, separate items of news reached the besiegers and the besieged. To Suleiman came the tidings that his favourite concubine, Hürrem, who would come to be known in Europe as Roxelana, had given birth to a child. Suleiman was already a father to a son from a previous concubine, Mahidevran, but the birth of a new child for the sultan was a cause for celebration and, for the defenders, allowed them a few hours' respite while the Ottomans celebrated the good news.

The birth would prove more important to the Ottomans than anyone realised at the time. The normal practice for an Ottoman sultan was to have relations with a concubine but once she gave birth to a healthy son, that relationship ceased. The concubine's role then shifted to that of mother to a potential heir. Given the law of fratricide that governed the inheritance of the throne, the mother also became her son's chief ally, looking to form alliances with the more powerful of the sultan's viziers so that, when the time came, he might have supporters in the struggle for the throne. The mother also became responsible for the education of her son, ensuring that he gained the necessary knowledge, skills and grace to rule such an empire. As the boy grew, she and he would leave Constantinople and move to a provincial posting where the boy could learn the practical exercise of power while keeping a weather eye on the Sublime Porte and the health of the ruling sultan.

That was the way it was supposed to be and the way it had been with Suleiman's eldest son and his mother.

But with Hürrem, it would be different. Suleiman did not put her aside after the birth of their son for the simple reason that he had completely and utterly fallen in love with her. Indeed, not only did he keep her in Constantinople, but they went on to have six children together and, in a final breaking with tradition, Suleiman even married her. For her sake, Suleiman, who had all the most beautiful and alluring women of his empire at his disposal, became a monogamous husband.

It is one of the great love stories in history.

The defenders also received news, from another ship that managed to evade the blockade, that a relief force was being readied at Messina in Sicily. But it was already the end of September. The European princes were reluctant and wary. The news, while received with joy, would prove false: with the lateness of the season, the princes took advantage of the worries that always attended sailing this late in the year to call off the mission. The campaigning season in the Mediterranean ran from mid to late spring to early autumn. Few captains were willing to risk long journeys across the sea from October onwards because of the risk of storms. Such a storm might wreck a whole fleet. And the risk wasn't just in the Mediterranean. A relief force from England did actually set sail in mid-October but the ship was lost in the Bay of Biscay.

Despite the promises, no further reinforcements would get through to Rhodes. The Knights were on their own.

As for the Turks, the new commander of the siege, Ahmed Pasha, chastened by the losses his army had suffered during its failed assaults, decided to adopt a new strategy. From now on, the Ottomans would concentrate on securing the trench network, allowing their men to make their way to the walls in relative safety. The artillery continued to bombard the breaches, seeking to widen and deepen them, while targeting the Knights' own artillery. Underground, miners worked to dig out the blocked tunnels and open routes to the walls.

It was a strategy of attrition and, as such, it was a strategy that would take time to work.

For the Knights, watching from their broken-down walls, there was nevertheless hope. For the season was dragging down. The weather had changed. The heat of summer had given way to cold and rain. If it was miserable for the besieged, it must surely be even worse for the besiegers whose only shelter were tents.

But the Knights' chief hope lay with General Winter. Surely, with his arrival, Suleiman would have to give up the siege? It was the standard Ottoman practice to return to Constantinople at the end of the campaigning season. With the Ottoman supply lines dependent upon shipping food and ammunition across the Rhodes strait, surely the sultan could not risk his supplies being cut off by bad weather, and he and his army becoming isolated on the island? Surely, he had to withdraw?

Indeed, Tadino himself was hopeful about the overall situation for the defenders for, on 10 October, he wrote a letter giving an account of the events of the previous few weeks and his assessment of how the defence stood.

> Dearest Brother,
> Since the departure of Fra' Antonio, events here have developed in such a way that, on the 3rd of September, while continuing the guard at the bastion of Saint Athanasius, I realized I could no longer prevent the Turkish mining operations. I immediately resolved to have a traverse constructed within the walls, and to block from the outside the areas where they might try to destroy us with their mines. This was carried out during the night.
>
> The next morning, on the 4th of the same month, the Turks ignited their mine. It destroyed the part of the bastion that I had sealed off with the traverse. That traverse, however, was what saved us. The Turks had already prepared their formations and launched a full assault. We fought for more than an hour over that traverse – without it, we could not have resisted their attack. We held out despite the full force of their artillery and the intense arquebus fire, enduring it with great effort, though it cost them dearly.
>
> On [a later date, possibly the 5th], they set off two more mines: one at the bastion of Auvergne, the other again at Saint Athanasius. Neither was effective, since I had counter-mines prepared in time. They also set off another mine at the bastion before I could erect a traverse, taking a small section of the outer work. They launched an immediate assault, managing to raise perhaps ten flags atop the traverse. Nonetheless, we repelled them with enormous losses on their side.

On the 18th, they ignited a mine at the bastion of Spain, and launched an assault both there and at Saint Athanasius. Again, their mines failed to take effect, and we repulsed their attack with honour.

On the 23rd, they ignited yet another mine, which also failed – its charge misfired. Though they had prepared their troops for a new assault, they lacked the courage to proceed.

On the 24th, about half an hour before dawn, they opened fire with all their artillery. Under the cover of smoke, some seventy banners were seen raised atop the batteries and walls. They succeeded in taking half of the bastion – specifically, that of Spain. The assault lasted for more than four continuous hours of close combat. By God's grace, we recaptured the bastion and drove them off with devastating losses and shame. So great was the carnage that, two days later, it was impossible to remain near the batteries because of the stench of the rotting corpses left in the trenches.

On the 6th of October, they attacked again at the bastion of Spain and managed once more to climb onto it. We immediately retook the position. In the meantime, they never ceased making fresh preparations – especially digging new mines. I swear, on my honour, that we have destroyed over 10,000 ducats' worth of their mining works. Without our countermeasures, Rhodes would surely have been lost.

Each day brings new artillery and other provisions, and never-ending mines. We have frequently encountered them hand-to-hand underground, and we have fought underground battles with artillery, muskets, and even fire. In every case, we have held our own.

They have piled up an enormous mound of earth over the edge of the moat to cover their approach. One would hardly believe it without seeing it. For three days now they have been in the moat, cutting through our wall. I am working to counter-cut it and am expecting at any moment to fight them there.

I cannot begin to describe the scale of the efforts we've made. Our men are worn down, and by all accounts their army is in a disordered state.

> The cause is their repeated losses, and they are now running short of munitions to continue bombarding the city. The siege seems to be nearing its end. Most of their forces have been withdrawing little by little each day. I assure you – according to many reliable men here – even a small Christian force could now inflict deep humiliation upon them.
>
> With God's help, I hope we shall prevail, to the honour of all Christian princes.
>
> I regret that you have not written to tell me of events in Italy. I have heard, however, that one of my nephews has been detained.
>
> Let it be in God's hands! The shame you mention is not mine – it is inflicted upon a faithful servant of his state. I had believed my service would not be repaid with such dishonour and disgrace. I commend myself to you in all things, with all that I have and can offer, and I pledge myself to your service.
>
> Written in Rhodes, on the 10th of October.[42]

Tadino's letter paints a vivid picture of the combat during the siege and, in particular, the close-quarters fighting that had taken place underground, in the network of tunnels that lay under the city. It had been brutal, unforgiving warfare.

What is also clear, from the final paragraph, is Tadino's sense of injustice at the Signoria's response to his coming to help the Religion. For Tadino, the call of his brothers in Christ outweighed the concerns of the Republic.

But Tadino also clearly believed that the besiegers were stretched just as tightly as the besieged. He could see the losses the Turks had incurred and the increasing reluctance of their soldiers to hurl themselves to their deaths against the walls of Rhodes.

But then, a day after Gabriele wrote this letter, disaster struck.

While inspecting the defences, Gabriele Tadino peered through an embrasure. On the far side of the moat, an Ottoman arquebusier saw the glint of movement in the shadow and, raising his primed gun to his shoulder, sighted along it. Tadino lingered at the opening, trying to see the extent of the damage.

The arquebusier squeezed the trigger.

The ball hit Tadino in the right eye. He had his head turned, so it did not travel out through the back of his skull but rather it bored diagonally through his head, emerging by his right ear.

Extraordinarily, Gabriele survived, although he hovered at the borders of death for some weeks. The man's indomitable will and astonishing vitality saw him back in action in six weeks. But for those six weeks, the Knights were without his help.

Their only hope lay in the sultan calling off the siege.

33

Facing General Winter

The autumn of 1522 was cold, wet and miserable. The wind blew in from the east and the men in the front lines shivered in their trenches and behind the earthworks. The wind reached cold fingers under the flaps of the tents and the guy ropes whistled and sang as the tents flared before it, like sails. Kurtoğlu's blockade, which had never been very secure, even after the admiral was bastinadoed, was all but abandoned as his ships sheltered in safe harbours. Any vessel attempting to make its way to the island was as much at risk from storm as from the Ottoman corsairs. Only in the brief passages of clear, cold weather did the supply ships dare to make the crossing from the mainland to the bays where the hungry army waited for their supplies.

In 1480, the Ottomans had given up the siege on 17 August after two months, three weeks and four days.

In 1522, 107 days had elapsed between the start of the siege and the day Tadino took an arquebus ball in the eye. That was three months and two weeks. It was also much later in the year. The weather had changed. The autumn storms had started.

To the Knights, peering through the battered embrasures and over the retrenchments at the bedraggled troops opposite, it must have seemed surely only a matter of time before the Ottomans gave up the siege.

But there was a difference between the two sieges. In 1480, Mehmed had not come to Rhodes to oversee the siege. This time, Suleiman was on the island himself.

The decision to continue the siege was the sultan's. The question is why he chose to continue the siege even though it had dragged on much longer than expected, and the advent of autumn and winter meant that there was the danger of his supply lines being cut as well as outbreaks of disease. Even for Suleiman, the inclement weather must have rendered the long-drawn-out siege unpleasant; for many of his men, it must have been positively purgatorial.

Unfortunately, the Ottoman sources are silent on the reasons for Suleiman's decision. We will have to examine the possibilities.

Some scholars have suggested that Suleiman needed a victory to fully secure his place on the throne. However, this seems unlikely, since there were no viable alternatives. His father had killed all his brothers and while Suleiman now had sons of his own, they were both very young; Mustafa, his eldest son, was six or seven while the son Roxelana had given him was only a year old. They were both too young to be used as figureheads by palace factions. Suleiman's rule was secure so far as rivals from his own family were concerned.

The prestige attached to the heirs of Osman also precluded a rival Turkish clan from making a bid for the throne of the empire, a prestige enhanced by the extraordinary growth of the empire in the last 50 years. Suleiman's rule was also secure with respect to rival Turkish clans.

It is true that, in later times, the Janissaries became something of a Turkish version of Rome's Praetorian Guard, able to raise and depose sultans should they fail to give the Janissaries what they regarded as their due. But Suleiman had been careful to pay the Janissaries the customary gift upon acceding to the throne, and the victory he had already won at Belgrade had successfully sated their desire for conquest and its consequent gold. There was no possibility of the Janissaries rising against him either.

So it was not fear driving Suleiman's decision to prolong the siege. If it was not fear, then it must have been something else. The possibilities here include the quite reasonable belief that victory was close. The walls had been breached, his sappers were steadily undermining the defences and the start of the winter storms meant that no relief force would dare sail to Rhodes. With this knowledge, it would not have been difficult for Suleiman to conclude that since he had stayed this long, he needed only to stay a while longer to achieve the victory he wanted.

Furthermore, the choice of Belgrade and Rhodes as his first two military campaigns showed a clear programme to set himself as the heir, and the better, of Mehmed. He had achieved the first objective by conquering Belgrade. While failing to conquer Rhodes would not be fatal to his reign, it would represent a significant loss of face. Staying a while longer to complete the siege and break the resistance of the Knights must have seemed a chance worth the taking.

So essentially the decision to continue the siege resulted from Suleiman's pride and ambition. While Suleiman was not as personally ruthless as his father, his ambition ran deeper and further. That ambition had further basis in the numerological lore that he had been taught when growing up. For he was the tenth sultan in the line of Osman and the number ten was an auspicious number for the Ottomans. Furthermore, his father had left him the sole heir to the empire, so he inherited without the blood guilt attached to his predecessors. Selim's conquests had also left him as guardian of the Holy Cities and in a uniquely powerful position.

It was as if his father had sat him on the throne in Constantinople and laid out the world before him, saying, 'This is all yours, for the taking.'

Suleiman meant to take it.

The Knights, while proving more obdurate than he had been led to believe, were not going to thwart his ambitions so early in his reign.

As for Gabriele Tadino, the arquebus ball that struck him in the eye meant the loss of his eye. But although gravely injured – even today, taking a bullet in the eye would be no small matter – he survived the immediate injury and began to recover. This might come as a surprise, as we tend to think of medical care at this time as, at best, rudimentary and often more likely to kill than to cure. However, medieval and very early modern medical treatment was, in some areas, far better than we think and the treatment of battlefield injuries was one of those areas.

For instance, Prince Henry, who would become Henry V, was shot in the face by an arrow at the Battle of Shrewsbury in 1403. Although the shaft was removed, the arrowhead became embedded in his cheek. The surgeon, John Bradmore, used special tongs to remove the arrowhead and then washed the wound with wine and cleaned it with a honey-based ointment. The wound healed cleanly and Prince Henry survived, although it must have been a hideously painful procedure, involving widening the wound so that Bradmore could insert the tongs. Honey would have been particularly effective as it acts as an antibiotic as well as drawing fluid, and thus infectious bacteria, out of the wound.

The sources tell us that, in Tadino's case, the ball that struck him in the eye exited by his right ear, so the doctors treating him did not have to remove anything from the wound; they simply had to stop the blood and prevent infection. Long practice with battlefield wounds meant that they were very good at stopping the blood while the Knights' doctors were better than almost everyone else at the time in preventing infections.

The very name of the Knights Hospitaller gives the clue that they had a more than ordinary interest in the practice of medicine. On Rhodes, they built their hospital at the eastern end of the Street of the Knights, the main city thoroughfare where each of the national contingents of the Knights had their own inn or *auberge*.

This was where they carried Gabriele after he was shot. The hospital was built around an enclosed courtyard. Two storeys of Romanesque arches looked out upon the courtyard, with the patients cared for on the first floor. There was a large ward with space for a hundred patients as well as separate rooms for individual patients. As Tadino was the most important patient in the entire hospital, he probably had a room to himself.

Although the germ theory of disease was yet to be developed, the Knights understood the importance of cleaning wounds to prevent infection and gangrene. This was one of the reasons that they imported so much wine before the siege: they knew they would need it to clean wounds. Honey and poultices were also used to draw infection out of wounds.

In the case of Tadino, the treatment worked.

It took six weeks, but at the end of that time he had recovered sufficiently to take up his duties once again. Indeed, being Tadino, he didn't start by just inspecting the creaking defences and offering suggestions; he insisted upon leading a fresh sortie against the Turkish sappers in the moat on 1 December, receiving a fresh wound in the knee for his troubles.

34

The Chancellor's Downfall

During the six weeks of his incapacity, Gabriele missed the most dramatic of the internal troubles that afflicted the Knights during the siege: the arrest, trial and execution of Fra' Andrea d'Amaral, the Chancellor of the Religion and second-in-command to the Grand Master.

D'Amaral's downfall began on 27 October. A sentry on the tower of St George, in the section of the wall defended by the Knights of the Auvergne, was huddled up against the chill. It had rained for two days solid. In such conditions, the Turkish sappers had had to forgo their efforts, while much of the earthworks that they had built along the top of the counterscarp had been washed away or weakened. It was a thoroughly miserable prospect, when the wretchedness of the conditions united the men fighting each other. But then the sentry spotted a cloaked figure on the rampart. It was dark but with his night-adjusted eyes, he saw that the man appeared to be bent over in the characteristic position of someone winding the cranequin of a crossbow.

There were no Turks out in the moat.

The sentry rushed down and stopped the man as he was about to fire the crossbow. Wrapped around the bolt was a message, addressed to Ayas Pasha, one of Suleiman's chief officers. But the real shock was the identity of the man caught in the act of sending information to the enemy. His name was Blasco Diaz and he was the personal servant and valet to Andrea d'Amaral, the chancellor. Diaz was Portuguese, a Jew who had converted to Christianity, and he had served d'Amaral for many years.

When first questioned, Diaz refused to answer any questions. But when put to the question – which meant being stretched on the rack – he started to talk at once, telling his interrogators that he had acted only on the instructions of the chancellor and that this was not the first time he had sent information to the Turks on the chancellor's behalf.

The message that he had been about to send had urged the Turks to continue with the siege, telling them that the garrison had only enough powder and shot to withstand one more assault and that the people of Rhodes were desperate for peace and would force the Grand Master to accept if the sultan were to offer him terms.

The news of the arrest of Diaz spread quickly.

Rumours were swirling around the city. Desperate hopes and desperate fears, chasing each other in a skein of confusion. One spy, the doctor Apella Renato, had already been arrested and executed. But suppose there was treachery in the highest ranks of the Religion? That would explain why, against all hopes and expectations, the Turks had continued the siege into autumn and were showing no signs of calling it off even when winter was approaching. That was something against all experience and to explain it there must be some other reason than just Suleiman's determination.

The Grand Master ordered that the chancellor be arrested. Andrea d'Amaral was taken to the Tower of St Nicholas. And then the accusations really started flying.

In the election that saw de L'Isle Adam elected Grand Master, d'Amaral had been his chief opponent. D'Amaral had been a Knight for 40 years, during which he had gained a reputation for arrogance and discipline. What he had not acquired were friends, although he had accumulated more than his fair share of enemies.

Some of the Portuguese Knights averred that, following his loss in the election, d'Amaral had stated that de L'Isle Adam would be the last Grand Master of the order and that he would go as far as selling his soul to bring ruin to him.

Other witnesses put forward similar stories, mainly composed of hearsay.

But in the febrile atmosphere of the siege, these accusations were enough for the Grand Master to authorise that the chancellor be put to the question.

Is it possible for a man to die from stubbornness? For sheer pigheadedness to make a man prefer death to saying anything in his own defence? Because it seems that this was the case with Fra' Andrea d'Amaral.

The evidence against him was all hearsay and circumstantial. It was his servant that was caught in the act of sending information to the enemy, but Blasco Diaz, as a Jewish convert to Christianity in the Iberian peninsula, had reason to hate Christians. Systematic persecution had led to most of the Jewish population of Spain converting to Christianity, but in 1492 Ferdinand and Isabella issued the Alhambra Decree, which ordered that all practising Jews be expelled from Castile and Aragon by 31 July. Many Spanish Jews emigrated to Portugal but there they soon came under pressure too, being given a deadline of October 1497 to convert or leave.

Blasco Diaz was one of those who chose to convert, at least in public, but these decrees certainly gave him sufficient motive to betray his employer. When put to the question, Diaz told the interrogators that he had sent the messages to the Turks only under the direction of his master, the chancellor. But we have only his word for that and, under torture, men will say anything to make the pain stop.

So it is possible that Diaz implicated his master purely to spread the blame and, by doing so, to get the interrogation to stop. In this, he succeeded. With feverish suspicions growing among the Knights and the Rhodians that there were high-level traitors among them, the accusation levelled against the chancellor fed into those suspicions.

Which is where the chancellor's stubbornness comes into play.

For when he was questioned, Andrea d'Amaral refused to make any answer to the accusations. He could have claimed that Diaz was acting on his own, without d'Amaral's knowledge. He could have said that this sort of internal division was exactly what the Turks wanted. But he said nothing. D'Amaral resolutely refused to answer any of the charges against him.

The Grand Master, however, was convinced of D'Amaral's guilt. He wrote to his nephew on 13 November 1522, saying:

> ... I tell you, my Nephew, that I have not been at war only with the Turks, but with one of the most senior members of our Council who, by reason of envy and a thirst for power, had long conspired to bring the Turk here and had promised to surrender this city to him.[43]

The two men were rivals not simply for the position of Grand Master; they disagreed fundamentally about what they were doing on Rhodes. De L'Isle Adam believed that the defence of Rhodes, to the last man if necessary, would shine such a light of sacrifice upon their deeds that it would enkindle a new spirit of unity among the princes and peoples of Europe, causing them to put aside their political differences and come together in a new crusade to expel the Turks from Constantinople and, eventually, reclaim the Holy Land for Christendom.

For three centuries the crusading ideal had taken the foremost place in the European imagination. It was not such a stupid notion that it might not be relit and the dramatic side of the Grand Master saw such a sacrifice – a sacrifice that he would share in – as the means to do so.

The chancellor saw no such possibility. So far as he was concerned, the only way to keep the crusading ideal alive lay in the Religion's survival; the princes of Europe were no longer prepared to put aside their ambitions to join in a crusade. D'Amaral was also clear-sighted enough to see that even should one of the European kings want to take up the Cross, he could no longer do so, for his brother kings would take advantage of his absence to attack his kingdom.

Thus the Religion's survival was paramount and, to achieve this, he was willing to negotiate a way off Rhodes with the sultan.

Under the pressure of the siege, the rivalry between de L'Isle Adam and d'Amaral had solidified into hatred. D'Amaral refused to give his rival the satisfaction of any answer, even an answer of innocence; most likely he believed any words he spoke would be futile and he was too proud a man to ask for anything from the man he believed was leading the order to its destruction.

> 'Am I, then, now to tell a lie and to sell my honour to save my old limbs from the pain of the rack?'[44]

The order's archives hold no record of the trial, but it came to the expected conclusion. The chancellor was found guilty and executed. His body was hung on the ramparts as a warning to other traitors. But for the watching Turks, it was sign of the increasing disunity within the city.

35

'Nothing in the World was Ever so Well Lost...'

Ahmed Pasha continued with his strategy of attrition. Supplies of powder within the city were running so low that gun crews had to seek permission from a senior officer before discharging their cannon. But the defence remained fierce, so much so that the Ottomans had to build parapets across the breaches they had made in the walls to protect their own men from the fire of the Knights behind the retrenchments, leaving the Turks in the ironic position of having to remake the walls that they had themselves broken.

Fighting continued through the misery and wet of October and into November. The weather was cruel and both attackers and defenders suffered from it. The Ottomans launched occasional attacks but the Knights were able to drive these back, at some losses to themselves. But the loss of supplies and, above all, the lack of labourers meant that there was less and less they could do to stop the Ottoman sappers and miners. Trenches now allowed the Turks reasonably clear access across the moat, while the war underground continued in its desperate close confines, but with fewer men to listen for the scritch scratch of Ottoman mining operations.

Both sides were exhausted. With the days drawing down towards the end of the year, the Turks could not summon the strength and fortitude to mount the final conclusive attack. Their soldiers had seen too many of their comrades die in previous assaults. But the Knights knew that there was no help coming. There was no way out.

The truth was, both sides were caught in clefts of expectation. The Grand Master had staked his hopes and reputation upon a defence to the death. To talk now, when so many had died, would seem a betrayal of those who had lain down their lives for the Religion. But while de L'Isle Adam was prepared to fight to the death, an increasing number of the Rhodians were coming to believe that they had done enough. They had resisted the sultan for nearly half a year. They had done their part. But for the sake of their children, their wives, their aged parents, they were beginning to look for some hope of living beyond the next few weeks.

Nor could Suleiman, the emperor who brooked no rival, admit to entering into negotiations with the Knights because to do so would suggest that he was unable to take Rhodes through the strength of his arms.

Both men were looking for a way through and a way out.

But if neither man could appear to his followers to be seeking to negotiate, perhaps there were others who could do so on their behalf?

On 3 December, two days after Tadino returned to duties, a Genoese merchant named Girolamo Monile, waving a flag of truce, appeared under the walls but was ordered away. Monile returned two days later, claiming that he wanted to speak to a Genoese in the city, and that he had a letter for the Grand Master. He was ordered off again.

The following day, it was the turn of an Albanian merchant.

The rumour of these approaches began to spread among the Rhodians, who went to their bishops, the Catholic bishop Balestrieri and the Orthodox bishop Clement, to ask them to intercede on their behalf with the Grand Master. The bishops, who had been stalwart in their support of the defence of the city thus far, consulted with some of the senior Knights and then went, in a body, to the Grand Master to ask him to talk, pointing out that the Rhodians might attempt to make their own peace with Suleiman if he didn't.

De L'Isle Adam was no more minded to talk after their representation than before but, with evidence of the increasing unease in the city, he realised that he needed to make a public demonstration of unity and determination to continue the defence. So he decided to convene the Council. This was a body that consisted of all the most senior Knights. The Grand Master probably expected his chief lieutenants to go along with his recommendation that they continue defending the city to the end. But he made the mistake of asking the men present for their honest assessment of the situation they were in.

The Prior of St Giles, who was responsible for the labour and the stores, reported that he was now so short of labour that cannon could not be moved from one part of the walls to another, nor did he have the men to repair the defences that the continuing Turkish bombardment broke. So far as powder was concerned, there was store enough only to repel one more Turkish assault.

Then the Grand Master turned to the man most responsible for the defence of the city, Gabriele Tadino. No one there could doubt Tadino's courage, nor his commitment to their cause, since he had given up his position with Venice to come to the aid of the Religion and had all but died in its service a few weeks ago.

> Gabriel Martingo [Tadino]... declared to the reverend lord and them of the council that seeing and considering the great beatings of shot that the town had suffered and after seeing the entering that the enemy had so large and they were within the town by their trenches both endelonge and overthwart. Seeing also that in two other places they were at the foot of the wall and that the most part of the knights and men of war and other were slain and hurt and powders wasted & that it was impossible for them to resist their enemy any more that without doubt the town was lost if there came no succour to help and resist the siege.[45]

Another senior Knight wound up the debate by saying to the Grand Master:

> As to succour from Europe either it will not come at all, or it will be too little and, by failing at the first encounter with Suleiman, will merely worsen our condition... Where all human hope is gone, it is our duty to try to come to terms, so that we may vindicate our loss at another time and place... Wise men surrender to necessity. No matter how praiseworthy our death, let us consider whether it may not be more damaging to the Holy Religion than our surrender.[46]

At these words in the Grand Council of the Knights, one could imagine the shade of the executed chancellor, Andrea d'Amaral, laughing with hollow satisfaction. Certainly, the counsel of his Council came as a terrible shock to de L'Isle Adam, so much so that he collapsed into a dead faint.

When the Grand Master had recovered sufficiently to rejoin the Council, he woke with the realisation that he no longer had the support of his brethren or the Rhodians. That even Gabriele should counsel that they come to terms had shaken de L'Isle Adam to the core. His old determination collapsed.

The Grand Master gave permission for negotiations to begin.

Talks began on 10 December and continued, fitfully, for the next two weeks, negotiations punctuated by outbreaks of artillery fire and a couple of desultory attacks on the breaches in the walls.

Suleiman first offered the Knights their lives, allowing them to leave in peace with their personal possessions and any Rhodians who wished to go with them.

By the end of the negotiations, the sultan's terms had become more generous. He would allow the Knights to leave with honour, bearing their personal weapons and their holy relics. He would provide them with ships to facilitate their withdrawal. The citizens of Rhodes were to be saved from the usual sack following a siege. Those who chose to remain would be free to continue to practise their religion and they would be free to leave the city for the next three years should the sultan's rule prove disagreeable to them.

The settlement was agreeable to both sides and, on 24 December, the Ottoman guns stopped firing.

In accordance with the agreement, the defenders sent 50 hostages to the Turkish camp: 25 Knights and 25 Rhodians.

The sultan and the Grand Master met each other, face to face, three times. According to one of the witnesses, following one meeting Suleiman said, 'It saddens me to be compelled to cast this brave old man out of his home.'[47] Suleiman was clearly impressed with de L'Isle Adam's dignity and probity because, on 27 December, he rode into Rhodes to formally claim the city as his own. But as he entered the city, he dismissed his bodyguard, telling them that his safety was guaranteed by the word of the Grand Master, a promise he regarded as sure.

It proved so to be. Suleiman, the sultan of the Ottoman Empire, rode among the enemies who had defied him for six long months and no hand was raised against him.

In general, the Turkish troops obeyed the terms of the agreement and refrained from loot, pillage and rape, although some of the accounts report isolated instances of men failing to keep to the agreement. In those cases, the Ottoman command punished the miscreants.

By the terms of the agreement, the Religion was allowed to carry away from Rhodes all their arms save their cannon, their possessions and their sacred relics.

But while the agreement told that all the Knights should be able to leave, subtle Ottoman enquiries after the Knights' military engineer had told them that an exception might be made in the case of Gabriele Tadino. Such knowledge as the Italian possessed was priceless and the Ottomans, ever keen to employ the best in service of the sultan, might well be tempted to prevent his departure.

To stop Tadino falling into the hands of the Turks, the Knights smuggled Gabriele away from Rhodes a couple of days before their general departure, hiding him on a brigantine that sailed from the harbour sometime between Christmas and New Year.

On 1 January 1523, the rest of the Knights followed. Many of their brethren they left dead on Rhodes. But among the surviving Knights on board the *Santa Maria* was a young man from Provençe named Jean Parisot de La Valette. When, 43 years later, Suleiman would renew his attack upon the Knights in their new fortress on Malta, Jean Parisot would be the Grand Master while Suleiman himself, by then old and ailing, sent his pashas to do his bidding rather than leading his armies in person. As the pashas struggled to subdue the Knights, they must have regretted their master's mercy all those years before.

When told of the fall of Rhodes, Charles V, who had so signally failed to send any help to the Knights, said, 'Nothing in the world was ever so well lost.'

But lost Rhodes was.

As the Knights sailed west, leaving their home behind, they knew their future was uncertain. Fra' Philippe Villiers de L'Isle Adam was all too aware that, to secure the future of the Religion, he needed to find them a new home, a place where they were beholden to none.

As the *Santa Maria* sailed west, much thought was spent upon where to go and whom to petition for that new home.

The Knights did not question their mission but, to the rest of Europe, they were becoming an anachronism, an embarrassing reminder of lost ideals.

'NOTHING IN THE WORLD WAS EVER SO WELL LOST...'

At the start of 1523, the Reformation was gathering pace. Martin Luther's translation of the New Testament into German was published on 21 September 1522 and he had solid support among some of the German princes. The whole idea of Christendom, united in faith, was splintering, just as the rivalries and conflicts between the different kingdoms were becoming more lethal through the new ways of war. The kingdoms themselves were more centralised, with authority and power increasingly invested in the king, where before the nobility could act almost independently of the monarch. Politics was becoming increasingly personal, and the personalities of the princes became the key to the politics of Europe. Where before there had been at least lip service to the idea of uniting in the defence of Christendom and against the infidel, that idea was no longer seriously entertained, although it continued to be trotted out in official pronouncements, usually as an excuse for attacking another European kingdom ('Just let us claim this city that is rightfully ours and then we will go off and defeat the Turk.').

Against this backdrop, Venice continued to try to walk its path of neutrality, willing to defend its key possessions against Ottoman expansion but otherwise preferring to do business with the Sublime Porte.

The papacy proposed crusades but did not have the money to fund them and no one took the pope's exhortations seriously unless the pope was willing to back them up with money.

The Knights remained committed to their calling as defenders of Christendom, but they no longer had a base from which to conduct that defence, while they had suffered great losses in their defence of Rhodes.

Suleiman, the sultan, had held his nerve and taken Rhodes as before he had taken Belgrade. Already he had outdone his ancestor, Mehmed. As the Sublime Porte gathered news of the increasing fissures between the kingdoms of Europe, with religion now adding to the split, the continued expansion of the empire westwards must have seemed the obvious choice.

There seemed little to stop him.

36

The Emperor's New Man

Gabriele Tadino left Rhodes in a hurry. The sultan was looking for a new military engineer and he had seen, first hand, Gabriele's expertise in the new arts of war.

On 5 January 1523, Tadino arrived on the Greek island of Zakynthos. Zakynthos lies west of the Peloponnese, so the ship had sailed past Crete and across the Aegean before making port. Tadino was clearly still *persona non grata* to Venice.

Tadino paused on Zakynthos only to write a letter. He addressed it to Daniele Renier, a Venetian patrician and member of the Council of Ten, the state body specifically concerned with intelligence. The letter is vivid with the shock of defeat and barely veiled disgust at how the Knights were left without aid from the so-called princes of Christendom.

> To the Most Illustrious and Honoured Lord, My Patron,
>
> In a previous letter, I informed Your Lordship of the reasons that had led me to proceed to Rhodes. Now, with the deepest sorrow, I must report that, on the 20th of December, His Most Reverend Lordship the Grand Master, together with his Sacred Council and the people of Rhodes, resolved to surrender the city to the Grand Turk, upon terms guaranteeing the safety of their persons and possessions, relying on promises which, it is to be hoped, will be honoured.
>
> Your Lordship may be assured that Rhodes was defended as bravely and honourably as any city ever besieged. At the time of the surrender, the Turks had already held a large part of the city for over a month. It would be long and difficult to describe all that passed, or the conditions in which we found ourselves.

Yet I affirm this with certainty: had even a thousand men of reinforcements arrived at any point in September – or even throughout October – Rhodes would never have been lost.

But so be it – God's will be done.

The poor Order has been abandoned, not only by all the Christian princes, but even, I must say, by its own members [this is presumably a reference to the treachery of Fra' Antonio d'Amaral, which clearly Tadino regarded as chiefly responsible for the Turks not giving up the siege in the autumn].

Yet I shall tell Your Lordship this: the Turks are not the warriors they are commonly believed to be.

On the 20th, the articles of surrender were agreed. That same evening, at half past midnight, hostages were sent to the Turkish camp: the Prior of Saint-Gilles and the Prior of Novara, accompanied by twenty-five knights and twenty-five leading citizens of the town. The capitulation articles had already been carried into the city.

The agreement stipulated that the Turkish army would withdraw four miles from the city, and that the fleet would go to Fischia.

Seeing this, I went to His Most Reverend Lordship the Grand Master and told him that, since there was no longer any possibility of fighting or repairing the city, it would be wise for me to seek my own safety, because for various reasons I believed that the Grand Turk would actively try to lay his hands on me.

Accordingly, His Lordship gave me, at midnight, a brigantine, and ordered me to go ahead to Messina, where, God willing, I shall eventually rejoin him.

Let me not fail to remind Your Lordship that if I have erred, I did not do so knowingly. On the contrary, I acted believing I was doing something pleasing to Your Lordship and to that most gracious State.

And so I remain, with all devotion, Your Lordship's faithful servant, and I humbly commend myself to your favour.

Your devoted servant,
Fra Gabriele Tadino da Martinengo.[48]

Boarding a fresh vessel, Tadino sailed across the Adriatic, arriving in the Italian town of Gallipoli, which is set into Italy's heel looking out into the Gulf of Taranto, the large bay between the heel and toe of Italy's boot.

From there, Tadino went to Naples, although the sources are not clear as to whether he sailed or went cross country. Sailors generally avoided long journeys during the winter months in the Mediterranean because of the uncertain weather at that time of year. That Tadino had found vessels ready to take him from Rhodes to Zakynthos, and then from Zakynthos to Gallipoli, suggests that he had gold sufficient to persuade ship masters to risk the winter weather, and that he had reason to hurry.

By early spring, Tadino was in Rome.

His destination suggests the reason for his haste.

The Knights had lost their base. They knew all too well what had happened to the Templars when they were left homeless following the fall of Acre. The Hospitallers had been saved that fate through their mastery of Rhodes. To ensure the continued existence of the order, they needed a new base. The place to go was Rome. There, Tadino could present to the pope the story of the Knights' defence against the Turk. Making sure that they got to tell their own story first was an important part of the Religion's strategy during the next few years. After Tadino's verbal report to Pope Adrian VI, a number of Knights who had taken part in the siege wrote their own accounts of events, ensuring that the preferred version of the siege should be heard by the princes of Europe.

The Knights dispatched Tadino as their first representative to the pope since his reputation was now Europe-wide. Moreover, as a man who had made his reputation outside the Religion, his testimony as to their conduct would carry greater weight than sending someone like Fra' Antonio Bosio.

The surviving members of the Religion followed more slowly in Tadino's wake. The Grand Master and many other Knights arrived in Civitavecchia, the port of Rome, which they made the order's temporary headquarters. On 1 September, Pope Adrian VI received Fra' Philippe Villiers de L'Isle Adam in private audience. Gabriele Tadino was probably there too. The Grand Master gave his own account of the siege to the pope, renewed the order's warnings about the rising danger of the Ottomans, and reiterated Tadino's plea that he help the Religion find a new base from which they could counter this threat.

THE EMPEROR'S NEW MAN

What neither the Grand Master nor Tadino knew during this meeting was that Pope Adrian would be dead in two weeks.

In recent times, papal conclaves have been reasonably brisk affairs. Indeed, through the 20th century and now into the 21st no conclave has lasted longer than five days. But that was not the case in the 16th century. Conclaves typically lasted a month or more. The longest, 1,006 days, started in 1268 and took nearly three years to come to a decision.

What was worse, there was no guarantee that the new pope would be as supportive of the Religion as Adrian VI had been. Having had to accept a foreign pope, and a Dutchman no less, it was unlikely that the mostly Italian cardinals would elect anyone other than an Italian next time round (and indeed they did not: Pope Clement VII, a Medici, was as Italian as you could get). Whatever promises Pope Adrian had given to de L'Isle Adam and Tadino died with him.

The Religion needed a new strategy and a new patron.

On 8 October, Tadino left Rome in service of the new strategy and in pursuit of a new patron.

The Grand Master had made Civitavecchia the temporary base for the Religion, so he was unable to leave. However, he dispatched Tadino, together with the persuasive Fra' Antonio Bosio and the Prior of Castile, Fra' Diego di Toledo, to Spain to meet the other emperor, Charles V. As such, it made perfect sense for the Religion's delegation to include a Spaniard. Fra' Antonio Bosio was a particularly gifted diplomat. And Tadino's fame was such that the emperor would want to see him in his own right.

They made the perfect team. But as they left Rome, they knew they had a difficult task ahead of them. While the emperor had the land and the wealth to grant them a demesne, it was their job to ensure that the gift, should it come, was not tied to too many obligations. The Knights knew all too well that royal gifts came with royal requirements. But for them to pursue their vocation, they needed an essentially free hand. They could not allow themselves to be turned into one of the fingers of the royal fist, any royal fist. Their vocation was as defenders of Christendom. Should they allow themselves to become too closely identified with one of the royal houses of Europe, then their vocation would be fatally compromised.

But they were going to seek the aid of the man who seemed set upon bringing all Christendom under his control. For such a man, it would surely seem a small thing to demand that the Knights join his cause. For if Christendom was united within, then it could more surely turn and face the enemy without.

Unfortunately, not all of Christendom was agreed as to who this leader should be. But Charles, Holy Roman Emperor, King of Spain, Archduke of Austria, Lord of the Netherlands and ruler of the new lands beyond the sea, had no doubt it should be him.

Like the rest of this generation of rulers, Charles had come to the throne as a young man. He was the youngest of the four princes whose suns rose over Europe at the start of the 16th century, being born on 24 February 1500, whereas Francis and Suleiman were both born in 1494 and Henry VIII in 1491. Of these, Henry proved largely a side show, and mainly of use as a lever against Francis. Charles's rivals would be Francis and Suleiman.

Where the other three men were bluff, healthy and, when young, very masculine rulers, Charles was smaller, frailer and younger. Already there were signs of the genetic debt to be paid from the marriage plans of the Habsburgs in his prognathous chin that he sought to disguise with his beard. Still, Charles's chin bore comparison to Francis's nose: they were both exceptional, although Francis carried off his nose better than Charles his chin.

Charles was 16 when he became king of Spain. But what he really wanted was to be elected Holy Roman Emperor. This title traced its lineage to Charlemagne, who was proclaimed and crowned Holy Roman Emperor by Pope Leo III on Christmas Day 800. Previously, the papacy had looked towards the emperors in Constantinople for political protection but a variety of reasons led Leo to look for a more conveniently placed protector. Charlemagne was both close enough and far enough to be ideal: close enough in that the Franks had taken control of northern Italy but far enough in that their main areas of interest and power were north of the Alps, meaning that they would leave the popes alone to get on with their business but they were close enough to come to their aid should the popes need them.

Charlemagne was the first emperor in the west since Romulus Augustulus was deposed in 476. Rome, as an ideal and a memory, still carried immense prestige, while New Rome, Constantinople, was the richest and most populous city in Europe. By accepting the title of emperor, Charlemagne was putting himself on the same level as the emperors in Constantinople, an equation that those emperors were not at all happy to accept.

Seven hundred years later, the title of Holy Roman Emperor had evolved into something that balanced between an honorific and a title. Most of the emperors of the previous two centuries had reigned rather than ruled, with power substantially held by the various princes and prince bishops of the Empire (roughly the area of modern-day Germany). However, Maximilian I, Charles's grandfather, succeeded in gathering more power to himself so that he did become the effective ruler of the Empire. However, the prestige attached to the title was just as much a reason for wanting to be emperor as the power, always somewhat circumscribed, that came with the title.

Both Francis and Charles had reasonable claims to being Holy Roman Emperor when Maximilian died. There were seven prince-electors whose votes would decide who would be the next Holy Roman Emperor. Charles and Francis spent eye-watering sums of money bribing the electors for their votes. For their part, the prince-electors took the utmost advantage of this royal largesse, although the prize for venality went to Albert of Brandenburg, the Elector of Mainz, who changed his vote six times during the two years of the contest, switching each time when promised a larger reward for his vote.

In the end, Charles spent more than Francis and won the election. He was crowned on 23 October 1520, but that was in Germany; to really be seen as emperor, Charles wanted to be invested with the title by the pope himself, as Charlemagne had been. The negotiations for this were long and complex, and the coronation still lay long in the future when the embassy from the Knights Hospitaller caught up with the emperor in Pamplona, Spain, on 4 December 1523.

Charles did sincerely see himself as the defender of Christendom. However, his ability to undertake this role was compromised, from his perspective, by the religious division that was engulfing the Empire, driven by that obstinate monk Martin Luther, and the stubborn refusal of the king of France to recognise Charles's legitimate claims in Italy. Once he got those matters sorted out, and his base secure, then he could turn to reclaiming the lands in the east that had been lost to Suleiman. But from his perspective, Charles could not amass his full strength against the Ottomans so long as Francis was waiting to take advantage of any absence, while the scandal of disunity was spreading among the German princes. The very definition of emperor told of a monarch reigning over a people with one faith, but now that faith was being divided.

The world was breaking apart and Charles was trying to get it all to stick back together again.

As part of those efforts, he met with the delegation from the Knights. He asked them about the defence of Rhodes. He quizzed them about the Ottomans, how they managed their army, managed their logistics, and how they had eventually broken the Knights' resistance.

And he asked them, at length, about how the Knights had held out so long against such odds.

In these conversations, Tadino played the major part, as he had led the defence. In fact, the emperor had a number of private audiences with Gabriele during the early months of 1524. During those audiences, Charles's appreciation of Tadino's talents grew until, at the start of spring, he made a proposition to Gabriele: that he come to work for him as the general commander of the Spanish artillery with the exceptional salary of 2,000 ducats a year.

It was an extraordinary offer. Tadino was not a nobleman. Normally, such a position would only be offered to someone of noble birth. Following the union of the Crowns of Aragon and Castile, Spain had reformed its currency, modelling the ducado after the Venetian ducat. The ducado was 23¾ carats and weighed 3.48 grammes. In today's world, that amount of gold would be worth about £275, so Charles was offering Gabriele an annual salary of £550,000. Good money by any standards!

However, money had never been Tadino's motivation. Honour, glory and recognition were what he sought. To be appointed commander of the Spanish artillery would give him both recognition and honour; the glory could come from the employment of that artillery against the emperor's enemies.

During those meetings, Charles must have said to Tadino what he said to so many other people: that he desired above all things to lead a crusade that would drive the Turk from Constantinople and reclaim the Holy Land for the church.

The 16th century was an era that placed much store in coincidences, so when Charles was elected Holy Roman Emperor at nearly the same time as Suleiman became the Ottoman emperor (23 October and 30 September 1520 respectively), observers came to see them as fate-linked rivals whose stars would inevitably rise and fall in competition against the other. No less a witness than Erasmus argued for this, seeing their accession to the thrones of empires in the West and East as the prelude to 'the final outcome, whether Charles will be the sole ruler of the whole world, or the Turks. The world can no longer support two suns.'[49]

Charles clearly saw himself as the defender of Christendom and had said as much in his correspondence, declaring that this was 'what I have wanted to do since I was a child, and also to fulfil the responsibilities of my imperial title as chief protector and defender of our Christian religion'.[50] He also promised in his letter that 'despite the vast costs and distractions that I face at present, on account of the war against the French, I have resolved to assemble a fleet as soon as I can to relieve Rhodes'.[51] Given his signal failure to actually do that, Charles probably said to Tadino that he had had every intention to keep to this, but that circumstances, and those circumstances were chiefly the French, had stopped him doing so.

As he would say to his brother six years later, when Suleiman was besieging Vienna, 'without the prior pacification of Italy, it could happen that as soon as I leave to succour you, Venice, Florence, Ferrara and Francesco Sforza will ally together, pool all their resources, and invite the French to support them'.[52]

Charles was the great stag attempting to defend Europe but stymied always by the dogs nipping at his heels, preventing him from concentrating all his forces against the Turks for fear of what his rivals would do behind his back.

If he could bring those rivals to heel, then he could commit to the great work of defending Christendom against the Turks.

That was the prospect that Charles placed before Tadino and it was one that Gabriele found deeply appealing. For the next few years, the Knights would be concerned with finding, settling and fortifying their new base. There would be little opportunity there for deeds of glory. As for the Knights who had accompanied Gabriele, that the emperor would want to appoint one of their own to such a senior position must have seemed like a God-sent opportunity to ensure that an advocate for the Religion would be employed where he would always have the emperor's ear. As commander of the Spanish artillery, Tadino would be able to pass on to the Knights the latest advances in the new science, as well as raising the Empire's cannon to a much higher plane of readiness for the attacks that they foresaw coming from the East. What's more, Tadino could also keep them connected to the latest information about the emperor, his plans and wishes. The Knights, as much as the Venetians, knew the advantages of having good sources of intelligence.

But whatever the decision, it was not Tadino's to make. Having made a vow of obedience to the Religion, he could not be released from it without the Grand Master's permission. So, in the spring of 1524, Tadino made his way back to Italy and presented himself to Fra' Philippe Villiers de L'Isle Adam to ask if he might be released into the service of the emperor.

The Grand Master gave Gabriele permission and he returned to Spain where he was proclaimed the general commander on 3 July 1524.

Charles needed a new, and battle-hardened, general of artillery. The war with France, which had paused on the deaths of Louis XII and Maximilian I, had started up again and it was about to become a highly personal struggle between two young kings.

37

Long Nose Versus Big Jaw, or 'All is lost save life and honour'

For Francis, king of France, the election of Charles as Holy Roman Emperor left his realm dangerously encircled.* Charles was King of Spain, Lord of the Netherlands and now Holy Roman Emperor. His claims ran down into northern Italy so that, should Charles make those claims stick, then France would be entirely encircled on land, with access only to the sea. All Francis's actions were geared towards breaking the Habsburg stranglehold on France.

But for Charles, the dominions he had been given through marriage and, finally, by taking out larger loans than Francis and buying the election as emperor were proofs of God's favour upon him and his house: God wished there to be a single emperor in Christendom, and one church, each supporting the other. All that was necessary for peace to reign once more was for the other, lesser monarchs to realise the pre-eminence of the emperor, adjust to his rightful claims, and then get on with ruling their own dominions. It was all so simple, really. It always came as a surprise to Charles that the other kings, most notably Francis, were not willing to accept something he saw as so obvious.

But at the start of their reigns, the two men remained wary and respectful of each other and the resources each could command. Open warfare between France and the Empire would be deeply costly even to any eventual victor. Francis, with his customary gallantry and

---

*The quote in the chapter title is from a letter Francis wrote to his mother after his defeat and capture.

gift for language, even turned the news of Charles's bid for the title of emperor into an allusion to courtly love: 'We must follow the example that one sometimes sees with two men who are in love with the same woman. Each exerts himself using all possible means to obtain her, but they do not for that reason fall out themselves.'[53]

(Francis was rather keen on most forms of love, having seven children with his queen and numerous mistresses, to the favourite of which he gave the title *Maîtresse-en-titre* or chief mistress.)

Even when Charles won the election, Francis, at least publicly, espoused the view that Charles would be so busy pacifying his Empire that he would not be a problem:

> Because his dominions are scattered in various places far from one another, and are as disobedient and difficult as we all know, [Charles] will be forced to hold and keep them without trying to acquire anything more. And because he owns so much, his care and concern must be to have peace, whatever the cost to him, to avoid the great and unsustainable expense that he would have to maintain if he goes to war.[54]

But by February 1521, Francis had changed his mind. He authorised the lord of Sedan to attack the Netherlands; he struck a secret deal with the deposed king of Navarre to help him regain his throne; he sponsored the duke of Guelders to attack Friesland; and he signed a secret treaty with the pope, Leo X, to free the kingdom of Naples from Spanish control while the pope himself agreed to refuse to crown Charles as emperor.

The struggle would occupy the rest of their reigns and all but tear Europe apart.

The papacy maintained its usual integrity, switching sides according to which side seemed weaker with respect to the Papal States. In 1522, Charles V landed in England on a state visit to Henry VIII. During the visit, and its accompanying pageantry, the two monarchs signed a secret treaty as part of the 'Great Enterprise' they had both agreed upon: they would jointly attack France, dismember the country and divide it up between them.

Henry did attack in 1523, an enterprise that cost him dearly – nearly two million ducats – to very little gain. So when Charles suggested that he would attack Provence from his possessions in Italy in 1524, Henry was not disposed to distract the French with a fresh attack.

However, even without explicit English support, Charles decided to go ahead. Although still a young man, he lived at a time when there were no guarantees of long life and intimations of mortality were natural to his melancholic personality. Often, when Charles found his course unclear, he sought to clarify his thinking by writing. He did so with respect to the attack upon France, which both makes clear his thinking and clears a window into his melancholic personality:

> The solution seems to be war... [but] how could we wage it? I lack the means to maintain my army right now... my friends have abandoned me and left me in the lurch because they do not want to see me more powerful... There are disadvantages to all courses of action, and some are impossible; but I wanted to write down my opinion in confidence... Since time is passing, and we are all going to die, I do not want to disappear from the world without leaving something memorable behind. Time lost today cannot be made up tomorrow, and until now I have done nothing that brings me honour. If I delay any more, it will take that much longer to recover... I do not want anything to prevent me from doing something important.[55]

Right at the forefront of the emperor's mind was the cost of war. Most of the soldiers he could raise were mercenaries who needed to be paid. The size of armies had increased hugely during the Italian Wars. To take the war to France, the other great power in Europe, he would need to raise, and keep in the field, armies that were tens of thousands strong.

Wars had an unpleasant habit of taking much longer than expected and costing much more than had been budgeted. Although Clausewitz had not yet written on war, the kings of the 16th century knew from experience that no plan survives contact with the enemy.[56]

But Charles was now determined to act. To carry out his plans, he called upon his new captain general of artillery as part of the push from Italy into France. The Imperial forces had succeeded in pushing the French out of Milan and indeed almost all of northern Italy by April 1524. To pursue them into France would be an expensive undertaking. Charles hoped that the army would be able to fund itself as it advanced, essentially by sacking and looting, and the Imperial forces did have some initial success, taking Aix-en-Provence. But the invasion stalled outside the walls of Marseille. Even with Tadino directing the artillery, the lessons of the last two decades had been learned by the defenders.

For his part, Francis was not going to let this chance pass him by either. With the Imperial army stalled outside Marseille, and no diversionary attack forthcoming from England, Francis assembled the army of France and marched to Avignon, 50 miles north of Marseille. When the Imperial forces received news of the approach of the French army, they realised that they were in danger of being trapped between two forces and lifted the siege on 29 September, retreating back towards Italy.

However, with the enemy on the retreat, and an army at his disposal, Francis had no intention of stopping at the border with Italy. He marched on and, by mid-October, he was outside Milan. The Imperial forces surrendered the city to the French – by this stage, just about everyone had given up counting how many times Milan had changed hands during the Italian Wars – with some seeking to rejoin the main Imperial forces in Italy and the rest, with Tadino among them, marching to Pavia, 20 miles south of Milan.

Francis decided, rather than chase the Imperial forces who had led him a merry dance all the way from Marseille, to advance on Pavia, where it seemed that half an army was ready to meet him in battle. The imbalance was marked. The Imperial commander in Pavia, Antonio de Leyva, had 300 men-at-arms and 5,000 infantry. The French army had 30,000 infantry, over 3,000 cavalry and the French field artillery. Francis was confident that, despite the lateness in the season, he could smash through the defences and take Pavia before making his winter quarters in Milan.

Learning of the advent of the French army, Antonio de Leyva immediately put Gabriele Tadino to work overseeing the digging of new trenches and the construction of gun emplacements and bunkers.

Arriving on the outskirts of Pavia, Francis set up three camps to isolate the city from reinforcements. Pavia sits on the north bank of the River Ticino, one of the main tributaries of the Po, which it joins five miles downstream. As such, the river provided a secure defence to the city's southern flank, so the main defences were the walls that ran from the river around the city.

Attempting to follow in the artillery steps of Charles VIII, Francis ordered his formidable field artillery to open fire on the city walls and the cannon soon opened a breach. But Tadino, with his recent experience of defending a city from such attacks, had the defenders ferry buckets of earth to fill the breach, the mounded soil acting as shock absorbers against the cannon fire.

However, with a breach made, the French were not going to wait. The assault, led by *francs-archers*, Italian *venturieri* and the men-at-arms, had German *Landsknechte* and Swiss infantry to follow up. But the attack foundered against the fire from the defenders, who used the hastily erected retrenchments that Tadino had engineered to hold the attackers in the breach and cut them down there. Gabriele's experience in Rhodes was bearing fruit.

With the first assault repulsed, the French resumed their artillery bombardment, looking to make new breaches as well as to widen the existing ones. The citizens of Pavia, mindful of the reputation of the French troops when they took a city by storm, were not surprisingly anxious about the situation they were in, while the Imperial soldiers were muttering about not having been paid. To stiffen their resolve, Antonio de Leyva melted down his personal gold and minted coins to pay his men, marked with the initials A and L. Such determination encouraged the citizens, who were further encouraged when paid to help with building and repairing the defences.

Two further assaults failed with heavy losses. With winter about to start, Francis realised that if he could not take the city soon he would either have to withdraw or settle down for a winter siege – no one's idea of fun.

The city walls had proved formidable but then one of the king's lieutenants came to him with a cunning plan. While the walls protected the east, north and west of Pavia, its southern flank was largely open, depending upon the river for defence. This Francis could see himself, but he didn't have a fleet of rivercraft to attempt a water landing, so what was his point?

Then the lieutenant pointed out that, a mile upstream of Pavia, the river split into two channels. The main one ran past Pavia but the lesser channel, called the Gravellone, ran to the north of the city before rejoining the main channel south of the city. The officer proposed that they should divert the river so that all its water flowed into the Gravellone, drying out the Ticino and exposing the city to direct attack from the south.

It was an ingenious idea and Francis adopted it enthusiastically, moving his sappers from the city and employing them as dam engineers. Learning of the French plans, Tadino shifted his attention to the riverbank and began digging trenches and building gun emplacements and earthworks to cover the city's exposed southern flank.

The French moved their artillery across the river and began shelling Tadino and the people working desperately to build defences along the riverside, while both sides watched the water level in the river start to fall.

The French sappers did a good job of diverting the river but just as it was beginning to dry out, and an assault became an imminent prospect, the defenders received meteorological aid: heavy rain that raised the level of the River Ticino upstream of the temporary dam so much that it overflowed the dam and breached it, running back down its normal course.

With both assault and drainage schemes having failed, Francis settled down to siege. He had the city cut off so that it could not receive supplies, whereas he had access to the resources of the area and Milan itself. So, as winter sieges go, it was not too difficult for the besiegers.

While sitting outside Pavia, Francis was turning his mind to his other aim in Italy. He had taken Milan and Pavia would surely be his in a few weeks. But he also had in mind the longstanding French claim to the Kingdom of Naples that had kicked off the Italian Wars 30 years earlier. With the Imperial forces divided and distracted, and a new if unwilling ally in Pope Clement VII, Francis dispatched one of his unlikelier officers, John Stewart, Duke of Albany and heir to the throne of Scotland, south with 5,000 infantry and 1,000 cavalry. After all, that still left him with 25,000 infantry alongside his cavalry and artillery. Besides, the Imperial soldiers in Pavia weren't going anywhere and nor were they getting any supplies. It was just a matter of time.

But it was not just Francis who knew that. So did Charles's officers in Italy. They were fast running out of funds to pay the army that they had recruited. Charles's standing orders to his generals were to avoid pitched battles and to attempt to achieve his ends by negotiation rather than risking everything on the risky dice of confrontation. But, as things stood, northern Italy would be lost to the Empire in a couple of months because the Imperial army would start fading away. First individual soldiers, then detachments, then some of the senior commanders would leave camp and either return home or, worse, contact the French to see if they had the money to pay for their services.

So rather than allow the French victory through sheer inaction, the Imperial commanders, led by Charles de Lannoy and the Marchise of Pescara, marched south towards Pavia. For three weeks, the two armies skirmished with each other without coming into full contact. The garrison was still cut off from the relieving Imperial army as the French had made their camp in the Visconti Park, the huge private hunting grounds of the Visconti and Sforza families, the lords of Milan, which stretched north of the city. During the siege, the French had fortified their camps, digging ditches, trenches and gun emplacements, and essentially turning the camp into an earthwork bastion. To attack the French in the camp would have been suicide, so the Imperial commanders, having decided to risk battle, knew that they had to lure the French out of camp and commit them to battle in open ground. To increase their chances of success, they also needed help from the garrison inside Pavia; a sally from the city into the French from the rear could turn the tide of the battle.

The history of the battle itself is complex, and made more complex by the Imperial commanders having initially set out with one plan only to find themselves doing something else entirely. But it was the boldness of the Marchise of Pescara's initial attack that opened up everything else. On the night of 23 February, Pescara led his men north and then broke through a breach they made in the wall of the Visconti Park. To conceal the noise of engineers hacking away at the wall with pickaxes, Imperial troops created a sonic diversion, bashing away at drums and playing trumpets nearer to the main French camp. The engineers managed to breach the wall and the Imperial troops started marching into the north of the great park. Because it was night, Lannoy and Pescara had ordered their men to wear white shirts over their usual multi-coloured tunics, so that they could be seen and recognised in the dark. Anyone who did not wear a shirt as part of their normal dress, such as the German mercenaries, pinned sheets of white paper on their chests.

The first column of Imperial troops made for a hunting tower, the Mirabello castle, which the French were using for their administrative staff, as a hospital, and a market for the sutlers who supplied the army. Not expecting an Imperial attack, the castle quickly fell to the Imperial forces.

Meanwhile, under the cover of the night-time February fog that rose from the river and rolled over the surrounding flood plain, the rest of the Imperial army crossed through the breach in the wall of the Visconti park.

As the eastern sky began to lighten, the night fog began to lift and the French suddenly realised that they had a battle on their hands.

But for Francis, this was not a moment for apprehension but rather for jubilation. He was to be given the opportunity to defeat his enemy on the field of battle.

For a man raised on chivalric literature, this was too good an opportunity to pass up and as the news spread of the Imperial onset, Francis put on his armour, mounted his horse and prepared to meet his destiny.

It turned out his destiny wasn't quite as he had imagined.

With the fog still obscuring the battlefield, it took the French some time to organise their forces but then, when the fog had lifted sufficiently for the French commanders to get a proper view of the disposition of the enemy, they saw a sight to gladden the heart of any cavalry commander: the Imperial cavalry, bunched together and out in the open.

Francis couched his lance and gave the order to charge. A thousand French heavy cavalry, armoured and magnificent, galloped across the fog-wet ground towards the Imperial forces, the king himself at the forefront of the charge. Francis was wearing a white surcoat and rich, colourful plumes flew from his helmet.

For a thousand years, the Frankish cavalry had reigned supreme on the battlefields of Europe. The paladins of Charlemagne had ridden towards the enemy just as the companions of Francis surrounded the king as he thundered forward on his specially trained horse.

The French knights crashed into the Imperial horse with the impact of an avalanche, shattering them. Francis himself slew the marquis of Sant'Angelo and the standard bearer of the count of Salm.

But in their charge, the French knights galloped right across the front line of their own artillery and arquebusiers. So that they didn't inadvertently kill their own king, the French artillery had to stop firing.

The Imperial arquebusiers had no such inhibitions. As the charge devolved into a general melee, they poured fire into the flanks of the roiling mass of men and horses, deliberately aiming for the animals to bring down the knights they were carrying. Then the Imperial infantry began to advance, cutting down the knights wherever they found them unhorsed.

Meanwhile, the garrison in Pavia, hearing the sounds of battle, realised that this was the pinch: either they prevailed or they were beaten. Antonio de Leyva and Gabriele Tadino led the garrison out from the city, attacking the mercenaries who had been left as a rearguard, before falling onto the rear of the French army. Their advent decisively separated Francis and his remaining knights from the rest of his army.

Assailed from in front and behind, the French army began to disintegrate. The Imperial forces poured arquebus and artillery fire at the French, concentrating particularly on the knights surrounding, and attempting to protect, King Francis.

Under the constant barrage, most of Francis's bodyguard were killed, including among their number some of the greatest men in France. Francis attempted to fight his way clear but his horse, wounded and dying, collapsed beneath him.

The Imperial infantry closed around the beleaguered king.

According to some accounts, the battle-roused soldiers were about to kill Francis when he yelled at them that he was the king. As the news of the capture of the king spread, Imperial commanders began to converge on the site, each eager for the honour of taking the surrender of the king of France.

In the end, credit was shared among a number of them, including Charles de Lannoy, the count of Salm and the *condottiero*, Cesare Hercolani.

But the credit lay with the whole Imperial army, which had decisively and comprehensively defeated the French.

As the gunpowder smoke slowly cleared, the Imperial forces looked out upon a scene they could not have imagined in their wildest dreams.

The French army had been almost completely destroyed. They had taken the French king prisoner. Almost all the French nobility present at the battle were either dead or prisoners too.

As the survivors looked out upon their bloodwork, and the battle-field scavengers began to strip the dead, it must have seemed a victory beyond hope.

The Battle of Pavia took place on 24 February 1525. Fourteen days later, a courier arrived in Madrid and was brought before the emperor.

> 'Sire, battle was joined before Pavia; the king of France is a prisoner in Your Majesty's power, and his entire army is destroyed.' Hearing just these words, [Charles] stood as if frozen, and repeated: 'The king of France is a prisoner in my power, and we won the battle?' Then, without saying anything more, and without trying to ascertain anything else for the time being, he retired into another room alone and fell to his knees before an image of Our Lady that he kept at the head of his bed.[57]

Charles had been granted a victory by heaven beyond his imagining. The question now arose, what was he going to do with his victory? Charles was not blind to the coincidence that the battle had taken place on his birthday; that his forces had won such a victory on that day naturally presented itself to his mind as proof of heaven's favour to him and his cause. In an official communique issued later, Charles's secretary made this connection explicit, stating that Charles had defeated Francis

> ... so that after the end of these civil wars (for that is what they should be called, since they are among Christians), he could seek out the Turks and Muslims in their own lands and, exalting our Holy Catholic faith as his ancestors had done, win the empire of Constantinople and the Holy City of Jerusalem, which are occupied because of our sins, so that (as many have prophesied) under this most Christian prince everyone may accept our Holy Catholic faith, and the words of our Redeemer may come true: let there be one flock and one shepherd.[58]

Such were the dizzying prospects that appeared now before Charles: the final end to the sniping against his claims as emperor, the unification of all Christians under his leadership, and then a renewed crusade, again under his leadership, to reconquer Constantinople and regain the Holy Land.

Unfortunately, not everyone was quite of the same mind that Charles should lead Christendom. Everyone did agree that Christendom should be united with one faith, but Martin Luther's split with the Catholic Church meant that not everyone agreed as to what that Christianity was that all should be united in.

Charles held Francis prisoner for over two years, finally releasing the French king on 17 March 1526 after he had signed the Treaty of Madrid, in which Francis formally gave up all claim to Milan and Naples. However, as soon as he was safely back in France, Francis repudiated the treaty as one signed under duress and therefore not legally binding.

So far as Francis was concerned, there was no world in which he would acknowledge Charles as superior to him and leader of Christendom. Indeed, the struggle for northern Italy would go on. But in the East, events were moving too, as the army of the sultan marched forth from Constantinople once again.

38

A Famous Victory and a Forgotten Siege

The king of France was a prisoner. The French army was defeated and much of it destroyed.

An opportunity for an Italian military engineer to take a holiday, perhaps? In the spring of 1525, Gabriele Tadino was between 45 and 47. He had been fighting, almost continually, since 1508. He had been shot in the eye, stabbed in the knee and suffered other injuries and illnesses sufficient to kill a less vital man many times over. If any man was due a rest, he was.

But no rest was forthcoming.

In April, there came the promulgation of the *Segunda ordenanza de las Guardas*, a document which laid out the standard features for the manufacture of Spanish artillery. As general commander of the Spanish artillery, Tadino must have been involved in establishing its parameters, although we don't know how much of the document he actually wrote.

Then, with the future standards for Spanish cannon established, Tadino took ship and sailed across the Mediterranean to Melilla. Melilla is a city on the north coast of Africa, in today's Morocco, that was then and still is a Spanish possession. (Ceuta, further to the west, is another Spanish possession on the coast of Morocco.)

Over the next year, Tadino took on the role of travelling defence consultant. In Melilla, he advised and oversaw the upgrade of the city's defences in light of the experience he had gained during the Italian Wars and in the defence of Rhodes. That his advice was successful is witnessed by the fact that Melilla has remained a Spanish possession to the present day.

Tadino's itinerary over the next few months is also a useful corrective to the idea that people at this time did not travel: the

Italian's route resembles a hyperactive interrailer with too much time on his hands.

From Melilla, he sailed back across the Mediterranean, landing in Perpignan, which then was part of Spain, where he inspected and improved the city's defences. He then crossed from the Mediterranean to the Atlantic coast to cast his eye over the defences of Fuenterrabia (also called Hondarribia) in the Basque country, and the nearby city of Donostia-San Sebastian.

During these fortification-finding trips, Tadino took a team of military engineers with him, including the Italians Antonio Bagherotto, Antonio Bosis and Benedetto da Ravenna. He was training a cadre of engineers in his methods so that they could go on and apply his knowledge in the reaches of the Empire that he could not reach.

While Tadino was working for the emperor, the Religion had not forgotten their brother. During this year, they contacted Tadino to tell him that a priory had fallen vacant and it was now his. That priory was Barletta, on the west coast of Italy, just below the spur of the Gargano. Having left his team of engineers behind to work on the defences of the key cities on the border between Spain and France, Tadino travelled to Italy to take possession of his priory.

The Hospitaller priories around Europe fulfilled a number of roles. They were bases away from the front line to where old brothers could retire. They were sources of funding because most priories came with associated land and properties that paid their revenue to the Religion. They were recruiting centres where young men who wanted to enter the order could come to test their vocation and be tested in turn.

As prior of Barletta, a title that Tadino would proudly claim for the rest of his life, Gabriele was entitled to the income of the priory as well as being titular master of the brothers living there.

Of course, Gabriele could not remain long in Barletta, but he must have ensured that the man he left in charge there was trustworthy.

From Barletta, Tadino crossed Italy to Naples and surveyed the defences and artillery of the kingdom.

All this travelling took up the spring and summer of 1526.

But further to the east, armies were marching.

The defeat at Pavia and the capture of their king had come, not surprisingly, as a dreadful shock to the French. For centuries they had been the pre-eminent power in Europe. Now they were encircled by the Empire and Francis was a prisoner of Charles. It did not take a strategic genius to see that they needed allies. But England was the old enemy, and Henry VIII still itched to claim back the possessions in France the English had lost. He was far more likely to take advantage of French discomfiture to try to take back Calais than enter into an alliance with France. Germany was part of the Empire, the papacy could not be trusted beyond its own political self-interest and the other Italian city states were much reduced in power following 30 years of war. The Christian kingdoms further east were either too far away or too weak to be serious threats to the Empire.

But there was another state to the east that certainly was powerful enough to be a threat to Charles's empire – and it was led by a man who had never acknowledged that Charles was an emperor for he reserved that title to himself.

An initial French embassy to Constantinople was sent soon after the Battle of Pavia but it did not arrive at the Sublime Porte. A second embassy was dispatched at the end of 1525 and it received a gracious, and most interested, reply from Suleiman.

It was the foundation for what would become the first formal treaty between a Christian kingdom and a Muslim empire, an alliance that would last until Napoleon invaded Egypt 262 years later.

Although the treaty was formally signed in 1536, the early contacts between the two powers encouraged Suleiman in his next turn towards the West. He had already taken Belgrade. Now he wanted the rest of Hungary.

On Monday 23 April 1526, Suleiman rode from Constantinople with his lifelong friend and new vizier, Ibrahim, by his side. Ibrahim was another slave child, most likely captured in a raid by the governor of Bosnia. Around 1514 he became part of Suleiman's household and the two became fast friends. As a signal mark of his favour and trust, Suleiman made Ibrahim his Grand Vizier in 1523. Ibrahim was probably born in 1495, making him and Suleiman very close in age; he was the first Grand Vizier that Suleiman had appointed himself, his predecessor being a holdover from the reign of Suleiman's father, Selim.

During the long advance up the Danube, Ibrahim acquitted himself extremely well, ensuring the steady progress of the army despite difficult weather conditions and spoiling attacks by the retreating

Hungarians. The first determined defence came from the fortress of Petrovaradin on the Danube. The sultan's diary laconically recorded the outcome: '[T]wo mines open a breach in the walls of the citadel; it is taken by assault; only twenty-five [of our] men killed. The Grand Vizir has 500 soldiers of the garrison decapitated; 300 others are sent off to slavery.'[59]

With their way now open, the Ottoman army marched on, their aim Budapest.

But the Hungarians had assembled their own army and decided to meet the Ottomans on the open fields of a place that would gain a name notorious in Hungarian history: Mohács.

The Hungarian army was riven by jealousy and dissension. King Louis II was young and no one trusted him to lead. In the event, the command was split between different nobles. Considerable reinforcements were on their way, but the Hungarian nobility persuaded Louis not to wait for their arrival but to face the Ottomans in open battle. After all, they had defeated the Ottomans before. They would surely do so again.

On 29 August, the armies met. A furious Hungarian cavalry charge drove into the Ottoman centre, nearly reaching the sultan himself. But the Ottomans had, in part, feigned this retreat so that they could open the flanks of the Hungarian army to their own counter-attack (although the ferocity of the initial attack took the Hungarians closer to Suleiman than the Ottomans would have wished: he was struck on the chest by an arquebus ball, but his cuirass deflected the shot).

The Ottoman flanks, employing volley fire from their arquebuses, mowed down the Hungarians and, after a couple of hours of furious fighting, the Hungarian army broke.

Young King Louis was unhorsed while trying to escape and drowned in one of the bogs that made the ground treacherous, his body only being found two weeks later.

In his diary, Suleiman noted: 'The Emperor, seated on a golden throne, receives the homage of the vizirs and the beys: massacre of 2000 prisoners: the rain falls in torrents.'[60]

It was the effective end of Hungary as an independent kingdom.

But nature abhors a vacuum and rulers can't abide seeing a country go without a government. Both Suleiman and Charles attempted to fill the gap left by the death of King Louis without an heir.

Suleiman installed a pasha in Buda, who ruled central Hungary. The fractious and entitled Hungarian nobility, whose squabbles and pride had landed Hungary in its mess, continued their fine record of putting their own interests first and proceeded to elect two different kings for the rest of Hungary: John Zápolya and Ferdinand, the younger brother of Charles. The country split into three: the Ottoman central regions; the northwest area, which became known as Royal Hungary, under the rule of the Habsburgs; and the Principality of Transylvania, which was nominally independent but acknowledged the sultan as overlord.

The Ottomans had turned the Black Sea into their lake, while the whole of south-eastern Europe was under their control. From Constantinople to Buda is 665 miles. The Ottomans effectively controlled everything within that arc. From Buda to Vienna was only another 130 miles. So relentless was the Ottoman advance, and so disunited and chaotic the Christian response, that it seemed only a matter of time before Vienna fell, opening the gate to central Europe.

Indeed, a perfect example of that disunited front was sent to Gabriele Tadino on 31 August 1526, just two days after the Battle of Mohács.

> Charles the Fifth
> By the favour of the divine Clemency Roman Emperor ever
> Augustus: To the Reverend, devoted, and beloved Gabriele
> Tadino etc.
>
> The Illustrious Doge of Genoa having informed us that he has a
> great need of your work for the defence and preservation of this
> our Imperial City; we wish to notify him that on such an occasion
> it is also to our advantage to follow his solicitations. We therefore
> exhort you that whenever you are requested and advised by
> the Doge himself, leave aside all other things in which you are
> occupied, present yourself to him, and that you attend to the
> defence of the aforementioned City with all care, faith, and action,
> and that you carry out all other things that you judge necessary
> for our interest, and appropriate for the same City of Genoa, and
> in carrying out our present commands you will do a most pleasing
> thing, and you will carry out our express will.

Given in our City of Granada on the last day of August in the year of our Lord one thousand five hundred and twenty-six, the eighth year of our empire.

Signed.

C. N.
M. Caes. & Cath. M.
Alphunsus Valdesius : &c.[61]

Charles wrote to Gabriele, telling him that he was urgently needed to take command of the defences of Genoa, upon which a French attack was imminently expected (admittedly, the news of the Battle of Mohács wouldn't have reached Charles when he wrote the letter but he certainly had time to reconsider and send a follow-up letter, although he never did). France and Francis were still the greater enemies than Suleiman, who had swept all before him.

Indeed, this was true for all the European kingdoms, who continued to be obsessed with the balance of power between them. On 22 May 1526, France, the pope, Venice, Florence and the Sforza family of Milan had signed up as members of the League of Cognac with the express aim of driving the Imperial forces from Italy and returning Milan, that most fought over of cities, to the control of the Sforza once again. The Italian Wars were about to kick into gear once again, this particular phase being known as the Wars of the League of Cognac.

On receiving Charles's letter, Tadino hired a felucca, a single-masted sailing boat known for its speed, from Naples and sailed directly to Genoa, arriving there before 15 September 1526. Given that Charles's letter was dispatched from Granada on 31 August, in less than two weeks the Imperial commission had been delivered and Tadino himself had arrived at his destination.

Genoa had been the proudly independent rival of Venice through the 13th and 14th centuries. In the 15th century, the Republic had often thrown in its lot with the Sforza family of Milan, but the first decades of the 16th century had been disastrous for the Republic, with France controlling the city for most of that time.

However, the Spanish had taken the city when the French were expelled from northern Italy in 1522. Now, the French wanted to take it back and the emperor expected Gabriele to stop them.

Amid the many sieges and battles of the Italian Wars, the siege of Genoa, which took place from the autumn of 1526 to August 1527, is almost entirely overlooked. In the standard textbooks about the wars, it barely rates a sentence and often it's completely ignored.

But for Gabriele, it was the most personally devastating of all the battles and sieges that he took part in.

Arriving in Genoa, Tadino went into action with his customary urgency, as confirmed by a letter dated 17 September sent by a French observer from their base at Portofino, along the coast from Genoa.

> Martinengo, who was in Rhodes, entered Genova and began to fortify it, and built bastions and fortifications with all speed. They repaired two bastions and cast a cannon which they had previously broken while attacking us; to do this they melted down many bells from the city.[62]

To prevent reinforcements and supplies getting to Genoa, the French occupied Portofino to the east and Savona to the west, while the famous admiral Andrea Doria patrolled the sea with his galleys, as well as a naval force lent by the pope and Venice. Doria exemplified the tortured loyalties of the time. A Genoese, he fought both with and against the French and the Empire, switching allegiances according to which side offered him better terms and a better deal for his native city.

Never one to meekly accept a siege, in October Tadino led a force of infantry from Genoa to attack the French forces at Portofino, but the attack failed and the Genoese had to retire back to the city. Tadino had intended the attack to both relieve the siege and to alleviate the dreadful supply situation in the city; Doria's naval blockade was, quite literally, beginning to starve the defenders.

The defenders, though, knew that the Imperial forces had put together a naval force to bring supplies through to Genoa. In November, a strong Spanish army set out from Cartagena: 20 escort galleys and 22 cargo ships carrying supplies, horses and 4,000 infantry. But a storm forced the fleet to take refuge in Corsica. On 19 November the fleet tried again to reach Genoa but on its way there, it was spotted by patrols from Doria's fleet. The Genoese admiral assembled his ships and sailed out to meet the relief convoy. The naval battle that took place resulted in the complete defeat of the Spanish fleet; those ships that weren't taken or sunk fled back to Naples.

Tadino's situation was not helped when disease broke out in the city. Couple that with the increasingly meagre rations that could be spared from the stores, and the prospect grew bleaker by the week.

The siege dragged on through the winter and into the spring. The Imperial forces could not relieve the city, but the French and their allies in the League of Cognac were content to wait rather than to attempt to storm it; let hunger and disease claim the defenders.

It was against this increasingly desperate backdrop that, in April, Gabriele decided to try to get a message out of the city to Milan. He found a messenger willing to try his luck in getting through the enemy lines. The messenger succeeded – it was, and still is, difficult to draw a siege so tight that no one can escape it – and a few days later, the messenger arrived in Milan with Tadino's plea that the Imperial commanders there send him some men and supplies so that he might resist longer.

But it was not just the Imperial commanders in Milan who got to hear this message: the efficient Venetian information service got to see it too, and transmitted Tadino's plea back to the Signoria.

Here there enters one of those ironies of history that would seem ridiculous if they were not true. For the man who took the report of this desperate plea back to Venice was Girolamo Tadino, Gabriele's older brother. Like his brother, Girolamo had entered the service of the Republic as a soldier and risen in its esteem but, unlike Gabriele, he had remained the Republic's faithful servant – until he saw the anguished plea for help from his younger brother.

Girolamo brought the news of the desperate straits the Imperial defence of Genoa had been reduced to back to the Republic, but then he decided that the ties of blood were tighter than those of his commission. Girolamo contacted another Tadino, cousin Fabrizio, and together they made their way back across Italy and, slipping through the lines, came to their brother's aid.

The sources are dry about their reunion, but it must have given the besieged Gabriele fresh heart that his brother and his cousin, together with the contingents of men they commanded, had given up their commissions with Venice to come to his help in his desperate situation.

But while these erstwhile soldiers of the Republic arrived to stiffen the garrison, there was no further help from the Imperial forces.

The siege dragged on until August. Then, the League of Cognac decided to bring it to an end.

A fresh army landed.

But then Tadino did something quite mad but completely characteristic. Rather than wait for the inevitable end, he decided to attack. With the men remaining to him, some 2,500 infantry and two cannon according to the accounts, he marched out of the city and engaged with the enemy, hoping to take them by surprise and cast them back into the sea before they could establish themselves properly in their bridgehead.

The battle wavered, the enemy fell back, but then a counter-attack smashed the resolve of Tadino's exhausted, starveling men. In the desperate fight, Gabriele saw his brother Girolamo and his cousin Fabrizio both killed.

With his army breaking, Tadino attempted to escape, finding a moored fishing boat and rowing out to sea, but the League troops, seeing the captain who had defied them for so long trying to get away, pursued him.

Exhausted and bereft from the deaths of Girolamo and Fabrizio, who had come to his aid only to die in his defence, Gabriele was taken prisoner.

He would remain a prisoner, held in the castle at Cremona, until May of 1527. Then, in an irony that would not have been lost on him, Gabriele, still a prisoner, was transferred to Brescia. His captors were demanding a ransom of 4,000 ducats for his release.

Jails were not healthy environments and Tadino had been ill-used the previous year. In July, he fell seriously ill, but when his captors tried to transfer him to a more salubrious location, Venice objected. La Serenissima had not forgotten, nor forgiven, Tadino's previous betrayal.

Tadino remained a prisoner from August 1527 to the end of October 1528. He was held in prison for 14 months.

39

Two Emperors is One Too Many

During his years as a military engineer, Gabriele Tadino had had an uncanny ability to be present at the most significant engagements of his time. He fought at the battles of Agnadello, Ravenna and Pavia, and he was there during the sieges of Padua and Brescia, as well as playing a crucial role in ensuring that the Knights escaped from Rhodes.

But the capture of Gabriele by the forces of the League of Cognac following the fall of Genoa meant that he was absent for possibly the single most infamous incident during the whole of the Italian Wars: the sack of Rome on 6 May 1527.

With Pope Clement VII a major player in the League of Cognac that had come together to force the Empire out of northern Italy, the emperor himself turned his attention to putting pressure on the pontiff to leave the League.

To that end, he put together a considerable force of German *Landsknechte* and Spanish infantry which were in northern Italy by the end of 1526. The Imperial army achieved some success against the League forces, but what it didn't receive was its pay.

This was where the split in Christendom brought about by the Reformation produced its first blood fruits. Many of the German *Landsknechte* were now followers of Martin Luther. Luther's tirade against the papacy had become steadily more strident. Following the publication of the papal bull *Exsurge Domine*, which had called upon Luther to recant his 95 theses, Luther had identified the pope with the Antichrist in 1520. His invective – and Luther had a gift for invective – did not tone down thereafter but grew more strident.

So when 10,000 German *Landsknechte*, in the pay of the Catholic Charles V but growing increasingly annoyed by his failure to actually pay them what he had promised, looked around them in Italy, an increasingly tempting target began to present itself: Rome.

The pope was the emperor's enemy, but he was also Luther's Antichrist. Rome itself was synonymous with wealth and excess. Rumours ran among the unpaid mercenaries, telling of roads paved with gold and palaces stuffed with treasure.

The putative commander of the Imperial army, Charles de Bourbon, found himself increasingly unable to control his restive troops. Charles himself was French. He was a prince of the blood and would have been a loyal servant to Francis if Francis had not attempted to strip him of the inheritance he felt was his due from his wife's estate following her early death. Their dispute grew so bitter that Charles had gone over to the side of Charles V in an attempt to regain what he saw as rightfully his – and possibly become king of France himself, should Francis be removed.

As a French royal prince, he was not an obvious fit when it came to negotiating with the prickly commanders of the German *Landsknechte*, always keen on receiving what they regarded as their negotiated due. With no money arriving from the Empire, they turned their sights upon Rome and began marching south.

De Bourbon wrote to the pope, advising him that he was unable to stop his army marching on the city, claiming that he was more the prisoner of his troops than their commander. Whether this was true or not is moot; it was a convenient fiction for de Bourbon and his men.

The Imperial army arrived at Rome on 5 May 1527.

At dawn on 6 May, the army attacked. The dawn mist gave the Imperial troops cover against the artillerymen stationed on the Castel Sant'Angelo and they were over the walls with only one significant loss: Charles de Bourbon himself.

De Bourbon had led the assault and, doing so, was shot and killed.

With his death, any restraints were removed. The sack was brutal, bloody and thorough. Clement himself managed to escape to Castel Sant'Angelo through the self-sacrifice of his Swiss Guard, but the city itself lay open to vengeful soldiers who had not been paid for six months and many of whom regarded the city they were entering as the Biblical Babylon.

Between 6,000 and 12,000 people were murdered. Unknown thousands of women were raped, with nuns being particular targets. Rome's population, over 55,000 before its sack, fell to 10,000 afterwards.

Culturally, the sack of Rome was a disaster too, bringing an abrupt end to the Italian Renaissance and sending the scholars who survived fleeing from the city.

Perhaps if Tadino had been part of that Imperial army he might have been able to prevent its disintegration into a looting rabble, but it's doubtful that even a man with his prestige would have been able to stop events without a wagon of gold ducats to pay the disaffected troops.

For his part, the emperor proclaimed himself innocent of but embarrassed by the actions of his troops. Charles did help towards restoring Rome when, eventually, the looting ceased, but he was not dissatisfied with the result of the sack: Pope Clement gave up any attempt to thwart Charles's will, becoming essentially a rubber stamp for the emperor's actions.

As such, the army had done what Charles wanted, although no doubt he would have preferred to achieve his ends without the actual sack of the city. In fact, such was the surrender of the pope to Charles's demands that he agreed to allow the investiture of Charles as Holy Roman Emperor in Rome at a date of his convenience.[63]

As for Gabriele, he must have heard the news about the sack of Rome while he was being held prisoner. Although he had no particular love for the papacy, having fought against the popes many times during the Italian Wars, no Italian could hear such news without being affected.

When Tadino was eventually freed in November 1528, he appears to have gone to Naples to resume his work there on the Imperial defences.

By this point, Gabriele was 50 years old. He had been shot, stabbed, slashed and generally injured many times, while the illness he had suffered during his recent captivity had almost killed him.

From our perspective, one can only marvel at the toughness of the men of this era, and their ability to survive and recover from injuries, without modern medical treatment, that would certainly kill us today. In particular, the fortitude required to withstand acute pain without much in the way of pain relief is remarkable.

But Gabriele was weary. His body was ill-used and it bore the scars of a lifetime of war.

For a while, he all but disappears from the historical record.

The likelihood is that he was simply trying to recuperate.

But in the east, cool grey eyes were gazing upon the growing conflict among the princes of Christendom while slowly and surely drawing up new plans.

In Hungary, John Zápolya, the rival claimant to the throne alongside Ferdinand, Charles's younger brother, had been defeated by the Habsburgs. Zápolya managed to escape to Transylvania, where he tried his luck again, only to be defeated for a second time. Realising that he needed to bring in some back-up to defeat the Habsburgs, Zápolya entered into secret negotiations with the Sublime Porte. At the end of the talks, he agreed that, for the sultan's support, he would become his vassal, pay an annual tribute, fight alongside Suleiman in his wars, permit Ottoman troops to be stationed in Hungary and, finally, he would allow the Ottomans to take ten per cent of the Hungarian people as slaves every ten years.

Clearly, Zápolya was prepared to lay down his people for the crown.

With Zápolya on board as a local ally and source of information, Suleiman began making his preparations. He initially aimed to march west in 1528, but the weather that spring and summer was so poor, with so much rain, that the necessary stores were either spoiled or never arrived.

But Suleiman was not to be put off so easily.

Meanwhile, in Hungary, Ferdinand, now king, was dealing with the usual Habsburg problem: a lack of money. Despite receiving intelligence that the Turks had called off a proposed attack in 1528, he did very little to prepare for a renewed attack the following year. There was, as usual, too little in the treasury, the German princes were on the brink of civil war, and his brother was, also as usual, preoccupied with France and Italy – as demonstrated by the way Charles sent Tadino to Naples, Milan, Barletta and the nearby coastal cities of Manfredonia and Trani, and finally Genoa, to upgrade the castle and city fortifications. If the brothers had seriously expected a full-scale Ottoman attack on their possessions in Hungary, they surely would have sent their most expert military engineer to Vienna to inspect, and improve, the dilapidated defences of Vienna.

In Constantinople, Suleiman started laying in fresh supplies and gathering his troops afresh as the winter ended and the spring of 1529 began. But the spring of 1529 proved almost as wet and trying as the previous year, delaying preparations. On 10 May, the army was finally ready to leave, and it marched from Constantinople.

However, the weather conditions did not improve. Heavy rain turned the roads into mud tracks, making it increasingly difficult to transport the heavy cannon that Suleiman had assembled to break down the walls of Vienna. Rivers were swollen, with many bridges swept away. The further they went, the harder it was to continue transporting the cannon and some of the heaviest pieces had to be abandoned lest the advance grind to a halt.

The weather also affected the troops, leading to outbreaks of illness among the miserable, marching men.

The Habsburg king, Ferdinand, gathered what intelligence he could. It was not clear what target the sultan had chosen. Buda, which had fallen to the Ottomans following the Battle of Mohács, had been retaken by Habsburg forces the following year and that seemed like a likely objective. Ferdinand left only a token force in the city, pulling what troops he had back to Vienna.

In August, the Ottoman army arrived at Mohács, the site of its great triumph three years earlier, where it was met by John Zápolya with 6,000 of his own troops. Together, they marched on to Buda, reaching the city on 7 September. The civilian population had largely fled, leaving the defence of the city to a thousand Hungarian and German troops under the command of Thomas Nadasky. Nadasky was determined to fight, despite being outnumbered pretty much one hundred to one. It took four days for the cannon that the Turks had managed to bring this far to open a breach in the walls. Their troops poured into the city. Nadasky, with his surviving men, retreated to the city's fortress but after a few days' defiance, his men, knowing no help would come, insisted on surrendering.

Suleiman installed his vassal, Zápolya, as master of Buda. But then came the question of what to do next. It was already early September. The march to Buda had been long and gruelling. The sultan could chalk Buda down as a victory – he had securely installed Zápolya in the city – and march back to Constantinople. But Vienna was 130 miles away. Taking Vienna would ensure that no attacks could be launched against Hungary without first retaking Vienna, while its position on the Danube would allow the Ottomans to control the vital trade that ran along the river, while also allowing them to resupply the city by river from Buda.

But all these coldly strategic reasons probably paled against one simple consideration. Vienna was the seat of the Habsburgs, the city from which they had gone out to marry their way to what they now called an empire. To take the city would deal a devastating blow to the man who also styled himself 'emperor'.

As such, despite the lateness of the season, Suleiman decided to march on to Vienna.

Ferdinand himself was not in the city. He left command of its defence to Nicholas, count of Salm. Nicholas was 70 but a vastly experienced soldier who had distinguished himself at the Battle of Pavia.

Arriving in Vienna, von Salm found the city walls in poor condition; little had been done to prepare them for the new age of gunpowder warfare. With little time to rectify the situation, Nicholas had his men dig earth embankments and trenches at the weakest spots, while siting his cannon on hastily constructed emplacements.

For the defence of the city, the count of Salm had about 20,000 men, including a strong contingent of *Landsknechte* and Spanish arquebusiers, but the defenders were hugely outnumbered by the approaching Ottoman forces.

However, the natural geography of the city offered Vienna some protection. The city had not yet crossed the river, so all its buildings were on the right bank and the wide river protected it from assaults on that front. The north was marshy while a tributary ran into the Danube, running along the southern walls of the city. The Wienerwald (Vienna Woods) covered the western approach to the city, leaving an attacking army largely limited to assaulting from the south-west. That was where the count of Salm concentrated his preparations and his best men.

On 27 September, the Ottoman army reached Vienna. They had made good time but it was very late in the campaigning season. However, the defenders knew that Suleiman had defied military convention while besieging Rhodes. They could not expect him to withdraw simply because the seasons were changing, particularly since it would be possible to ship supplies up the Danube from Buda to the army besieging Vienna.

The sultan had brought about a hundred thousand men to the walls of the city. With him was his Grand Vizier, Ibrahim, who acted as the chief executive to Suleiman's chairman of the board of directors.

As the Ottoman tents went up outside the city, the defenders, seeing the extent of the tent city, realised just how great was the army that Suleiman had brought with him. But they must have been encouraged by one thing they did not see: the great siege cannon that had broken the walls of Constantinople and that had breached the defences of Rhodes. The conditions had been so bad that the Ottomans had had to leave all their largest cannon behind. They still had many smaller cannon, but they did not have the big wall-breakers that could have quickly smashed the city's walls.

Nevertheless, Suleiman sent a group of prisoners as his emissaries into the city, asking its surrender and promising them their lives and properties should they do so. However, should the city resist, then the city would be utterly destroyed. Those who survived the sack would be enslaved and the very ground upon which Vienna had once stood would be salted, that it stand as a desolate testament to defying his will.

Suleiman gave notice to the defenders that on Michaelmas, 29 September, he would breakfast in the city that counted St Michael as its patron saint.

In answer, von Salm returned to the Ottoman camp an equal number of Turkish prisoners, but on the morning of 29 September he sent another prisoner with a further message for the sultan: his breakfast was getting cold.

The Turkish threats were a standard part of Ottoman psychological warfare. Suleiman himself was no bloodthirsty conqueror and, when he promised mercy, he almost always delivered it. But time was flowing past – the Danube running past the Turkish tents gave liquid testament to that – and he needed to force a quick outcome to the siege.

Without their heavy cannon, the Turkish miners and sappers were given the task of undermining the walls. They set to quickly and were soon within range. However, von Salm organised regular sorties from the city to attack the sappers and the miners, while counter-mining efforts from within the city managed to intercept most of the Turkish tunnels. In this, the defenders were helped when one of the sappers defected to the defenders, claiming to have been born a Christian and wanting to return to his religion. He told von Salm the location of two mines which had reached the walls. With this information, the defenders were able to counter-mine and stop that attack.

A larger sally on 3 October by up to 8,000 men had initial success but developed into a confused melee, with the Imperial troops in the end suffering losses they could not afford and only just retreating in time. Von Salm would be more cautious in future.

Shortly afterwards, the defenders were bolstered by a message, delivered by a courier who had swum across the Danube, saying that Ferdinand was assembling an army and would arrive in a week to relieve the city. In truth, Ferdinand was still far away and his army was far too small to face Suleiman's forces in open battle, but the message renewed the heart of the garrison.

The Ottomans continued their mining operations while mounting distracting assaults, and at about 9am on 10 October, the eleventh day of the siege, they finally succeeded in opening a breach in the wall near one of the city's gates. The immediate assault almost carried the breach, with an Ottoman standard bearer managing to raise his standard on the city wall. But he was brought down by an arquebus ball and the garrison pushed the assault back.

Despite his age, von Salm personally led many of these counter-attacks. Whenever a Turkish attack was defeated, the bells of St Stephen's Cathedral were rung in joy and gratitude, their peal running silver across the wet and miserable ranks of Ottoman troops stuck outside the city.

For the weather was deteriorating, with the first frosts now punctuating the autumn storms. The surrounding countryside had been picked clean by scavenging parties while river-borne supplies were proving insufficient to keep the massive army fed. Disease was rife and dissatisfaction was growing even among the highly disciplined Ottoman troops.

The sultan's Janissaries asked for a meeting to discuss the situation of the siege with Suleiman. It was 12 October. If they remained outside the walls of Vienna much longer, they would be stuck there: retreating to Constantinople in winter would be impossible. There were three options: take the city as planned within the next few days, retreat in the next few days, or start planning and preparing for a winter siege.

Suleiman had succeeded in every campaign he had embarked upon. He did not intend to fail this time. The decision was made to attack.

Not wasting any time, the assault began as the council of war ended. The Turks succeeded in making another breach but they were again forced back. Ottoman commanders launched further attacks on 12 October but they were all beaten back.

Following the failure of the day's attacks, Suleiman summoned his commanders again on the night of the 13th for a further council. The sultan was still not willing to give up. They would make a final, all-out assault the following day, attacking at dawn.

Although the war council agreed to the sultan's commands, the cold, wet and exhausted Ottoman troops, even the Janissaries, were far less keen to throw themselves against the walls again and they had to be bribed with payments of 20 ducats each to agree to try.

When the trumpets and drums sounded to summon the men forward for this last try, the normally compliant Ottoman troops proved reluctant, many having to be forced forward at sword point. Suleiman offered huge rewards and promotions to any men who succeeded in breaching the defences, which produced some enthusiasm, and a successful mine did create another breach, to which the Ottoman soldiers directed their fire, trying to clear it for their advancing troops.

But once again, Nicholas von Salm led the defence personally, throwing back the attackers. Such was the violence of the cannon fire – the Ottomans were using the field artillery they had managed to bring through the mud to Vienna to sweep the breach – that von Salm was hit and wounded by stone shrapnel. Although the count continued fighting, the wound did not heal properly and he died from his wounds in May the following year.

But the resistance of von Salm and his men was enough to prevent this final attack succeeding. With two all-out assaults having failed and the weather worsening, Suleiman decided to call off the siege.

On 15 October, the Ottoman army started its long march back to Constantinople. They finally reached the city on 28 November, having suffered considerable losses on the way due to the weather and to harrying by pursuing Habsburg forces.

However, in a masterful display of 16th-century spin, the Grand Vizier, Ibrahim, declared the expedition a victory as the sultan had marched on Vienna with the honourable aim of meeting, and defeating, Ferdinand in fair battle and, since Ferdinand had declined to test his mettle in battle, therefore the sultan was the moral winner of the campaign.

In reality, Suleiman's first great attempt to open the road into central Europe had failed.

But where was Gabriele while all this was going on? After all, he had immense experience in fighting the Turks, particularly in a siege. Surely he would have brought great expertise to the defence.

Unfortunately, we simply don't know what Tadino was doing nor where he was during the siege and indeed for the whole of the next year, 1530. We know that Gabriele was in Genoa in August 1529 with Charles. But after that there is a complete hole in our sources for the next year. From Genoa, he could have reached Vienna before the sultan arrived, but it would have been a difficult journey and we don't have any accounts of him being present at the siege – although if he was a late arrival, sent as an advisor rather than as a commander, then it is possible he would not have been included among the fairly sketchy records of the siege. And the efficiency with which the defenders defeated the Turkish mining effort does suggest the presence of an expert military engineer.

But, sadly, we just don't know.

Tadino was now 50 years old. Perhaps he took a sabbatical. Perhaps he was ill. Or perhaps he was there, at the siege, lending his knowledge to the defenders.

In the final stage of his life, Tadino's knowledge would be sought out by many people, but by one man in particular, an old friend whom Tadino had known when he was a poor boy: Niccolò Tartaglia.

40

WHEN AN OLD SOLDIER LEAVES THE FIELD

On 24 February 1530, Pope Clement VII crowned Charles Holy Roman Emperor in Bologna. It was Charles's birthday. He was 30.

The coronation marked something of a high point in Charles's power. The following 26 years of his reign were troubled and while he certainly did not fall from power – at 56, ailing and weary, he abdicated his many thrones and retired to a monastery – the next two decades were largely spent trying to stop the inherently fissiparous territories that made up the Habsburg Empire splitting away.

Gabriele Tadino was there to see the coronation of the man he had served so faithfully these last eight years, enduring imprisonment and injury on his behalf.

That he had done so showed how the nature of loyalty was slowly changing in Europe.

Today, we generally express loyalty to an idea: most often a nation but sometimes an ideology. Americans swear an oath to the Constitution of the United States. Loyalty, for the last couple of hundred years, has become fixed upon the ideas and ideals of nation states, rather than the particular person in charge of the nation at any one time. For some people today, loyalty has become even more impersonal, focusing perhaps on an ideology or a supranational body such as the European Union or the United Nations.

In the medieval world, it was the exact opposite. Then, loyalty was personal and local. People were loyal to the lord they personally served and to the particular patch of land and community in which they lived. There were no 'Englishmen' or 'Italians'; there might be Men of Kent or Ferrarese.

As a boy and young man, this was the world where Tadino's loyalties lay. He learned to defend his local town. However, as he grew older, he became a soldier of Venice. That was the state to which the Martinenghesi and the Bergamaschi owed their loyalty but, being a republic, it was a more abstract loyalty than those who followed the king of France. It was, nevertheless, fiercely particular; in both the Stato da Màr and the Stato da Tera, Venice essentially sought to recreate Venice abroad.

Loyalty to the Republic was often mediated through loyalty to particular commanders. The *condottieri* who fought for the Republic, and the other Italian city states, generally had cohorts of men who followed them personally. These were soldiers who cleaved to an older idea of loyalty, to a particular leader and to fortune, for some men seemed fortune's favoured child and to follow these men was to walk in fortune's shadow.

Although they have left little trace in the historical record, Tadino appears to have had an entourage of followers and fellow travellers during the Venetian phase of his career. That the obligations of loyalty were reciprocal is shown by the kidnap plot, when Tadino found himself the unwitting accomplice of the mad marriage scheme of Camillo da Barco.

But in the second phase of his military career, Tadino's loyalties shifted dramatically. Despite explicit orders from his Venetian employers, Gabriele deserted his post on Candia and went to Rhodes to aid the Knights.

Gabriele was not a Knight when he arrived on Rhodes. So far as we know, he had had no dealing with the Religion before this. But upon hearing a call to come to the defence of Christendom, he decided that his loyalty lay more with the Knights, men he had never met, than with the Signoria, which paid his wages and whose members he did know.

This was a shift to a more impersonal, but also a deeply personal, loyalty. Impersonal, because Christendom transcended any of the local loyalties that transcribed most people's allegiances. But it was also deeply personal because religious faith was the foundation of Gabriele's identity, as it was for most of his contemporaries.

Tadino remained loyal to the Religion to the end of his life. In the portrait that Titian painted of him in 1548, when he was 60, Gabriele is depicted wearing the robes and insignia of the Knights Hospitaller.

But when he entered the service of Charles V, Tadino's loyalties became more mixed, mirroring the wider shift of loyalty and symbols that were occurring throughout Europe. For loyalty to Charles was both personal and institutional; to his person, to the Empire and to the ideal of Christendom to which Charles presented himself as guardian and defender. Thus Tadino, who had left his post on Candia to defend Christendom, could become a staunch servant of the emperor even in his many wars against other Christian powers and not just on the occasions when he confronted the Turks.

However, it was as the defender of the faith that Gabriele was able to square his service to the emperor with his continued service as a brother of the Knights Hospitaller. The Grand Master was happy for Tadino to continue in service to the emperor because that service gave Gabriele regular opportunities to remind Charles of the order's need for a new base, and his promise that he would help them find such a base.

The negotiations were long and delicate. The main sticking point was the order's need to ensure that it did not become a pawn in the power politics of Europe, and in particular a card for the emperor to play against France. Many of the order's brethren were French, including the Grand Master himself. Should they accept an agreement that drew them into the battles of France and the Empire, then it would surely spell the disintegration of the order.

Fra' Philippe had put out some feelers to King Francis to see if the French king could provide them with a suitable base, but the suggestions they received from France were such that, in short order, the Knights would be reduced to an irrelevance. So far as Fra' Philippe was concerned, their new base would be temporary, a stopping place before they eventually reconquered Rhodes. As such, their new home had to be somewhere from which it would be feasible to launch a fleet to retake Rhodes. Francis had no such territories available.

But Charles had.

To be precise, these were the island of Malta and its smaller offshoot, Gozo, as well as the port of Tripoli on the North African coast, which had been conquered by Spain in 1510. The islands command the passage between the eastern and western Mediterranean where the sea narrows to fit between Sicily and an upspur of Africa. For the Knights, with their command of sea-borne warfare, the islands were an excellent base. They were not so keen on having to guard Tripoli, but it was part of the deal and it had a good harbour. A reasonable price to pay for the security of a base in which the order would be sovereign.

For that was what Charles was offering the order in exchange for a symbolic annual gift in token of their freedom from the normal service to the monarch. That annual gift was a falcon, to be paid on the Feast of All Saints (1 November): the Maltese Falcon that, in Dashiell Hammet's seminal private eye novel, became a gold falcon rather than a flesh and feather bird.

In 1530, Charles officially gave Malta, Gozo and Tripoli into the keeping of the Knights. The grant, which the order has preserved, is also notable for the extraordinary number of titles that Charles had acquired:

> ever Augustus, Emperor of the Romans; Joanna his mother, and the same Charles being, by the Grace of God Monarchs of Castile, Aragon, the Two Sicilies, Jerusalem, Hungary, Dalmatia, Croatia, Leòn, Navarre, Granada, Toledo, Valencia, Gallicia, Majorca, Seville, Sardinia, Cordoba, Corsica, Murcia, Algarve, Algeria, Gibraltar, the Canary Islands; also the Islands and Continent of India and of the Oceans; Archduke of Austria, Duke of Burgundy and of Brabant; Count of Barcelona, of Flanders and of Tyrol, Lord of Biscay and of Molina, Duke of Athens and of Neopatria; Count of Rousillon and of Catalonia, Marquis of La Mancha and of Ghent.[64]

The grant itself was, in the end, wholehearted.

> [W]e grant, and of our liberality we bountifully bestow upon the aforesaid Very Reverend Grand Master of the Religion and Order of Saint John of Jerusalem, in feudal perpetuity, noble, free and unencumbered, our cities, castles, places and islands of Tripoli, Malta and Gozo, with all their cities, castles, places and island territories; with pure and mixed jurisdiction, right, and property of useful government; with power of life and death over males and females residing within their limits, and with the laws, constitutions, and rights now existing amongst the inhabitants; together with all other laws and rights, exemptions, privileges, revenues and other immunities whatsoever; so that they may hereafter hold

them in feudal tenure from us, as Kings of both Sicilies, and from our successors in the same kingdom, reigning at the time, under the sole payment of a falcon; which every year, on the Feast of All Saints, shall be presented by the person or persons duly authorised for that purpose, into the hands of the Viceroy or President, who may at that time be administering the government, in sign and recognition of feudal tenure; and having made that payment, they shall remain exempt and free from all other service claimable by law, and by custom performed by feudal vassals.[65]

The Religion had a home again.

Fra' Philippe Villiers de L'Isle Adam arrived on Malta on 26 October 1530. The Knights weren't immediately impressed by their new base. Compared to Rhodes, Malta was a bleak, semi-arid desert with almost no trees and practically no defences. What was worse, its capital and main centre of population was Mdina, in the centre of the island, far from the coast. This was deliberate on the part of the islanders, who were suffering greatly from the Muslim corsairs of North Africa, but it was useless for the Religion, which based its power upon its war galleys.

However, Malta did have good harbours on its north and eastern coasts, while the south coast was protected by high cliffs. If the order could build a new stronghold at one of those harbours, it would have a strong and well-protected base from which to continue: the last Crusaders.

That is what the order did, using its remaining funds and calling in favours and loans in order to pay for the building and recruitment. For their part, the Maltese, who had scratched out a poor living before the Religion's arrival, found much work from their new masters and so tolerated their arrival.

Suleiman had spent much money and more lives in removing the Order of Knights of the Hospital of St John of Jerusalem from Rhodes, but now they had a new base from which to continue harassing and raiding Ottoman shipping and bases in the eastern Mediterranean, while making it difficult for the Ottoman navy to link up with the Muslim corsairs of the Barbary Coast (modern-day Morocco, Algeria and Tunisia, and, after the Ottomans reconquered it in 1551, Tripoli in Libya). The threat from the order would grow during the next decades, from an irritant, to a sore, rising to a cancer that required removal once and for all.

For Suleiman, the Knights had been a problem that he thought resolved as a young man, only to have to return to them when he was old. The problem would prove intractable.

In 1565, the sultan was too old to accompany his army on such a long journey or to endure the rigours of another siege. When news finally reached Constantinople of the failure of the siege, Suleiman must have remembered the siege of 1522 when, young and strong, and magnanimous in his strength, he had allowed the Knights to sail away from Rhodes. The memory of the man who had stalled all his efforts to take Rhodes by storm and destroy the Knights must also have returned to his mind, that Italian military engineer who had escaped his grasp.

Gabriele was indeed crucial in ensuring that the Knights escaped Rhodes as a still living order. But when they moved to Malta, he did not join them. He had become the emperor's man. That was not an undertaking he could easily forgo, even if he had wanted to. But it served the Religion as well to have such an advocate close to Charles.

But for Tadino, there were other reasons to remain in the emperor's service. For as a Knight of Christendom, he saw that the tide from the east, which had ebbed back a little, was beginning to rise again.

In 1531, reports from Constantinople told that the sultan was gathering his army for a new strike west. However, the weather during the spring of 1531 was so appalling that Suleiman had to abandon his plans for that year. But his plans were postponed, not cancelled.

In 1532, Suleiman marched west once again.

The long awaited clash of emperors was suddenly a real prospect. For Suleiman had delivered a personal challenge to Charles before he left Constantinople.

> The king of Spain has for a long time declared his wish to go against the Turks; but I by the grace of God am proceeding with my army against him. If he is great of heart, let him await me in the field, and then, whatever God wills, shall be. If, however, he does not wish to wait for me, let him send tribute.[66]

Having received Suleiman's challenge, Charles wrote to his wife, 'In the light of duty, I have to defend the faith and the Christian religion in person.'[67]

The showdown was on.

Gabriele was one of the men given the task of preparing the ground for the coming heavyweight contest: logistics, defences, supplies. These were all accumulated in a frenzy of preparation, while Charles, through some delicate negotiations, managed to persuade his fractious Lutheran subjects in Germany to contribute their men to the cause of the defence of Christendom against the Turk.

Charles marched with a considerable army towards Vienna where his brother was waiting for him. Together, they waited for news of Suleiman.

He never arrived.

The Turkish march stalled in front of the fortress of Güns in central Hungary. The garrison, which consisted of only 800 men, was commanded by Nikola Jurišić, a Croatian. The defenders had no cannon and only a few guns; the hundred thousand strong Ottoman army, which this time had managed to successfully transport its cannon into Hungary, was expected to roll over the fortress in a day or two at most.

Instead, the Turks were stuck outside Güns for over four weeks, from 5 to 30 August. The defenders withstood everything the Turks could throw at them: constant bombardment, mines and 19 assaults.

The Grand Vizier, Ibrahim, was so impressed by the conduct of the defenders that he personally guaranteed safe conduct to Jurišić. By this point, Jurišić had run out of powder and half his men were dead. He agreed. Ibrahim kept his word. He received Jurišić graciously and congratulated him on his conduct.

There are two different accounts of the final events of the siege. One states that Ibrahim offered Jurišić excellent terms to surrender but that Jurišić replied that, as the fortress did not belong to him but to Ferdinand, he could not give it up. The other version says that Ibrahim asked that Jurišić allow a symbolic surrender and that Jurišić acceded to that: a single Ottoman flag bearer was allowed into the fortress and, climbing to the top, waved the Ottoman standard from the tower in symbolic victory. But, the flag having been waved, the Ottoman troops withdrew from Güns and turned east.

The Ottoman army was in the field. The Habsburg army was in Vienna. The two could meet and settle the matter once and for all.

But Charles did not leave Vienna.

For his part, Suleiman did not force the issue by marching on the city.

The two emperors glared at each other, separated by about a hundred miles. When faced with the decision of what to do, the lateness of the season, and the risk inherent in offering battle to a comparable army, weighed on both men's minds.

Suleiman retreated.

Charles never ventured out from Vienna.

The risk was too great. Each might have ventured the risk if they could lure the other into a battle on ground of their choosing. Most probably, Suleiman's decision to harry the territory east of Güns was in part designed to lure Charles out into a battle on ground that would favour the Ottomans.

For his part, Charles would probably only have decided upon battle if forced to it by Suleiman's appearance outside Vienna. While he had assembled a good army, it was still smaller than the Ottoman forces. To succeed, he would have needed the force multiplier of defending fixed positions.

It was the closest the two men who both claimed the title 'emperor' would ever come.

Following the withdrawal of the Turkish forces, Charles marched back to Italy, ever the focus of his efforts. Gabriele, in command of the artillery, went with him.

On 7 November, the army reached Mantua. While there, Charles officially invested Ludovico Ariosto as poet. Ariosto had written *Orlando Furioso*, an epic poem of chivalric love, unrequited love and paladins as everyone wished they had been, in 1516, and it had been a huge success.

As the Imperial army marched through northern Italy, Tadino had the chance to visit his old home in Martinengo. There, he met his nephew, Camillo, son of Girolamo who was killed in Genoa, and his nephew asked for his uncle's help in looking after the family's land and possessions. Tadino was in his fifties. He had been wounded by shot, sword, illness and long war. He was weary and spent. It was time to rest and care for the family that he had left.

But before he could retire, there was one matter that had still not been put to rest.

Gabriele requested an audience with the emperor. The two men had spoken frequently through the years he had spent in his service.

They were not friends – no man of his rank could befriend Charles – but they knew each other well and the emperor respected Tadino's opinions and, when he could, acceded to his requests.

Gabriele had one final request.

He asked Charles to write to Venice on his behalf to ask the Signoria to forgive his desertion of his post in Candia. In the ten years that had passed since then, the Signoria had neither forgiven nor forgotten his betrayal.

Charles was 32. He already suffered from gout but he was otherwise healthy and vital. The man standing before him, an empty socket where his right eye had been, bore the marks of a lifetime of service, but his hair was still black and the eye that remained gazed steadily at the emperor whom he had served in defence of Christendom.

Charles wrote the letter.

The Signoria, receiving such a request from such a hand, acceded to it.

The Republic pardoned the engineer. He was now free to live and travel through Venetian territory without fear of retribution for his past actions.

On 8 April 1533, in Genoa, Charles signed the document releasing Gabriele Tadino from his service. Tadino had suffered much for the emperor in Genoa, so it was a good place in which to end his service.

By June, Tadino was back in Martinengo. There, he lived quietly for some years, managing his assets and looking after his nephew, Camillo. Gabriele was about 55. He had spent his adult life at war and the peace must have been welcome – but perhaps a little boring.

Because when, in 1535, Charles asked Gabriele to return to his service, he did so with little hesitation.

The Barbary corsair, Hayreddin Barbarossa, had captured Tunis on 16 August 1534, expelling the previous ruler, Muley Hasan, who had kept his city and its excellent port from the endemic piracy of the Barbary Coast. Hayreddin Barbarossa, the greatest, most ruthless and most daring of the corsairs, had no such compunction and began enthusiastically raiding coastal towns in Sicily and Italy.

In response, Charles decided to attack Tunis. Tadino acted as one of his advisors for the planned expedition: a difficult and dangerous mission, as any amphibious assault must be.

However, the attack was successful. Barbarossa was defeated, although the corsair captain managed to escape and would prove as great a thorn in Charles's side as the Knights were in Suleiman's.

This would prove the last military engagement of Gabriele's life. However, Tadino continued to serve as an advisor both to Charles and to his brother, Ferdinand. He had already advised Ferdinand on how best to improve the defences of Vienna during the campaigns of 1532 and, after the Ottoman withdrawal, he had given further counsel on the siting of border fortresses. Tadino continued to act as an adviser to Ferdinand for the next decade, helping shape the Habsburg fortresses at Komárom, Győr, and Zemun in Hungary, and Kostajnica and Koprivnica in what is now Croatia, as well as advising on garrison sizes and training, improvements in logistics and the best place to put fortresses with respect to the local terrain. As such, Gabriele played an important role in strengthening the border between the Habsburg and Ottoman empires.

This work was very different from his previous, hands-on style, but there was a reason for the change. Gabriele was getting old and the marks left on him from a lifetime of soldiering were proving increasingly wearisome. Returning to Martinengo, Gabriele renounced military service for good. He had seen enough of death. He could wait now until he met the reaper face to face.

But there was still one matter left unresolved from his former life: La Serenissima. The Republic to whom he had given so much of his life and in whose service he had suffered so much had, at Charles's request, forgiven him, but he had not dared to go back.

Now, however, the Republic asked him to come back.

The Ottomans were pressing hard in the eastern Mediterranean. The Signoria foresaw that, despite their most fervent wish to retain neutrality, the time was soon coming when they would have to go to war with the Sublime Porte. They knew all too well that the resources available to Constantinople were far greater than those that Venice could call upon, but they also knew how Gabriele had forestalled the sultan on Rhodes and how the preparations in Hungary had stopped his advance on Vienna.

So now the Signoria called Tadino back to Venice to ask his advice on how best they could defend the Republic's possessions. Gabriele had become a consultant – with all the perks that come from that.

Although Gabriele was Martinenghesi, Venice was the city that had his heart. Returning there, it worked its spell upon him once again. In 1537, he settled permanently in the city. Apart from short trips, he would not leave it again.

Gabriele's decision was encouraged by the old friend he met in Venice: Niccolò Tartaglia. The young boy whom he had first met in Brescia in the most desperate of circumstances had become a scholar of renown and, what was almost as unlikely, he was no longer the dirt-poor urchin that Tadino remembered but a teacher of mathematics – although still quite poor. What made this the more unlikely was that Tartaglia was almost entirely self-taught. At 14, he had earned enough money to pay for a teacher to teach him how to read and write, but his money ran out by the time they got to the letter 'k'. Tartaglia later wrote, 'From that day, I never returned to a tutor, but continued to labour by myself over the works of dead men, accompanied only by the daughter of poverty that is called industry.'[68]

Tartaglia made much of his money from selling solutions to mathematical problems to artillerymen, who could quite clearly see the mathematical underpinning of their new way of war. But now, when the questions arrived, he had sitting at his table a man who had as much practical experience with the problems of ballistics as anyone in the world: the erstwhile general commander of the Spanish artillery.

In his answers, Tartaglia drew on Tadino's knowledge and, for his part, Gabriele was happy to share his experience. Indeed, so close did their collaboration become that when Tartaglia wrote his seminal book on ballistics, *Nova Scientia* (*New Science*), which was published in 1537, it's clear that Tadino influenced it greatly. Perhaps the most obvious fruit of Tadino's practical knowledge was Tartaglia's demonstration that the greatest range of a cannon could be achieved by elevating the barrel to an angle of 45 degrees to the horizontal.

The *Nova Scientia* was immensely influential among practical gunners and Galileo himself referred to it constantly when doing his own work on projectiles.

In 1546, Tartaglia followed *Nova Scientia* with *Quesiti et Inventioni Diversi* (*Various Questions and Inventions*). The book was a remarkable tour through arithmetic, algebra, geometry, ballistics and the theory of fortification and, like many similar books written during the 16th and 17th centuries (such as Galileo's *Dialogue Concerning the Two Chief World Systems*), Tartaglia wrote it as a dialogue, with a number of interlocutors asking questions and giving answers. The man who answered the questions on ballistics, fortifications and military tactics in Tartaglia's book was Gabriele Tadino.

Tadino had taught and trained a number of younger military engineers, particularly during his service to the emperor, but now, through Tartaglia's book, he made the distilled experience of his years as an engineer available to anyone who read *Quesiti et Inventioni Diversi*.

The following year, 1538, the Signoria paid for the great painter, Tiziano Vecelli, better known to us as Titian, to paint Tadino's portrait. During the same year, a commemorative medal, showing Tadino's face in profile, was also minted. The coincidence of both memorials suggests that Tadino's friends in Venice had arranged for these to be done to commemorate a significant anniversary and the most likely candidate would be to mark Gabriele's 60th birthday. If that was the case, then he was born in 1478.

In Titian's portrait, Gabriele sits at a slight angle to the viewer, putting his nose into semi-profile and partly obscuring his ruined right eye. Tadino is dressed in the formal robes of the Knights Hospitaller, wearing a black tunic with the white cross of the order embroidered on his chest. He has a fur cloak over his shoulders and his left hand rests upon the jewelled hilt of a sword. His beard is still black without any hint of grey but a hat covers his hair. His nose is proudly hooked, a proboscis to bear comparison with that of Francis of France. In the background to his right, a row of cannon stand pointing out of the frame, with a bucolic landscape stretching into the distance.

It is a fine portrait of a striking man. Looking at it, one sees a man who would not suffer fools, whose temper was quick but whose wit was quicker. A good friend and a bad enemy.

Tadino spent the few years left to him in Venice. He had money and enough to live on, having been granted a pension by the emperor, but at the end of May 1543 Tadino fell ill, possibly from a stroke.

Gabriele had seen many men die. He knew his end was near. So, on 30 May 1543, he wrote his will. In it, he declared his nephew, Camillo, his chief heir, stating he was as a son to him. In the will, he confirmed a gift of property given to his brother, Gian Francesco, but with the stipulation that after Gian Francesco's death the property was to go to Camillo. Tadino also made provision in his will that his sister, Tranquilla, receive a hundred ducats a year for the rest of her life, as well as leaving small bequests to various people in his service, and legacies to three monasteries.

On 4 June 1453, Gabriele Tadino died in Venice. He was buried in the Church of St John and St Paul, but his tomb and mortal remains were lost in a later remodelling of the church and he has no extant memorial or grave.

It is, perhaps, appropriate that a man who had given such service to the Republic, but who had also incurred such anger from the Signoria, should be buried in the city but lost to civic memory.

If there should be any memorial to Gabriele Tadino, the foremost military engineer of his age, it lay in the long war between the Habsburgs and the Ottomans for control of the Mediterranean, their war for the heart of the world that he had done so much to ensure did not end in the first decades of the 16th century with an Ottoman victory.

But wars for control of the sea leave no marks, only the shifting waves, and Gabriele Tadino himself slipped beneath the waves of time, all but forgotten, his exploits and his importance largely unknown even in his own home town.

I hope this book might do something to change that. In the final chapter, I will look at why Gabriele Tadino matters and what his life tells us today.

41

THE LAST KNIGHT OF CHRISTENDOM: THE FIRST MAN OF THE MODERN WORLD

Thank you, dear reader, for coming this far with me. It's been a journey through a different and often confusing landscape, among people who in some ways are very different from today. But having come this far, you might be wondering if this book might have been better called *The Man Who Slowed Down the Sultan*. I must admit, I do have some sympathy with you (but would you have bought the book if it was called that?). Slowing down Suleiman was no mean feat in itself, particularly when you consider how riddled with existing tunnels Rhodes was. The fact that Gabriele Tadino managed to stop the Ottomans from completely mining the walls is a testament both to his ability and innovations as a military engineer and his skill in organising the Knights' resources to counter the far greater manpower the Turks had at their disposal. But of course, fighting Suleiman to what was, effectively, a draw meant that the Knights were able to withdraw from Rhodes as a still intact organisation and fighting force. If Rhodes had been lost to storm, there would not have been a Knight left alive to escape. The Knights who ran the Religion's different *langues* around Europe would, no doubt, have attempted to continue but such a catastrophic loss would have left the Knights Hospitaller bereft of men, their base and their reputation; the Religion would have ebbed away within a generation.

Gabriele Tadino's presence on Rhodes during those six months of 1522 was vital. Without him, the Knights would not have been able to stop the Ottoman miners, many more breaches would have been created in the walls, and the city would have fallen. With him, the surviving Knights, with their colours and their relics, retreated from Rhodes with a reputation still high enough to give them the negotiating space to find a new base. Those negotiations were eased by having Gabriele Tadino become a trusted servant of the emperor with regular access to Charles in person. The Habsburgs were the first bureaucratic kings in Europe, conducting much of their business by letter and memo, but there were still undeniable advantages in having someone who could speak to the king, face to face, on your behalf.

It was the Knights' defence of Rhodes and Tadino's advocacy that ensured they obtained their new base on Malta and under the sort of terms that allowed them to continue in the business of crusading – or piracy, as the Ottomans, not without some justification, saw it. Among the Knights who arrived on Malta was a young man named Jean Parisot de la Valette who had been among the defenders of Rhodes. When, in 1565, the aged sultan decided to finally make an end of these troublesome knights, it was Fra' Jean who led the defence of Malta as the Grand Master of the Religion.

Suleiman was 69 when he decided to finish his unfinished business with the Religion. Tadino had been dead for over 20 years. But Suleiman himself was no longer the young, confident monarch who had allowed the Knights to sail away from Rhodes with honour. He had suffered, and caused, family tragedy. He had lost Roxelana, the woman he had loved truly and to the exclusion of all others. The Empire was still strong, the single greatest power in Europe and the Near East, but despite its resources Suleiman had not been able to achieve all his aims. As the saying goes, all political lives end in failure, but Suleiman, as he felt his strength beginning to fail, was determined to clear up one of the failures of his early strength and magnanimity. Allowing the Knights to retreat and regroup had left them perched athwart the Ottoman plans to win control of the Mediterranean.

This war for the heart of the world had played out throughout his reign during his long struggle with Charles, 'the king of Spain', and then Charles's son and heir, Philip II. While modern historians generally assert, with some complacence, that the logistical challenges facing powers set at opposite ends of the Mediterranean ensured that neither could have achieved mastery of the whole sea, such was not the belief of the men engaged in this titanic struggle. I suspect that they were more right than historians looking at graphs and charts, for these ignore the effect of morale, confidence and that greatest of game changers, victory.

Should the Ottoman galleys have returned to Constantinople in 1565 with the news that they had taken Malta and destroyed the Knights, then Suleiman's last year would have taken on a different hue entirely. The highly effective Barbary corsairs who worked for the Ottomans could have taken control of Malta, dominating the channel between Sicily and North Africa, while creating a new and effective base for naval operations in the western Mediterranean.

That the Ottoman siege failed was vital for the security of the coasts of Spain, France and Italy. Although raids from the Barbary pirates continued, they would not graduate to becoming existential threats.

This, in itself, makes Gabriele Tadino worth writing about. But it's only a facet of his importance. What makes him more important is the key role he played in the transition from the Middle Ages to the modern world. This all began when Gabriele was about 16 and Charles VIII invaded Italy, setting off the Italian Wars and unwittingly signalling the end of the Middle Ages.

There were many different signals for the change from the medieval to the modern, from the printing press, voyages of discovery, the heliocentric view and so on, but one of the most compelling is the military changes. Essentially, gunpowder and cannon took over from swords and arrows. But that was just the surface change. What was more important was the social change that this brought about. Medieval society was fundamentally hierarchical, with its lords spiritual, lords temporal and the commons. While there were various philosophical and theological underpinnings to this social structure, one of its key supports was power: the nobility, trained for war and protected by the best armour and wielding the best weapons, were able to deal out death in a way that no untrained man could match. This in part explains the horror that was felt by the French at the way the English employed longbowmen, all commoners, to destroy the cream of the French nobility during the Hundred Years' War. French knights had for centuries been the epitome of European martial culture, their pre-eminence sealed by the romances that made the profession of arms something more than just the dealing of death: even blood-stained warriors looked for a chance of redemption within their calling, and found it in the ideal of the knight that was exemplified in the romances, even if that ideal was rarely encountered in person or on the battlefield.

However, even the challenge to the status quo posed by English longbowmen was overcome by better armour: the plate armour of the 15th century was incredibly effective at deflecting and defending against arrows and other projectiles. The man wearing it was like a tank upon the battlefield, impregnable and powerful, the embodiment of the power of the elite.

And then a little round hole appeared in his breast plate and he toppled over, face down in the mud.

Where arrows bounced off plate armour, arquebus balls punched right through, and through the man wearing it. And it was not just arquebuses. A cannonball would all but vaporise the best suit of armour, leaving the wearer a scattering of tin-covered limbs, helmeted head rolling on the floor.

The new gunpowder weapons paid even less respect to social class than longbows. At least a bowman had to train for years to master his weapon. An arquebusier could be trained in a matter of a few weeks, and the same was true for a cannon crew. And while armour had been improved to defend against the longbow and the crossbow, there was nothing that could be done to protect a knight against the impact of a cannonball. No shield was going to deflect a 20-pound ball of iron fired at a thousand feet a second.

This changed utterly the dynamics on the battlefield. But it had just as profound an effect upon social structures. In the Middle Ages, and indeed in pretty well all recorded history, the nobility reserved to itself the greatest power to kill (an exception was Rome, where the army was professional). A medieval knight could be brought down by a group of peasants, but they would have a tough fight of it and many would die in the attempt. So the social strata were reinforced by the capacity for violence that the nobility could employ against the commons.

However, with the invention of gunpowder weapons, there began the process of levelling out that, in the end, ground down the old social divisions. The capacity for violence was evened out: a commoner with an arquebus could kill a prince of the blood, and there was no suit of armour or training that would protect the prince against such an ignominious end.

So the change to gunpowder warfare acted as an accelerant to the other social changes that took place in the following centuries, changes that eventually brought down monarchies in bloody revolutions to replace them with the democratic slaughter of the world wars.

It was the military engineers who were the midwives to this momentous change in its early decades. While the arquebus had its place on the battlefield, castles still remained as the physical embodiment of power. But when cannon started shredding the high walls and towers, tumbling the powers that had previously lorded over all their surroundings, it was the engineers who directed the cannon and who dug tunnels under the walls to set mines there. Most of the early military engineers were Italian, for during the six decades of the Italian Wars the tactics and strategies of attack and defence were tested, refined and perfected. Italian engineers became expensive exports, travelling all over Europe to exchange their knowledge for payment from the various kings looking to bolster their power.

However, there was a paradox in these changes that played out over the next two centuries in Europe. While gunpowder weapons in the end brought about a democratisation of power, their early effect was the exact opposite: the concentration of power on kings.

During the Middle Ages, the king was only slightly more powerful than his nobles, leading to a diffusion of power from the centre. Indeed, most of the wars of the Middle Ages were not between countries but within countries, as barons tried to assert their independence of the king while the king tried to bring his barons back under his control.

But the arrival and increasing importance of gunpowder weapons, and cannon in particular, led to the concentration of power in the king. This was because the new weapons, particularly cannon, were expensive and what was even more expensive was the building of the sorts of defences and fortresses that could withstand cannon fire. Where before a baron might be able to quickly put up a castle and defy the king's army from within its ramparts (which might just be a wooden palisade above an earth rampart), the new gunpowder fortresses were incredibly expensive to make and only a very few of the nobility had the money to make and man them. But kings did have the money, and the consolidation of power that these fortresses and armies provided made them richer, accelerating the concentration of power in their hands.

So we have a paradox. Gunpowder weapons eventually brought about a levelling of social hierarchies through their democratisation of the means of dealing out violence, but in their first centuries of dominance they effectively increased the powers of Europe's kings, leading to the increasingly centralised monarchies of the 17th century that claimed divine mandate for the rule of the king. These monarchies collapsed amid revolutions that were driven, in part, by the ability of men who were not of the nobility to kill the nobility.

It was Italian military engineers who drove this technology through its birth in fire and stone during the Italian Wars, and the most important of these engineers was Gabriele Tadino. His importance lay in a number of areas.

Firstly, through years of practical experience he developed a unique understanding of the new arts of war, in particular the use of artillery and the building of defences against that artillery.

Because of his employment by Charles V, Gabriele then played an important part in spreading this knowledge through the rest of Europe. He was personally responsible for revising the manufacturing standards for the Spanish artillery through his work on the *Segunda ordenanza de las Guardas*, the orders governing how Spanish cannon were to be manufactured and used in future. Also while working for Charles, Tadino supervised the rebuilding of the defences of many towns and fortresses, teaching other engineers his methods while doing so.

During the 1530s, Gabriele also acted as an advisor to Charles's brother, Ferdinand, the ruler of the Habsburgs' eastern territories. He was instrumental in siting and strengthening the border fortresses that were becoming a key part of the Habsburg defence strategy against further Ottoman assaults. The gallant defence of Güns had shown how important border fortresses could be. Tadino's inspection tours and advice not only established many of these fortresses, but his training of local engineers ensured that they would be built with all the knowledge and craft that his years of practical learning had accrued. This knowledge was then passed onwards, in space and time, ensuring that the *trace italienne* became the standard method of fortification for the next three hundred years.

So Gabriele Tadino played a key role in stabilising the previously quite fluid border between the Habsburgs and the Ottomans, while ensuring that the Knights Hospitaller remained in the game as well.

Tadino's ideas and experience were further broadcast through his friendship with Niccolò Tartaglia. Tartaglia used Tadino's knowledge to illustrate and expand on the arguments in his books, while the inclusion of Tadino as an interlocutor in his *Quesiti* ensured that Tadino's ideas spread beyond their natural orbit in Italy and among the servants of the Habsburgs, reaching the growing cadre of engineers who worked outside the Empire and Italy.

Another fascinating aspect of his career is how he illustrates the changing nature of European identity and loyalties during this period. During his early career he was a faithful servant of Venice. Venice was not his home, but the Martinenghesi had become supporters of the Republic and Gabriele fought for Venice through its trials in the first decades of the Italian Wars, a true *condottiero*.

However, when the call came from the Knights asking him to help them, Tadino had no doubt where his greater loyalty lay: with the defence of Christendom.

On the wider stage, that loyalty was fast fracturing. Christendom was in the process of tearing itself apart in the Reformation while the increasingly powerful European states were starting to stake greater claims to their peoples' loyalty. Henry VIII declared himself the leader of the church in England. The kings of France, in their struggle with the Habsburgs, decided to embrace the principle that 'the enemy of my enemy is my friend' even when that friend was the Islamic Ottoman Empire. National loyalties began increasingly to trump confessional identities. But Gabriele represented the old chivalric ideals of Europe, ideals that flowed from the Faith and from medieval romances. He was Roland at the pass, Galahad in search of the Grail, Orlando mad with love. Those ideals now had rivals, but they still moved many men and Gabriele was one of them. It was loyalty to those old ideals that ensured Europe's survival against the Ottomans.

But then, in one of those ironic twists of which history is so fond, the competition inherent in the new ideals of the nation state ensured that the countries of Europe would compete against each other through the next four centuries, that competition driving European development forward so that by the 19th century the Ottomans were no longer any sort of threat. Indeed, the danger had reversed so much that 19th-century journalism is full of essays posing the question what to do about the 'sick man of Europe'. The Ottomans, for their part, had settled into the long lassitude of a civilisation past its peak and they would have happily stayed there if not for their misfortune of bordering an increasingly rapacious Europe.

Gabriele Tadino's life straddled this change, lying athwart the medieval and the modern, Christendom and a Europe divided into warring nation states, the knight and the professional soldier. He embodied aspects of both, and lived and died at the highest pitch of both sets of competing ideals. But while a man might combine both perspectives, cultures cannot.

Europe changed but Gabriele didn't. He lived, and died, the last knight of Christendom and the first man of the modern world.

NOTES

1. There's no single agreed date for the end of the Middle Ages, in part because that age ended at different times in different parts of Europe. Italy was the first European country to enter the modern period, with 1453, the date of the fall of Constantinople, often given as an alternative for the end of the Middle Ages since the flood of Greek-speaking refugees bringing precious manuscripts in their luggage helped inspire the humanists of the Quattrocento. In Spain, 1492 is often taken as the end of the Middle Ages as that was the year the Reconquista ended, with the fall of Granada, while across the Atlantic Christopher Columbus discovered the New World. For France, the reign of Francis I marked a decisive shift from medieval models of kingship, while in England and Germany the end of the Middle Ages is more associated with the Reformation, and the splits with Rome engineered by Henry VIII and Martin Luther. But the one universal event through all these changes was the adoption of gunpowder weapons, which is why I favour 1494 as the year the Middle Ages ended.
2. His plots earned Louis the epithets 'the Cunning' and 'the Universal Spider'.
3. For ease, 'Italy' is used throughout the book to designate the geographical area of the modern nation, even though it was separate kingdoms until the 19th century.
4. Quattrocento means four hundred. It derives from *millequattrocento*, or 1400, the Italian word for the century in which Renaissance humanism reached its peak in Italy. Its use is confusing for English speakers as the Quattrocento refers to what we would call the 15th century.
5. Rome's population fell to its lowest level following the Black Death and while the papacy itself had decamped to Avignon in France. In the mid-14th century the city's population may even have fallen below 10,000.
6. The truly large cities in this era were outside Europe. Beijing, with possibly a million inhabitants, was the biggest city in the world, but Vijayanagara in India, Cairo in Egypt, Nanjing in China, Tenochtitlán in America and Gaur in Bengal all had larger populations than Constantinople.
7. I am sad to report that while Sixtus the Fifth reigned from 1585 to 1590, we still await a Sixtus the Sixth.
8. Machiavelli, *The Prince*, transl. Rufus Goodwin (Dante University Press, 2003), p.77.
9. In an amorous age, Francesco Gonzago was famous for his sexual appetites, so much so that his own sister-in-law volunteered to find him a

suitable '*femmina di partito*' ('party girl') with whom to enjoy one victory, in part to try to ensure that her sister not be exposed to the new disease, the *malfrancese* ('French disease') that was sweeping through Europe. We now call *malfrancese* syphilis and, on this occasion, the French were only partly to blame: Charles VIII's army had brought it with them when it swept south through Italy and then settled the disease firmly in Naples during the army's winter stay there. Beatrice d'Este's efforts proved ultimately in vain, as Francesco died from syphilis in 1519.

10 On a personal note, my Italian grandmother took to spending the winter with us in London because the weather was better for her arthritis here than on the east coast of the Po plain.

11 Massimo Predonzani & Vincenzo Alberici, *The Italian Wars* (Warwick: Helion & Company, 2021), volume 2, p.56; author's translation.

12 *The Italian Wars*, volume 2, p.56; author's translation.

13 *The Italian Wars*, volume 2, p.60.

14 A *passo* was five Roman feet, or about 1.5 metres.

15 *Badessa* is the Italian word for 'abbess'.

16 Halberds were typically five or six feet long, with a head made of an axe and a spike, so they could be used as both thrusting and cutting weapons. Pikes were much longer, some three times the length of a halberd, with a steel spike at the end.

17 Guido Tadini, *Vita di Gabriele Tadino* (Ateneo di Scienze, Lettere ed Arti, Bergamo, 1973), p.22; translated by the author.

18 *Kanunname-i Âl-i Osmān (Law Code of the Ottoman Dynasty attributed to Mehmed II)*, as preserved in Vienna (Austrian National Library, Cod. HO 143, et al.).

19 Roger Crowley, *City of Fortune: How Venice Won and Lost a Naval Empire* (London: Faber & Faber 2012), p.310. The author acknowledges author Roger Crowley and publisher Faber and Faber Ltd for granting permission to quote from *City of Fortune* in this book.

20 Ibid., p.314.

21 From the diary of Girolamo Priuli, quoted in *City of Fortune* by Roger Crowley, p.369.

22 Marco Minio, *Relazione di Marco Minio, oratore alla Porta Ottomana, fatta leggere in Pregadi li 8 Aprile 1522*, in *Le relazioni degli ambasciatori veneti al Senato. Serie III: Le relazioni degli stati ottomani*, vol. 3, ed. Eugenio Albèri (Firenze: Società Editrice Fiorentina, 1855), p.72.

23 Minio, *Relazione di Marco Minio*, pp.69–119.

24 Spoons might seem incongruous accoutrements for the most feared troops in Europe, but Janissaries were organised in companies called *orta*s. Each *orta* had a *kazan taşıyıcısı* ('pot bearer') whose job it was to carry the *kazan*, the communal cooking pot that each *orta* used to prepare its meals. The spoon was the implement with which each Janissary partook of the food in the *kazan*.

25 Anthony Bridge, *Suleiman the Magnificent: Scourge of Heaven* (Hippocrene, 1988), p.42.
26 Bridge, *Suleiman the Magnificent*, p.48.
27 Ibid., p.49.
28 This was starkly demonstrated by the Reformation, where the support of various German princes allowed Martin Luther's reformed church to take hold and establish itself; no such latitude would have been permitted within Suleiman's empire.
29 Ashley Giles, the England spin bowler during the 2005 Ashes series that saw England finally win back the Ashes from Australia during five epic test matches, had a testimonial year with his county, Warwickshire, the year before. As part of the merchandise produced to celebrate his ten years with the club, Giles had some mugs made that were to be printed with the legend, 'King of Spin'. Unfortunately, the typesetter got it wrong, and the mugs produced were emblazoned 'King of Spain'. The nickname stuck, leading even King Juan Carlos to remark, 'I do not know who this Ashley Giles is, but I can assure him that *I* am the King of Spain'.
30 Eric Brockman, *The Two Sieges of Rhodes: The Knights of St John at War, 1480–1522* (Barnes & Noble, 1996), p.114.
31 Brockman, *The Two Sieges of Rhodes*, pp.117–18.
32 A new pope, Adrian VI, had been elected on 9 January 1522. Adrian was a Dutchman and he was cut from a very different cloth from the Renaissance popes who had preceded him: austere, incorrupt, dedicated to reforming the abuses of the church, his short pontificate accomplished almost nothing of note, his attempts at reform stymied by the bureaucracy of the church and his own lack of resources. Adrian VI was buried in the church of Santa Maria dell'Anima in Rome and his epitaph reads, 'Alas, even with the best of men, how much depends on the times in which he lives' (Brockman, *The Two Sieges of Rhodes*, p.118).
33 The counterscarp was the face of the outer side of a defending ditch or moat. The counterscarp of the moat that surrounded the walls of Rhodes was dug to be as vertical as possible. That meant that attackers had to make a steep descent into the moat and then, in the moat, they were exposed to fire from the defender while the attackers would be unable to directly support them with counter fire.
34 Antonio Bosio, *Relazione della difesa di Rodi nel 1522*. Manuscript, Archivio Storico dell'Ordine di Malta, Rome.
35 Suleiman arrived on Rhodes on 28 July 1522.
36 Neville Lytton, *The Press and the General Staff* (Collins, 1921), p.97.
37 Quentin Hughes and Athanassios Migos, 'Rhodes: The Turkish Sieges', *Fort: The International Journal of Fortification and Military Architecture*, 21 (pp.3–17) (1993), p.15.

38 Hughes and Migos, 'Rhodes', p.17; translated by Roger Vella Bonavita.
39 Jacques de Bourbon, *Grande et Merveilleuse & Trescruelle Oppugnation de la noble Cite de Rhodes*, quoted in Jonathan Davies, *The Sieges of Rhodes, 1480 and 1522* (Helion & Company, 2024), p.187. The author acknowledges author Jonathan Davies and publisher Helion & Company for granting permission to quote from *The Sieges of Rhodes, 1480 and 1522* in this book.
40 Guido Tadini, *Vita di Gabriele Tadino* (Ateneo di Scienze, Lettere ed Arti, Bergamo, 1973), pp.30–31; translated by the author.
41 Quoted in Davies, *The Siege of Rhodes*, p.188.
42 Tadini, *Vita di Gabriele Tadino*, pp.31–34; translated by the author.
43 Brockman, *The Two Sieges of Rhodes*, p.145.
44 Ibid., p.142.
45 Davies, *The Sieges of Rhodes*, p.202.
46 Brockman, *The Two Sieges of Rhodes*, p.150.
47 Ibid., p.153.
48 Tadini, *Vita di Gabriele Tadino*, pp.36–37; translated by the author.
49 Geoffrey Parker, *Emperor: A New Life of Charles V* (Yale University Press, 2020), p.189.
50 Parker, *Emperor*, p.189.
51 Ibid., p.189.
52 Ibid., pp.189–90.
53 Ibid., p.130.
54 Ibid., p.131.
55 Ibid., p.146.
56 In fact, the original quote was by the Prussian general Helmuth von Moltke, who wrote in an 1871 essay: 'Kein Operationsplan reicht mit einiger Sicherheit über das erste Zusammentreffen mit der feindlichen Hauptmacht hinaus' ('No plan of operations extends with any certainty beyond the first encounter with the main enemy forces'). *Moltkes Militärische Werke: II. Die Thätigkeit als Chef des Generalstabes der Armee im Frieden. (Moltke's Military Works: II. Activity as Chief of the Army General Staff in Peacetime) Zweiter Teil (Second Part), Aufsatz vom Jahre 1871 Über Strategie (Article from 1871 on strategy)* (Ernst Siegfried Mittler und Sohn, 1900).
57 Parker, *Emperor*, p.149.
58 Ibid., p.152.
59 Quote from Suleiman the Magnificent. https://ia800609.us.archive.org/7/items/in.ernet.dli.2015.87496/2015.87496.Suleiman-The-Magnificent-1520-1566_text.pdf
60 Ibid.
61 Giambattista Gallizioli, *Memorie per Servire alla Storia della Vita di Gabriele Tadino*, pp.81–82; translated by the author.
62 Tadini, *Vita di Gabriele Tadino*, p.89.

63 Pope Clement VII crowned Charles as Holy Roman Emperor on 24 February 1530. However, the coronation, at Charles's request, took place in Bologna rather than Rome. Rome itself bore too many scars from its sack, and too many Romans blamed Charles for what had happened for the coronation to be guaranteed to be trouble free there.
64 https://web.archive.org/web/20131020083710/http://www.regalis.com/malta/deedCharles.pdf
65 Ibid.
66 Roger Crowley, *Empires of the Sea: The Final Battle for the Mediterranean, 1521–1580* (Faber & Faber, 2013), p.53. The author acknowledges author Roger Crowley and publisher Faber and Faber Ltd for granting permission to quote from *Empires of the Sea* in this book.
67 Ibid.
68 *Niccolò Tartaglia*, Arnoldo Masotti in the *Dictionary of Scientific Biography*.

BIBLIOGRAPHY

Having come with me this far in tracing the life of Gabriele Tadino da Martinengo, you will have noticed that there are periods where his life is well documented and others shrouded in obscurity. Tadino's first biographer, Giambattista Gallizioli, who published his life of Gabriele in 1783, suffered no such dearth of sources; his, fairly brief, work is full of allusions to family documents and letters that would have filled in the more obscure areas of Gabriele's life. Unfortunately, Gallizioli often does no more than sketch in what he read in these family documents and, on other occasions, he mentions he has read them but, to the great frustration of later historians, does not deign to tell the reader what he read in them.

It's frustrating because all those letters and documents were lost in 1797. The French Revolutionary Army, led by a general named Napoleon Bonaparte, had marched into Italy the previous year and the young general had won a string of brilliant victories, establishing his name and fame in France and stirring the first intimations beyond that someone unusual was on the rise.

In the final act of the campaign, Bonaparte dissolved the Republic of Venice, ending its 1,100-year independent history. The territory Venice controlled in mainland Italy was parcelled out, and the area around Martinengo became part of the short-lived Republic of Crema.

Among the citizens of Martinengo was Count Luigi Tadini, whose title revealed how well the Tadino family had done in the centuries after Gabriele's death. However, in a burst of revolutionary enthusiasm, Count Luigi decided to burnish his revolutionary credentials by declaring himself a republican and burning the family documents in the great fire that the revolutionaries laid up in the town square to burn away the old age and usher in the new age of revolution.

So we lost all the family documents and letters that Gallizioli had read but failed to transcribe – leaving some considerable gaps in Gabriele's life. I have tried to fill in these gaps as best I can in this book, but some have proved impossible to fill, in particular, what Tadino was doing in 1529, when Suleiman laid siege to Vienna. It seems unlikely that he played no part in the siege but the family documents that might have revealed his role – in particular, the letters in cypher that he received from the emperor – all went up in smoke while Count Luigi attempted to reinvent himself as Citizen Tadini.

That does leave a big hole for the historian. Luckily, other primary sources allow us to fill in most of the lacunae, while the careful work of generations of historians has brought the importance of the Italian Wars into clear focus. More recently, some excellent Turkish historians have cast new light upon the Ottoman Empire and, for our purposes, the reign of Suleiman the Lawgiver, as he's known in his home country.

In this bibliography, I list the main sources I consulted on the life of Gabriele Tadino. But in order to understand his life, it was also necessary to understand the times in which he lived, so after that I include a partial bibliography and further reading ideas for interested readers on the context in which Gabriele lived, arranged under topics.

MAIN SOURCES FOR THE LIFE OF GABRIELE TADINO

Belotti, Bortolo. *Storia di Bergamo e dei Bergamaschi*. Bergamo: Poligrafiche Bolis, 1959.

Boldoni, Sigismondo. *Epistolarum liber*. Milan, 1651.

Bosio, Giacomo. *Dell'historia della sacra Religione et illustrissima militia di San Giovanni Gierosolimitano*. Rome, 1594.

Caccia, Ferdinando. 'Gabriele Tadino.' In *Vite di eccellenti architetti militari*, in appendice a F. M. Tassi, *Vite de' pittori, scultori e architetti bergamaschi*, Bergamo, 1793.

Gallizioli, Giovanni Battista. *Memorie per servire alla storia della vita di Gabriele Tadino priore di Barletta*. Bergamo, 1783.

Promis, Carlo. 'Gabriele Tadini di Martinengo.' *Miscellanea di Storia Italiana* 14 (1874).

Sanudo, Marin. *I Diarii*. Edited by Rinaldo Fulin, Federico Stefani, et al. Vol. 26. Venice: Visentini, 1879–1902.

Tadini, Guido. *Vita di Gabriele Tadino da Martinengo priore di Barletta*. Bergamo: Ateneo di scienze, lettere ed arti, 1973.

Tartaglia, Niccolò. *Quesiti et inventioni diverse*. Brescia: Ateneo de Brescia, 1959.

THE ITALIAN WARS AND THE NEW GUNPOWDER WEAPONS

Black, Jeremy. *A Military Revolution? Military Change and European Society, 1550–1800*. Basingstoke: Macmillan / Humanities Press, 1991.

Duffy, Christopher. *Siege Warfare: The Fortress in the Early Modern World 1494–1660*. London: Routledge & Kegan Paul, 1996.

Guicciardini, Francesco. *The History of Italy*. Translated by Sydney Alexander. Princeton: Princeton University Press, 1964.

Guilmartin, John F., Jr. *Gunpowder and Galleys: Changing Technology and Mediterranean Warfare at Sea in the Sixteenth Century*. Rev. ed. Annapolis, MD: Naval Institute Press, 2003.

Knecht, R. J. *Renaissance Warrior and Patron: The Reign of Francis I.* Cambridge: Cambridge University Press, 1994.
Mallett, Michael. *Mercenaries and their Masters.* Barnsley: Pen & Sword, 2019.
Mallett, Michael and Christine Shaw. *The Italian Wars 1494–1559: War, State and Society in Early Modern Europe.* 2nd ed. London: Routledge, 2019.
Oman, Charles. *A History of the Art of War in the Sixteenth Century.* London: Methuen, 1937.
Parker, Geoffrey. *The Military Revolution: Military Innovation and the Rise of the West, 1500–1800.* Rev. ed. Cambridge: Cambridge University Press, 1996.
Parrott, David. *The Business of War: Military Enterprise and Military Revolution in Early Modern Europe.* Cambridge: Cambridge University Press, 2012.
Predonzani, Massimo and Vincenzo Alberici. *The Italian Wars, Volume 1: The Expedition of Charles VIII into Italy and the Battle of Fornovo, 1495.* Solihull: Helion & Company, 2019.
Predonzani, Massimo and Vincenzo Alberici. *The Italian Wars, Volume 2: Agnadello 1509, Ravenna 1512, Marignano 1515.* Solihull: Helion & Company, 2021.
Predonzani, Massimo and Vincenzo Alberici. *The Italian Wars, Volume 3: Francis I and the Battle of Pavia 1525.* Solihull: Helion & Company, 2022.
Rogers, Clifford J., ed. *The Military Revolution Debate: Readings on the Military Transformation of Early Modern Europe.* Boulder, CO: Westview Press, 1995.
Romane, Julian. *The First and Second Italian Wars 1494–1504: Fearless Knights, Ruthless Princes and the Coming of Gunpowder Armies.* Barnsley: Pen & Sword, 2020.

THE RENAISSANCE

This is a vast topic and one with more facets than Leonardo's drawing of Vitruvian man. As such, this is just a suggestion for some key texts, although anyone wanting to learn more about the revolution in education that took place in Italy in the Quattrocento which then spread throughout Europe has to start with Paul Grendler's book, *Schooling in Renaissance Italy*.

Burckhardt, Jacob. *The Civilization of the Renaissance in Italy.* Translated by S. G. C. Middlemore. Revised edition. London: Phaidon, 1990.
Grendler, Paul F. *Schooling in Renaissance Italy: Literacy and Learning, 1300–1600.* Baltimore: Johns Hopkins University Press, 1989.

Najemy, John M., ed. *Italy in the Age of the Renaissance, 1300–1550*. Oxford: Oxford University Press, 2004.
Plumb, J. H. *The Penguin Book of the Renaissance*. London: Penguin, 2001.

VENICE

While there's not quite so much about Venice, it's a close-run race. Here are some suggestions for further reading about the Most Serene Republic.

Ackroyd, Peter. *Venice: Pure City*. London: Chatto & Windus, 2009.
Chambers, David and Brian Pullan, eds. *Venice: A Documentary History, 1450–1630*. Toronto: University of Toronto Press, 2001.
Crowley, Roger. *City of Fortune: How Venice Ruled the Seas*. London: Faber & Faber Ltd, 2011.
Finlay, Robert. *Politics in Renaissance Venice*. New Brunswick, NJ: Rutgers University Press, 1980.
Lane, Frederic C. *Venice: A Maritime Republic*. Baltimore: Johns Hopkins University Press, 1973.
Mallett, Michael E. and John R. Hale. *The Military Organization of a Renaissance State: Venice c. 1400–1617*. Cambridge: Cambridge University Press, 1984.

THE KNIGHTS HOSPITALLER AND THE SIEGE OF RHODES

Primary sources

Bourbon, Jacques de. *La grande et merveilleuse et trescruelle oppugnation de la noble cité de Rhodes*. Paris: Pierre Vidoue for Gilles de Gourmont, 1525.
Fontanus, Jacques. *De bello Rhodio libri tres*. Rome: apud Ioannem Secerium, 1527.
Guichard, Thomas. *Oratio habita ab eloquentissimo viro F. Thoma Guichardo Rhodio, iuris utriusque doctore*. Rome, 1524.

Secondary sources

Bosio, Antonio. *Historia della sacra religione et illustrissima militia di San Giovanni Battista*. Rome: 1594–1602.
Brockman, Eric. *The Two Sieges of Rhodes, 1480–1522*. London: J. Murray; reprint, New York: Barnes & Noble, 1995/1996.
Carr, John C. *The Knights Hospitaller: A Military History of the Knights of St John*. Barnsley: Pen & Sword, 2016.
Davies, Jonathan. *The Sieges of Rhodes, 1480 and 1522 (From Retinue to Regiment 1453–1618)*. Ramsbury: Helion & Company, 2024.

Nicolle, David. *Knights of Jerusalem: The Crusading Order of Hospitallers 1100–1565*. Oxford: Osprey (World of the Warrior series), 2008.

Nossov, Konstantin. *The Fortress of Rhodes 1309–1522* (Fortress series, no. 96). Oxford: Osprey Publishing, 2010.

Sire, H. J. A. *The Knights of Malta*. New Haven: Yale University Press, 1994.

Smith, Robert Douglas and Kelly DeVries. *Rhodes Besieged: A New History*. Stroud: The History Press, 2012.

CHARLES V AND THE HABSBURG EMPIRE

Blockmans, Wim. *Emperor Charles V, 1500–1558*. Oxford: Oxford University Press, 2002.

Crowley, Roger. *Empires of the Sea: The Final Battle for the Mediterranean 1521–1580*. London: Faber & Faber Ltd, 2008.

Kamen, Henry. *Empire: How Spain Became a World Power, 1492–1763*. HarperCollins, 2003.

Mitchell, A. Wess. *The Grand Strategy of the Habsburg Empire*. Princeton: Princeton University Press, 2018.

Norwich, John Julius. *Four Princes: Henry VIII, Francis I, Charles V, Suleiman the Magnificent and the Obsessions that Forged Modern Europe*. New York: Random House, 2017.

Parker, Geoffrey. *Emperor: A New Life of Charles V*. New Haven: Yale University Press, 2019.

Rady, Martyn. *The Emperor Charles V* (Seminar Studies in History). Harlow: Pearson Education, 2004.

Reston Jr., James. *Defenders of the Faith: Charles V, Suleiman the Magnificent, and the Battle for Europe, 1520–1536*. New York: Doubleday, 2009.

Rodríguez-Salgado, María. *The Changing Face of Empire: Charles V, Philip II and Habsburg Authority, 1551–1559*. Cambridge: Cambridge University Press, 2008.

Thomas, Hugh. *The Golden Empire: Spain, Charles V, and the Creation of America*. New York: Random House, 2010.

Tracy, James D. *Emperor Charles V, Impresario of War*. Cambridge: Cambridge University Press, 2002.

SULEIMAN THE MAGNIFICENT AND THE OTTOMAN EMPIRE

There's a whole world of little explored scholarship about the Ottoman Empire out there, with some notable Turkish historians contributing hugely to the field. I've only included Halil İnalcık in this list as his work is most widely available in English but I hope more work will be translated soon.

Bridge, Antony. *Suleiman the Magnificent: Scourge of Heaven*. London: Granada, 1983.
Clot, André. *Suleiman the Magnificent: The Man, His Life, His Epoch*. London: Saqi Books, 1992.
De Bellaigue, Christopher. *The Lion House: The Coming of a King*. New York: Farrar, Straus and Giroux, 2022.
De Bellaigue, Christopher. *The Golden Throne: The Curse of a King*. London: The Bodley Head, 2025.
Goffman, Daniel. *The Ottoman Empire and Early Modern Europe*. Cambridge: Cambridge University Press, 2001.
Goodwin, Jason. *Lords of the Horizons: A History of the Ottoman Empire*. New York: Henry Holt and Company, 1999.
İnalcık, Halil. *An Economic and Social History of the Ottoman Empire, 1300–1600*. Cambridge: Cambridge University Press, 1994.
İnalcık, Halil. *The Ottoman Empire: The Classical Age, 1300–1600*. London: Weidenfeld & Nicolson, 1973.
Kinross, Lord. *The Ottoman Centuries: The Rise and Fall of the Turkish Empire*. New York: Morrow, 1977.
Peirce, Leslie P. *Empress of the East: How a European Slave Girl Became Queen of the Ottoman Empire*. London: Icon, 2017.

ACKNOWLEDGEMENTS

Pretty well every writer starts off his acknowledgements by stating the book you've just read was the result of many people's work. And while I did debate stating that, no, this is all my own work, I have to admit that it isn't. Many people did help in bringing *The Man Who Stopped the Sultan* to publication and here I get the chance to thank them (while crossing my fingers that I haven't forgotten anyone).

I'm going to start with my mother, Paolina Perello, as she was when she first arrived in London aged 18 and not speaking a word of English. It was my mother who taught me to read and who inculcated the love of books that has been the defining characteristic of my life. It was in order to learn more about my Italian background that I started investigating the history of Italy, the disastrous series of wars that blighted and divided the country, and the extraordinary history of the military engineer who played such a key role role in these events.

So this book is very much for my mother, Paolina Perello Albert – after all, who else would an Italian boy dedicate his book to than his mamma!

Still even Italian boys grow up, so I also want to thank my dear wife, Harriet, who has helped, encouraged, criticised and praised, my first editor and my most perspicacious reader. My boys, Theo, Matthew and Isaac, are the best sons a father could hope for and I thank them for, well, everything, with a particular note to thank Isaac for cajoling us into getting a dog. Barnaby has ensured that I get away from my desk (actually an ironing board) twice a day, breathe fresh air and talk to fellow dog-walkers.

In researching this book, Sonny Topsom proved invaluable, chasing down obscure texts, finding things that I had missed and single-handedly ensuring that I finished the book three years earlier than I would have. Should any reader be looking for a researcher, I wholeheartedly recommend him (get in touch with me via my website and I will pass on his contact details).

My agent, Robert Dudley, has been my consistent champion; a friend and an encourager, he made this book possible.

At Osprey, I want to thank Kate Moore, who commissioned the book and has been its unflagging supporter. Gemma White saw the book through editing to production, coping gracefully with my last-minute changes. Venetia Bridges polished my rough prose into something much finer through her meticulous copyediting (a medievalist, we both lament the loss of the old St Peter's), and Julie Frederick went through everything with the keenest eye to get the text ready for publication. Chris Raine was the production controller, the man responsible for the look and feel of the text, while Stewart Larking produced the beautiful cover which will lure many unwitting readers into the world of Gabriele Tadino.

Any remaining errors are entirely my own.

Finally, dear reader, I would like to thank you. In a world where there are so many other calls on attention and (limited) time, I am grateful that you chose to pick up this book and read it. If I might further ask for a review, positive or negative, then my gratitude shall truly overflow. If you have enjoyed learning about Gabriele Tadino's life and times, then I hope you will have a look at my historical fiction novel, *The War for the Heart of the World: the Last Crusaders*, which tells the story of the defence of Rhodes.

INDEX

Adrian VI, Pope 14, 228–229
Africa 145–146, 148–149, 174, 246, 267, 269, 280
Ahmed Pasha 158, 207, 220
Alexander VI, Pope 45–46, 67, 73–74
Alexandria 132–134, 144
Alps 42, 56, 59, 61, 65, 91, 99, 108, 230
Anatolia 52, 163
Anne, 'Madame la Grande' 36–40, 48
Aragon 13, 18–20, 41, 46, 48, 66, 134, 148, 173, 183, 186, 195–196, 203–204, 218, 232, 268
arquebusiers 19–20, 89–90, 101, 126, 131, 184, 186, 196, 199, 201, 210, 243, 260, 281
artillery 8, 14–15, 23, 29, 45, 47, 49, 66, 83–84, 88–91, 94–95, 97, 100, 105–106, 118, 126, 130–131, 166, 176, 178, 182, 183, 185–187, 189, 194–196, 198–200, 207–209, 223, 232, 234, 239, 237–240, 243, 246–247, 263, 272, 275, 283
Averoldo, Altobello 117–118, 129
Avignon 77, 174, 238
Avogadro, Luigi 95–96, 100, 102

bailo 87, 130, 142, 144, 150
Balkans 8, 83, 137, 139, 178, 189
Barbaran, Fra' Juan de 19–20
Barbarossa, Hayreddin 273–274
Barco, Camillo da 110–111, 113–118, 120, 129, 266
Barco, Theofilo da 110, 113–114, 116, 118, 120, 129
Barletta 15, 180, 247, 258
bastions 7, 15, 19, 23–24, 68, 88, 127, 158, 165, 176, 183–184, 186, 189–190, 193–194, 200–201, 203–204, 204–205, 208–209, 241, 252
battles:
 Agnadello 13, 85–88, 99–100, 102, 125, 255

Fornovo 47, 59
Mohács 15, 249–251, 259
Pavia 8, 14, 238, 244, 247–248, 255, 260
Ravenna 107–108, 125, 255
Belgrade 14, 155, 158–159, 162, 181, 213–214, 225, 248
Bergamaschi 62–63, 93, 95, 122, 266
Bergamo 13, 22, 30–32, 54, 60–64, 69–70, 95, 97, 100, 102, 109, 122
blockade 23, 96, 142, 167–168, 177, 186, 197, 207, 212, 252
Bologna 15, 33–34, 54, 81, 95–96, 100, 265
Boniface of Montserrat 134–135
Bosio, Fra' Antonio 14, 165–166, 168, 170, 193, 228–229
Bourbon, Jacques de 185, 195, 200, 204
Bramante, Donato 77–78
Brescia 13, 15, 32, 94–104, 108–110, 115, 117–118, 120, 122, 129–130, 167, 254–255, 275
brigantines 169–170, 177, 180, 224, 227
Brittany 37–40
Buda 250, 259–261
Budapest 155, 249
Byzantine 43, 52, 121, 133, 135

Candia 14–15, 22, 130–131, 133–135, 150, 165–170, 198–199, 226, 266–267, 273
cannon 8–9, 18–19, 22–24, 28–29, 35, 38, 41–45, 47–48, 59–60, 62, 66, 68, 88–91, 94, 105, 127, 130, 138, 158, 176, 182–185, 187–189, 203, 220, 222, 224, 234, 239, 246, 252, 254, 259–261, 271, 275–276, 280–283
Caprioli 110–115
Capua 67–68
Carapazio, Basil 186
Castile 13, 38, 48, 52, 148, 173, 218, 229, 232, 268

Ceri, Renzo da 92–93
Charlemagne 230–231, 242
Charles V 8, 13–15, 22, 41, 148, 153, 160, 224, 229, 236, 256, 267, 283
Charles VIII 8, 13, 34–35, 45, 50, 56, 62, 66, 69, 73, 123, 239, 280
Christendom 22, 79, 88, 124–125, 141, 153–154, 156, 160, 162, 164–167, 194, 219, 225–226, 229–231, 233, 235, 245, 255, 258, 266–267, 270–271, 273, 278, 284–285
Christianity 77, 79, 216, 218, 245
Citolo da Perugia 88–89
Civitavecchia 14, 228–229
Clement VII, Pope 229, 240, 255, 265
Çoban Mustafa Pasha 178, 180–181, 200–201, 203–205
Colleoni, Captain Bartolomeo 27–31, 70, 110, 120
Colleoni family 26, 119–120
Colonna, Fabrizio 105
condottieri 9, 13, 26, 31, 47, 49, 52, 60, 63, 70, 88, 92–93, 110, 120, 122, 130, 167, 243, 266, 284
Constantine XI 43, 188
Constantinople 13, 21–22, 35, 42–43, 53, 57, 121, 130, 133–135, 138, 141–144, 149–151, 153–156, 161–163, 165, 175, 181, 188, 206–208, 214, 219, 230–232, 244–245, 248, 250, 259–263, 270, 274, 280
Conversano (Zorzi da Conversano), Giorgio di 169–170, 180, 199
Council of Ten 14, 93–94, 226
courtiers 36–37, 40
Crema 32, 109, 122
Cremona 15, 52, 109, 254
Croatia 131, 268, 274
crossbow 201, 216, 281
Crusades 21, 52, 123, 133–134, 149, 167, 171–172, 269
curtain wall 7, 183–184, 187, 203
Cyprus 14, 22, 130, 173

d'Alviano, Bartolomeo 83–85
d'Amaral, Fra' Andrea 163, 216–219, 222
d'Aubusson, Pierre 202
devshirme 139, 178
Dias, Bartolomeu 13, 145–146

Diaz, Blasco 216–218
digging 18, 23, 38, 88, 126, 130, 183, 187–190, 192–195, 209, 238, 240–241
ducats 73, 90, 92, 102, 122, 134, 144, 147, 150, 180, 209, 232, 236, 254, 257, 263, 277
Duomo Vecchio 99, 103

earthworks 127, 186, 195, 212, 216, 240–241
education 33, 36, 51, 54, 136, 140, 175, 206
Egypt 133, 137, 144, 147, 162, 248
embankments 88, 127, 260
embrasures 176, 183–186, 210, 212
Emiliano, Paolantonio 166–167
enfilading (flanking) fire 7, 23, 91, 127, 176, 183–184, 198, 204
England 7, 22, 38, 57, 59, 70–71, 104, 123, 128, 148, 165, 173, 175–176, 183, 186, 193, 195–196, 200, 205, 207, 236, 238, 248, 284
Euclid 52–54
Europe 22, 30, 33–35, 41–42, 46–47, 49–50, 52–53, 57, 59, 67, 82, 99, 102, 121, 124, 127–128, 144, 146–148, 160, 162, 165, 167, 172–173, 175–176, 189, 194, 206, 219, 222, 224–225, 228–231, 233, 236–237, 242, 247, 250, 264–265, 267, 278–279, 282–285
execution 66, 102, 139, 141, 147, 157, 174, 202, 204, 216–217, 219, 222

fausse braye 7, 184
Ferdinand I of Habsburg 250, 258–260, 262, 264, 271, 274, 283
Ferdinand II of Aragon 46, 66–67, 74, 82, 86, 108
Ferrante, Ferdinand I of Naples 13, 41, 67, 148, 218
Ferrara 13, 31, 61, 70–71, 96, 118–120, 233
Florence 24, 28–29, 44–45, 50, 54, 56–58, 61, 70, 233, 251
Florentines 45, 66, 143
Foix, Gaston de 8, 94–97, 100–102, 104–108
Fort of St Nicholas 177, 179

INDEX

fortifications 23, 30, 49, 60, 122, 126–127, 130, 164, 166, 168, 178, 180, 182, 184, 186, 188–189, 193–194, 252, 258, 276

fortresses 21, 28–29, 42–45, 67, 87, 127, 131, 138, 155, 158–159, 162–163, 172, 190, 224, 249, 259, 271, 274, 282–283

France 7–8, 13, 36–38, 43, 45–48, 52, 58–59, 63, 67–68, 70–71, 73, 77, 86, 101–102, 104, 108–109, 119, 121–124, 128, 153, 160–161, 173–174, 234–238, 243, 245, 247–248, 251, 258, 267, 280

Francesco, Gian 32, 34, 276

Francis I 7, 13, 22, 128, 147, 153, 160, 256

French army 42, 46, 67, 84, 94–95, 100, 102, 104, 107–108, 238, 243–244, 246

galleys 22, 131–133, 136–137, 141–142, 151, 163, 165, 169–170, 174, 177, 179, 252, 269, 280

Gallipoli 14, 136, 151, 163, 227–228

Genoa 15, 22, 57, 73, 108, 148, 250–253, 255, 258, 264, 272–273

Genoese 134, 143, 175, 221, 252

Germany 65, 86, 148, 160, 173, 185, 193, 231, 248, 271

Giotto 78, 80

gold 57–58, 108, 115, 133–134, 137, 144, 150–152, 160, 166, 213, 228, 232, 239, 249, 256–257, 268

Gozo 267–268

Granada 67, 251, 268

Grand Cross 23, 180, 198

Gravellone 239–240

Greece 52, 134, 137

Gritti, Andrea 86–88, 94–97, 100–101

gun emplacements 238, 240–241

gunners 43, 184–185, 188, 194–195, 201, 275

gunpowder 19, 61, 89, 126, 165, 187–188, 243, 280

Güns 271–272, 283

Habsburgs 68, 230, 250, 258, 260, 277, 279, 283–284

halberds 126, 193

harbours 169, 177, 179–180, 186, 197, 224, 268–269

heirs 36–37, 39–40, 48, 128, 138, 161, 206, 213–214, 240, 249, 276, 279

Henry VIII 22, 104, 128, 148, 153, 230, 236, 248, 284

Holy Land 21, 82, 123–125, 154, 163, 172–173, 219, 232, 245

Holy Roman Empire 70–71, 82, 94, 128, 160–161, 173

Hundred Years' War 43, 57, 280

Hungarian army 157, 249

Hungary 38, 83, 153, 155, 157, 162, 173, 248–250, 258, 260, 268, 271, 274

Hürrem (Roxelana) 206, 213, 279

Ibrahim 248, 261, 264, 271

India 13, 147, 268

infantry 9, 70, 83, 88, 101, 105–107, 110, 126, 130, 238–240, 243, 252, 254–255

Innocent VIII, Pope 73

iron 19, 44, 182, 185, 281

Islam 52, 125, 138–139, 149–150, 153, 155, 284

Italian Wars 8–9, 21, 23, 48, 50, 56, 62, 65–66, 68–71, 92, 96, 102–103, 105, 107, 109, 118, 121–122, 124–127, 130, 167, 182, 237–238, 240, 246, 251–252, 255, 257, 280, 282–284

Italy 7, 13, 22–24, 33, 35, 38, 40, 42, 44–51, 53–59, 61–63, 65–66, 68–71, 73, 76, 81–82, 86, 94, 99–100, 104, 107–108, 114, 120–125, 130–131, 148, 173, 176, 191, 194, 210, 227–228, 230–231, 233–235, 237–238, 240–241, 245, 247, 251, 253, 255–256, 258, 272–273, 280, 284

Quattrocento 50, 54, 58–59, 123

Janissaries 7, 18, 20, 139, 151, 156–157, 178, 181, 203–204, 213, 262–263

Jerusalem 123, 149, 162, 171–172, 244, 268

Julius II (Giuliano della Rovere), Pope 71–72, 74–82, 86, 93, 108, 120–121, 123

Jurišic, Nikola 271

Knights Hospitaller 7, 14, 19, 21–22, 123, 149, 162, 167, 171–173, 180, 185, 215, 228, 231, 247, 266–267, 269, 276, 278, 284
  Grand Masters 7, 14, 18–20, 23, 162–165, 167–168, 171–175, 177, 180–182, 194, 196, 201–203, 216–224, 226–229, 234, 267–268, 279
Knights Templar 21, 162, 172, 174, 228
Kurtoglu Muslihiddin Reis 167, 179, 197

Landsknechte 8–9, 86–87, 89–91, 104, 106, 122, 239, 255–256, 260
langues 172–176, 193, 278
Lannoy, Charles de 241, 243
Latin 36, 52, 54, 133, 135, 175, 183
League of Cambrai 71, 74, 83, 85–86, 94, 121
  War of 13, 63, 70, 81, 120
League of Cognac 56, 251, 253–255
Leo X, Pope 155, 236
Levant 133–135, 147–149, 163, 174
Leyva, Antonio de 238–239, 243
Lombardy 57, 61, 66, 85–86, 99, 102, 108
looting 47, 58, 102, 106, 108, 223, 237, 257
Louis XII, King 48, 66, 73–74, 83, 128, 234
Luther, Martin 13, 35, 75, 156, 225, 231, 245, 255–256

Machiavelli 85, 124
Malta 149, 190, 224, 267–270, 279–280
Mantua 47, 61, 96, 100, 272
Marseille 14, 42, 238
Martinenghesi 24, 63, 266, 275, 284
Martinengo 15, 22, 24, 26, 31–32, 51, 53–54, 60, 62, 69, 111, 272–274
mathematics 52–54, 103, 275
Maximilian I 37, 63, 65, 74, 86–87, 231, 234
medicine 32–34, 51, 215
Mediterranean 21–22, 48, 56, 61, 137, 144, 146, 148–149, 169, 174–175, 177, 207, 228, 246–247, 267, 269, 274, 277, 279–280

Mehmed II 'the Conqueror' 13, 21–22, 43, 140–144, 147, 155, 157, 159, 161, 175, 181, 188, 212, 214, 225
Melilla 246–247
men-at-arms 20, 60, 83–84, 88, 101, 105–107, 113, 132, 172, 181, 238
mercenaries 20–21, 49, 67, 76, 84, 86–87, 90, 166–167, 181, 237, 242–243, 256
merchants 54, 57, 86, 133–134, 137, 140–141, 143, 163, 166, 175, 179, 221
Michelangelo 13, 77–80
Middle Ages 35, 48, 79, 132, 187, 280–282
Milan 31, 46, 56–58, 61–63, 66–67, 70, 109, 125, 237–238, 240–241, 245, 251, 253, 258
military engineers 13, 17, 21, 23, 51, 60, 62–64, 129, 167, 176, 184, 188, 191, 224, 226, 246–247, 255, 259, 264, 270, 276–278, 282–283
mines 18–20, 90–91, 150, 178–179, 187–191, 193–194, 199–201, 208–209, 249, 262–263, 271, 282
Minio, Marco 150–155
moats 7, 88–89, 158–159, 165, 176, 182–185, 188, 190–191, 195–196, 199–201, 209–210, 215–216, 220

Naples 13–14, 24, 29, 33, 41–42, 45–46, 48, 50, 57–59, 61–62, 66–68, 188, 228, 245, 247, 251–252, 257–258
Napoleon 62, 68, 248
Navarre 70, 236, 268
Negroponte 133–134, 144

Osman 138–139, 150, 213–214
Ottoman Empire 21–22, 139, 147–148, 154, 163, 166, 191, 223, 274, 284
Ottomans 15, 21–22, 35, 43, 82, 131, 134–142, 148–150, 155, 158, 178, 181, 185–186, 188–190, 195, 200–201, 206–207, 212, 214, 220, 224, 228, 232, 249–250, 258–263, 269, 272, 274, 277–280, 284–285
Outremer 123, 133, 162, 172

Pamplona 14, 231
Papal States 42, 45–46, 56, 61, 63, 67, 70–72, 74, 76, 92, 120–121, 124, 236

INDEX

Paris 33, 57, 104, 161
pashas 140, 153–154, 156–158, 189, 201, 203–205, 216, 224, 250
Pavia 238–241, 243–244
Peloponnese 134–135, 144, 226
Philip the Fair 162, 174
pikemen 83, 126
pirates 134, 149, 163, 175, 198
  Barbary 174, 280
Pisa 47, 61, 66, 134, 188
Pitigliano, Niccolò di 84–85
Portugal 144, 147, 173, 218
prince-electors 160–161, 231

ramparts 42, 44, 201, 216, 219, 282
rape 68, 102, 157, 223, 257
Raphael 77, 79–81, 151
Ravenna 81, 104, 121
Reformation 35, 79, 156, 225, 255, 284
reinforcements 47, 85, 131, 167, 196–197, 207, 227, 238, 249, 252
religion 8, 167–168, 173–176, 179–182, 184–185, 190, 193–194, 202–203, 210, 216–217, 219, 221–222, 224, 228–229, 234, 247, 266, 268–270, 278–279
Renaissance 7, 50, 53, 57, 72–73, 75, 79, 81, 132, 151, 257
Renato, Apella 201–202, 217
retrenchments 23, 90–91, 198, 203, 212, 220, 239
Rhodes 14, 17–18, 21–23, 123, 149, 162–163, 165–170, 173–178, 180–183, 185–187, 189–191, 193–195, 198–202, 207–210, 212–215, 217, 219, 221, 223–228, 232–233, 239, 246, 252, 255, 260–261, 266–267, 269–270, 274, 278–279
Roman Empire 21, 35, 50, 56, 59, 70–71, 82, 94, 104, 121, 128, 160–161, 173
Rome 14–15, 29, 46–47, 57, 67, 72–74, 77–78, 104, 120–121, 151, 153–154, 161, 174, 213, 228–230, 255–257, 281

Safavids 147, 155
sailors 141–142, 144–145, 166–167, 174, 177, 181, 197, 228

sappers 18, 130, 178, 187, 195–196, 213, 215–216, 220, 240, 261–262
Scaramosa, Beneto 169–170, 180, 199
Scotland 70–71, 173, 240
Selim 'the Grim' 147, 155, 178, 202, 214, 248
servants 19, 29, 31, 129, 137, 151–152, 170, 210, 216, 218, 227, 253, 256, 267, 279, 284
Sforza, Ludovico 41, 65
Sicily 46, 52, 148–149, 207, 267, 273, 280
sieges:
  Genoa 15, 252
  Padua 13, 86, 91
Siena 47, 58, 61
Signoria 15, 28–29, 88, 93–94, 118, 129–131, 143, 146, 150–151, 154, 168, 198, 210, 253, 266, 273–274, 276–277
silver 17, 58, 110, 152, 192, 262
Sistine Chapel 13, 79–80, 151
Sixtus IV (Francesco Della Rovere), Pope 72–73
slaves 18, 136–137, 139, 151, 156–157, 160, 162–163, 168, 179, 186, 194, 204, 248–249, 258, 261
Spain 8, 14, 22, 52, 67, 74, 124, 128, 148, 160–161, 209, 218, 229–232, 234–235, 247, 267, 270, 279–280
spices 132–135, 144, 146–147
St Peter's Basilica 77–79, 120
Stato da Màr 61, 82–83, 129–130, 134–135, 143–144, 166, 266
Stato da Tera 61–62, 70, 74, 82, 86–87, 99, 266
Sublime Porte 9, 87, 140, 143–144, 150, 155, 160, 166, 168, 190, 202, 206, 225, 248, 258, 274
Suleiman 7–8, 13–15, 21–22, 131, 147–158, 161–165, 178, 180–181, 189–191, 197, 201–208, 212–214, 216–217, 221–225, 230, 232–233, 248–251, 258–264, 269–272, 274, 278–280
supplies 95, 165–167, 178, 181, 197, 203, 208, 212, 220, 240, 252–253, 259, 261–262, 271
surrender 14, 66, 68, 87, 99–102, 108, 159, 163, 218, 222, 226–227, 238, 243, 257, 259, 261, 271

swords 98–99, 103, 112, 156, 162, 182, 193, 201, 263, 272, 276, 280
Syria 52, 147, 162

Tadino, Clemente 25–27, 29–33, 51–53, 60, 69–70
Tadino, Gabriele 8, 13–15, 17–28, 30–34, 51–55, 60–64, 69–70, 83, 85, 87–95, 97–100, 102–103, 109–120, 122, 129–132, 166–170, 176, 179–182, 185, 187, 191–196, 198–201, 203–204, 208, 210–212, 214–216, 221–224, 226–229, 232–234, 238–240, 243, 246–247, 250–255, 257–258, 264–267, 270–280, 283–285
Tadino, Girolamo 32, 34, 253–254, 272
Tadino, Tranquilla 32–33, 277
Tartaglia, Niccolò 15, 99, 103, 120, 264, 275–276, 284
taxes 31, 48, 50, 99, 135, 139, 147, 150, 158, 173, 178
teaching 33–34, 52–53, 60, 283
tenaille 7, 176, 183–187, 190
terre plein 176, 183, 186–187, 203
Titian (Tiziano Vecelli) 8, 15, 266, 276
Toledo 52, 229, 268
torture 139, 143, 174, 202, 218, 252
trace italienne 127, 130, 283
trade routes 129, 134–135
training 23, 33, 60, 126, 140, 191, 247, 274, 281, 283
trenches 49, 184, 187, 193, 195–197, 199–201, 207, 209, 212, 220, 222, 238, 240–241, 260

trials 13, 21, 30, 42, 117, 216, 219, 284
Tripoli 133, 267–269
Tunis 15, 273
tunnels 17–20, 23, 130, 187–188, 190–193, 204, 207, 210, 262, 278, 282
Turks 17, 19, 21–22, 74, 82, 123–124, 138, 141–142, 154–155, 159, 168, 177–178, 181, 185–186, 189–193, 195–204, 207–208, 210, 216–220, 224–228, 232–233, 244, 258–259, 263–264, 267, 270–271, 278

University of Bologna 33–34, 54

Valette, Jean Parisot de la 224, 279
Venice 13–15, 22–23, 29, 31, 46, 54, 56–58, 61–64, 69–71, 74, 76, 82–83, 85–86, 92–93, 99–100, 102–103, 109, 114, 117–119, 122, 124, 129–135, 137–138, 140–142, 144–147, 150, 153–155, 163, 166–168, 198, 222, 225–226, 233, 251–254, 266, 273–277, 284
Verona 13, 93, 118, 122
Vienna 15, 155, 233, 250, 259–264, 271–272, 274
Villiers de L'Isle Adam, Philippe 162–163, 165, 167, 180, 196–197, 201, 217, 219, 221–224, 228–229, 234, 269

Zakynthos 14, 226, 228
Zápolya, John 250, 258–259